"People of faith often find themselves immersed in a chaotic and uncertain culture. In that arena, it can prove overwhelming to navigate the seemingly gray areas where principle and conviction collide with life's messy realities. Erisman and Pope's *Living with Purpose in a Polarizing World* reminds us that we are not the first to encounter such conflict. Leaning on the experiences, triumphs, and failures of characters in biblical times, we can draw encouragement that we are not alone in that struggle. Indeed, we can learn to find a way forward—one of grace and mercy for ourselves and the world around us, even when the path appears dark."

—Hon. Toby Barker, mayor, City of Hattiesburg, Mississippi

"Our world is seemingly fueled and animated by radical and extremist views on the Right and Left, which may infect our families, workplaces, places of worship, and neighborhoods because these are a microcosm of our polarized world. Fortunately, Albert Erisman and Randy Pope explain and model 'another way' forward, informed by the sensible principles they gleaned by carefully studying familiar Old Testament and New Testament characters in their particular historical-cultural contexts, to bridge this polarization gap. The church, and our polarized world, owes much gratitude to these two brothers because 'another way' is the way of Christ Jesus."

—Luke Bobo, director of bioethics, Kansas City University

"Erisman and Pope provide thoughtful retellings of biblical narratives, offer insightful reflections on how those narratives might inform our current polarized cultural context, and present contemporary and constructive examples from their own experiences. Particularly for Christians tempted to assimilate, withdraw, seek power, or react in anger or fear, this book offers a better way. Whether you agree with their particular conclusions or not, their approach to engaging in a spirited dialogue with Scripture and one another is a terrific example for all of us."

—Uli Chi, senior fellow, De Pree Center for Leadership
Author of *The Wise Leader*

"Erisman and Pope provide biblical exemplars of how Christians ought to live in a world that is characterized by disunity and polarization. Yet in Jesus Christ, Christians are called to embody 'faithful presence.' If you are asking, 'How do I walk with God in a post-Christian world?,' grab this book and join the excursion into 'faithful presence' as you seek to cooperate with God in bearing witness to the world."

—JoAnn Flett, executive director, Center for Faithful Business

T0038028

"Al and Randy have crafted a well-written, thought-provoking, encouraging, and timely book that asserts that the Christian assignment from God is to live with purpose in an increasingly secular society. Using twelve case studies from the Scriptures interspersed with examples from modern times, they make the compelling case that our purpose is to serve God in all aspects of our lives as long as we live. When I read something I want to savor and remember, I read a chapter or so at a time, put it aside for reflection, and then go back to it the following day. It takes longer to finish that way, but for me it's effective. It was a delightful way to approach the manuscript—a truly inspirational message!"

—William Colbert, city attorney
Sanford, Oviedo, and Webster, Florida

"How should Christians live in a polarized world that doesn't seem to value a faith perspective? How should we navigate relationships with other believers when their perspectives differ from our own? Al Erisman and Randy Pope address these questions by turning to well-known characters from Scripture who model ways that Christians can engage in our own cultural moment. Applying these lessons to their own relationship, they demonstrate what it means to navigate difficult issues without alienating others. I can think of few people I trust as much as Al and Randy to provide guidance for whole-life discipleship."

—Denise Daniels, Hudson T. Harrison Professor
of Entrepreneurship, Wheaton College
Co-author of *Working in the Presence of God:*
Spiritual Practices for Everyday Work

"*Living with Purpose in a Polarizing World* is truly an extraordinary exploration of practical life lessons from twelve biblical characters who lived and worked creatively and redemptively in varied challenging, conflicted, sometimes even hostile environments. Christians will be inspired and encouraged over and over. Non-Christian readers will be introduced to a way of life, biblical teaching, and Christian faith far different from the deformations and stereotypes in today's culture and its media. This book is truly gospel—good news—that deserves to be read, studied, and gifted to as wide an audience as possible in our polarizing, often deteriorating, world."

—David W. Gill, president, International Jacques Ellul Society
Professor (retired), Gordon-Conwell Theological Seminary and North
Park University, Author of *Workplace Discipleship 101: A Primer*

"I was encouraged by the practical, scriptural advice on how we are walk with God in an increasingly post-Christian world. I was challenged by their call to seek the world's good and to cooperate with God in his work of redemption and restoration. They encourage readers to follow Jesus in every aspect of our lives, which they call 'whole-life discipleship.' In whole-life discipleship, work assignments are not incidental to our faithful walk but integral to it. Equally intriguing is the realization that Al and Randy lived out their call for respectful, humble engagement as they collaborated in writing this book. Well done!"

—Scott Griffin, VP, Information Technology, Boeing (retired)
Former moderator, Evangelical Presbyterian Church

"A huge contribution toward making society a little more civilized than it is at present, representing the potential even to reverse the current tendency toward barbarism. An inspirational and practical guide arising from an examination of concrete examples taken from the Bible of notable individuals who also lived in a polarizing culture. Transformatively useful at a personal level for Christians, I am sure, but also for non-Christians like me who are happy to learn and not merely be prepared to scoff."

—Prabhu Guptara, distinguished professor
Global Business, Management and Public Policy, India
Publisher, Salt Desert Media, Cambridge, UK

"*Living with Purpose in a Polarizing World* is a terrific book that is both timely and eternal. The authors initially provide some helpful summary insights, analysis, and suggestions. They then proceed in the following chapters to examine the lives of twelve biblical characters. This structure allows them to illuminate the points initially made and, more importantly to me, facilitate readers to discover applications to their own circumstances from the lives of these heroes of the faith. I recommend this book to all who desire to live a life of love and purpose in these challenging times."

—Scott Hardman, chair, Alexander Hutton

"Analyzing the lives of twelve biblical figures, Al Erisman and Randy Pope explore what it means to walk faithfully in a polarized culture. Rejecting both withdrawal and assimilation, they call readers to seek truth, build trust, and engage honestly. I recommend the book to anyone trying to live biblically in these challenging times."

—Alec Hill, president emeritus, InterVarsity Christian Fellowship USA

"This book offers a potent and timely invitation for believers to engage with conviction and grace in our ever-evolving society. With its deep insights and steadfast adherence to enduring truths, this book serves as an indispensable beacon, guiding readers through the complexities of modern faith with the wisdom of biblical narratives and the unswerving light of gospel truth."

—Baolerhu Ligden, founder and executive director
Asia Leadership Development Network

"Erisman and Pope address one of the great challenges of our day in which the global family of nations is multi-polar and the common experience in the American setting is the multiplication of polarizing issues. The challenge for Christians is how to live with purpose is such a world. There is no better place to turn for guidance than the biblical characters embedded in non-Western and ancient cultures to gain guidance for today. The authors have mined for wisdom and uncovered gems for those of us seeking to walk faithfully and purposely in our challenging Euro-American worlds."

—Bill Lowrey, director of peacemaking (retired)
World Vision International

"*Living with Purpose in a Polarizing World* is a prophetic word manifested in the biblical narratives of the great men and women of the Scriptures. It challenges readers to look deeply into the present through the eyes of those who have gone before and the deep dive of the authors' intensity to seek truth within the reality of our very present culture. Each of the narratives present readers with thought-provoking analysis and interpretations in order to navigate the polarizing world we live in while partnering with God to spur one another on toward love and good work."

—Nancy Alderson McDonnell, president and CEO
Value of the Person Consultants

"For over fifty years, I have lived and worked in Mississippi encouraging the Christian community to work across socioeconomic as well as racial barriers. My prayer is that all who read this book would begin to see themselves as Christians first with a mission to invite others to give their lives to Christ and be reconciled to him and to one another. Sometimes, we need to learn how to agree to disagree without becoming enemies. I encourage Christians to read this book and dare to declare, 'If God can love them, why can't I?'"

—Dolphus Weary, founder, Mission Mississippi
and R.E.A.L. Christian Foundation

"Many Christians today seem to be overwhelmed by the cultural chaos in which we live, and the putative paths forward urged on us by many pundits often seem at odds with how Jesus lived and ministered with both truth and compassion in a culture that was often hostile. Al Erisman and Randy Pope's wonderful new book is an important contribution to the conversation about how Christians can be salt and light today. Looking to Scripture, they show us characters who were not just in a 'religious corner' but were men and women seeking to follow God wholeheartedly within the context of careers and families, navigating their culture, making difficult choices, and representing God to those around them in a way that models both righteousness and love. Timely, insightful, and practical!"

—Brian McGreevy, assistant to the rector
St. Philip's Church, Charleston, South Carolina

"Al and Randy have written an important and timely book for Christians who want a biblical approach to be salt and light in the divisive times we live in. And what better way to do this than by looking at the lives of men and women in the Bible who lived through similar times and drawing on the timeless spiritual lessons they teach us."

—The Honorable Edmund C. Moy, former White House staff
and director of the United States Mint (2006–2011)

"Al Erisman and Randy Pope have hit it out of the park with *Living in a Polarizing World*. Christians wrestle mightily, and often hopelessly, with the growing gap between a Christian worldview and life in contemporary culture. Just like the early church, which found favor in a pre-Christian society, today's church must learn to earn favor in a largely post-Christian society. Erisman and Pope use biblical examples in history as well as current conditions and opportunities to point the church toward constructive engagement. Rather than believing we are compelled toward the Right or the Left in culture, we can move toward the centrality of Christ by serving society as 'salt and light'—as endearing personalities and enlightening contributors. The church can do much better than resignation and assimilation, withdrawal and retrenchment, fear, power seeking, or anger! I heartily recommend this book as a practical primer for shifting the spiritual climate and accelerating the kingdom's advancement."

—Chuck Proudfit, president, At Work on Purpose

"I've written a lot about working in 'exile' and the challenges that believers face in this post-Christian world and how it can be tempting to either assimilate or isolate into Christian bubbles. But in *Living with Purpose in a Polarizing World*, the authors give us a different path forward. By examining the lives of people from Scripture who were in secular occupations but were able to work *with* God to bring about redemption in their situations, they show how it is through our work that we have opportunities to represent Christ to those around us. This is an important work and one I will be returning to as a guide to navigating today's world in a way that ultimately points people to Jesus."

—Jordan Raynor, bestselling author of *The Sacredness of Secular Work* and *Redeeming Your Time*

"Too often the church has been classified as a volunteer organization, but in showing us a path forward in conflict-filled times, Al and Randy help us understand that we are those who have been given assignments by God to live faithfully where we have been placed intentionally. This is not another analysis of how we got here but a guide for moving forward."

—Fred Smith, founder, The Gathering

"If ever there were a book for today, this is it! Al Erisman and Randy Pope have crafted a vitally relevant book on how to live in a post-Christian world. They do this by weaving together several stories of people in the Old and New Testaments who faced similar situations. Its wise reflections at the end can help us to navigate the cultural, moral, and spiritual ambiguities we face daily. Richly researched, this book is a gold mine for people struggling to be authentic Christians in a secularized business, not-for-profit, or even a hostile culture. A gift!"

—R. Paul Stevens, president and chair, Institute for Marketplace Transformation Professor emeritus, Marketplace Theology, Regent College

"Christians need help navigating the complexities of living, serving, and working faithfully in our fragmenting world. Some pundits claim to know the best way to engage our changing culture: assimilate, retreat, fight, or leverage power. Erisman and Pope describe a better path—a life of faithful service that cooperates with God's heart and ambitions for the world. Drawing on their long-term friendship, their love of the Bible and the people who populate its pages, and their seasoned marketplace experience, they are trusted guides to help us navigate the complexities of a polarizing world."

—John Terrill, executive director, Upper House and the Stephen & Laurel Brown Foundation

"We are not alone! This treasured book reveals a crystal-clear picture of how those from biblical times faced many of the conundrums we wrestle with today. Who knew? I was literally in tears thinking, *This is me!* How did Al and Randy know what I am struggling with today in my workplace, in my community, at church and home? The authors have provided a pathway for me to get into the word of God and consider it from a totally new perspective so that I can live faithfully in the world knowing that 'if we truly believe the other person is made in the image of God, then we should try.'"

—Julia Underwood, distinguished professor, dean and accreditation liaison officer, California Institute of Advanced Management

"We are hard-wired to seek a life of meaning and purpose, but the blueprints of that pathway to purpose are very blurry. In the introduction of *Living with Purpose*, the authors cite Hebrews 12:1–2. These are special Bible verses for me because I 'randomly' heard them twice the day after my whistleblowing role at Enron was announced by the US Congress. Those verses state that we have a race marked out for us and that we have a spiritual cheering squad as we run that race, *but* we must remain focused on the things that matter and discard the burdensome distractions that hinder our race. Erisman and Pope provide excellent commentary and analysis of twelve biblical characters who ran a successful race despite challenging and sometimes harrowing distractions. Our polarized world is a distraction from our purpose, and the biblical life stories examined by the authors provide not only encouragement to us but also a clearer blueprint to living out our chosen purpose."

—Sherron Watkins, Enron whistleblower, *Time* Person of the Year

"Johann Bengel, the great eighteenth-century biblical scholar, once wrote: 'Apply yourself wholly to the text, apply the text wholly to yourself.' The authors fully embraced this framework as their guiding principle. The book is thoughtful, insightful, and filled with profound reflections and practical wisdom that are relevant and applicable to our cultural context. By deeply engaging the stories of well-known biblical characters, the book challenges us with the complexity of the human condition and how this manifests itself in leaders throughout history. It also encourages us with stories of genuine transformation for those whose hearts, souls, minds, and strength are formed by their relationship to God."

—Don Flow, chair and CEO, Flow Automotive Companies

"In a world marked by polarization and pain, Al and Randy have gifted us with an insightful look into the successes and failures of a dozen key men and women in the Bible. Building on the work of others who have wrestled with how Christians should respond to a post-Christian culture, they powerfully demonstrate that the common paths of resignation, withdrawal, fear, power-seeking, and anger are fruitless. Instead, this book provides wise counsel that will not only heal the divisions of the church but of the world, if we are willing to listen and follow it."

—Mark Washington, national director, MBA Ministry, InterVarsity Christian Fellowship/USA

Living with Purpose
in a Polarizing World

Living with Purpose in a Polarizing World

Guidance from Biblical Narratives

ALBERT M. ERISMAN
& RANDY POPE

HENDRICKSON PUBLISHERS · THEOLOGY OF WORK · PROJECT

Living with Purpose in a Polarizing World: Guidance from Biblical Narratives

Published by Hendrickson Publishers
Hendrickson Publishers, LLC
P. O. Box 3473
Peabody, Massachusetts 01961-3473
www.hendricksonpublishers.com

ISBN 978-1-4964-8715-5

Cover photo by Galvna Andrushko via Adobe Stock Photo.

Printed in the United States of America

First Printing — June 2024

Let this mind be in you that was also in Christ Jesus.

(Phil. 2:5 KJV)

Contents

A Tale of Two Gardens

By Malcolm Guite

God gave us all a garden once
And walked with us at eve
That we might know him face to face
With no need to believe.

But we denied and hid from him
Concealing our own shame
Yet he still came to look for us
And call us each by name.

He found us where we hid from him
He clothed us in his grace
But still we turned our backs on him
And would not see his face.

So now he comes to us again
Not as a Lord most high
But weak and helpless as we are
That we might hear him cry.

And he who clothed us in our need
Lies naked in the straw
That we might wrap him in our rags
Whom once we fled in awe.

The strongest comes in weakness now
A stranger to our door
The king forsakes his palaces
And dwells amongst the poor.

And where we hurt he hurts with us
And when we weep he cries
He knows the heart of all our hurts
The inside of our sighs.

He does not look down from above
But gazes up at us
That we might take him in our arms
Who always cradles us.

And if we welcome him again
With open hands and heart
He'll plant his garden deep in us
The end from which we start.

And in that garden there's a tomb
Whose stone is rolled away
Where we and all we've ever loved
Were lowered in the clay.

But Lo! the tomb is empty now
And, clothed in living light,
His ransomed people walk with One
Who came on Christmas night.

So come Lord Jesus, find in me
The child you came to save
Stoop tenderly with wounded hands
And lift me from my grave.

Be with us all Emmanuel
And keep us close and true
Be with us till that Kingdom comes
Where we will be with you.

Introduction

We keep on assuming that we know the play. We do not know the play. We do not even know whether we are in Act I or Act V. We do not know who are the major and who the minor characters are. The Author knows. . . . But we, never seeing the play from outside, never meeting any characters except the tiny minority who are "on" in the same scenes as ourselves, wholly ignorant of the future and very imperfectly informed about the past, cannot tell at what moment the [Second Coming of Christ] will come. That it will come when it ought, we may be sure; but we waste our time in guessing when that will be. . . . We are led to expect that the Author will have something to say to each of us on the part that each of us has played. The playing it well is what matters infinitely.

— C. S. Lewis, "The World's Last Night"

Recently, a friend of Al's at church offered this perspective on living as a Christian in an increasingly secular culture: "It is really hard to be a Christian business leader in America today. Our world is rapidly becoming anti-Christian. It is increasingly difficult to even admit you are a Christian let alone share anything about your faith in this post-Christian world."

Although the Seattle area, where Al attends church, and Hattiesburg, Mississippi, where Randy attends church, are culturally very different from each other, the sentiments that Al's friend shared with him are felt by many Christians in south Mississippi as well. Paul Williams makes this point in his recent book *Exiles on Mission: How Christians Can Thrive in a Post-Christian World*:

Culture is now not simply increasingly pagan but is pagan with an anti-Christian flavor. Christianity is typically derided as the enemy of free thought and rational science by secular critics like Richard Dawkins but is at the same time blamed for its part in the rise of modern science and the market economy by advocates of the environmental movement. Christians who work for justice in the social arena can easily be critiqued by those who fear a renewed attempt at a Christian theocracy or those who recall the previous entanglement of missions with colonialism. Tainting everything is the ongoing scandal of institutional child sexual abuse.[1]

In other words, the feeling of Christians that they are "under siege" by the dominant secular culture has some basis in fact and is compounded by Christians' own bad behavior.

In our time today, Christians lack a plan for how to respond to a culture that has dramatically changed. As Randy talked about the book he and Al were writing, his friend commented that "Christians are absolutely clueless about how to respond to the end of Christendom."

This feeling of exile has not only led Christians to be confused about how they should respond to the general culture, but it has also led to Christians arguing among themselves about how they should live in the culture as it exists today. This division may also be a factor in the decline of Christian witness to the world, since Jesus said,

"My prayer is not for them alone. I pray also for those who will believe in me through their message, that all of them may be one, Father, just as you are in me and I am in you. May they also be in us so that the world may believe that you have sent me." (John 17:20–21)

Before we respond as victims of our circumstances, we need to remember three things.

First, though we believe there were many good things that "Christendom" brought to our general culture, we must look honestly at both the good and the bad in our history as Christians rather than seeing life in Christendom through rose-colored glasses. We sometimes tend to sugarcoat the past, remembering the good things and missing the darker side. Ecclesiastes reminds us, "Do not say, 'Why were the old days better than these?' For it is not wise to ask such questions" (Eccles. 7:10). John Perkins, an esteemed African American leader and author, brought this to his audience's attention in his sermon at Westminster Chapel in Washington in the early 1990s: "Some of you might wish you were back in the 1950s when life was simpler. Not me. I would be in the back of the bus." Many of our Christian brothers and sisters have experienced hardship in society for a long time.

Second, in many places in the world today, Christians are killed for their faith. *Christianity Today* identified the top fifty countries in the world where persecution is worst.[2] No country in the West made the list. Even as we recognize Western culture in general is becoming increasingly suspicious of—and even hostile toward—Christians, we still can practice our faith without fear of physical persecution and, as Hebrews 11 tells us, that has not always been the case:

> There were others who were tortured, refusing to be released so that they might gain an even better resurrection. Some faced jeers and flogging, and even chains and imprisonment. They were put to death by stoning; they were sawed in two; they were killed by the sword. They went about in sheepskins and goatskins, destitute, persecuted and mistreated—the world was not worthy of them. They wandered in deserts and mountains, living in caves and in holes in the ground. (Heb. 11:35b–38)

Our challenges look quite mild compared to others in the world or those from biblical times.

Finally, it is crucial that we acknowledge God's sovereignty in placing us here in the twenty-first century. God has deliberately placed us in our current time and place, and we need to faithfully carry out the assignments he has given us.

Early in J. R. R. Tolkien's *The Lord of the Rings*, Gandalf tells Frodo Baggins the story of the One Ring and Sauron's plans to recover it. When Frodo complains, "I wish it need not have happened in my time," Gandalf responds, "So do I, and so do all who live to see such times. But that is not for them to decide. All we have to decide is what to do with the time that is given us."[3] So it is with us as well.

Where, then, do we find the path forward in this new world? Job was correct when he said, "No bird of prey knows that hidden path, no falcon's eye has seen it. Proud beasts do not set foot on it, and no lion prowls there" (28:7–8). It won't be a path of our own invention. In Isaiah 55:8–9, we are reminded, " 'For my thoughts are not your thoughts, neither are your ways my ways,' declares the LORD. 'As the heavens are higher than the earth, so are my ways higher than your ways and my thoughts than your thoughts.' "

But we can gain glimpses of the path by examining the lives of biblical characters who walked before us. Many of the biblical narratives portray a path of walking with God in cultures that were at best indifferent or, more often, hostile to the worship and values of God. Although these characters lived in different cultures and in different times in history, they all sought to demonstrate a "faithful presence," as James Davison Hunter calls it.[4]

———

How do we walk with God in an increasingly post-Christian world? There are many ways to respond to this challenge, but in recent years we have seen five major responses.

Resignation and Assimilation

In this view, we are to simply accept the changes in the culture and, as Ross Douthat writes, "reconcile [ourselves] to the new dispensation, accepting that the 'modern age is not a sacral, but a secular age,' that the state can no longer be treated 'as the secular arm of the spiritual power,' that the 'freedom of individual conscience' is one of the 'crucial assets' of our civilization, and place [our] hope in the church's liberty, its opportunity to act as 'spiritual leaven.' "[5] This is similar to H. Richard Niebuhr's "Christ of Culture," which "identifies changes in contemporary society *with* the advancement of the kingdom of God."[6]

One version of resignation and assimilation is what has been termed "moralistic therapeutic deism," which seems, at best, "Christianity Lite": God exists and created the world and cares about it, he wants people to be "nice" and "fair" to other people, the central goal of life is to be happy and feel good about ourselves, God is not particularly involved in our lives except when he is needed to resolve a problem, and "good people go to heaven when they die."[7]

Withdrawal and Retrenchment

Another strategy has been to hunker down in a community of like-minded believers and create a parallel *polis*—a "separate but porous" Christian culture existing alongside the dominant culture, particularly focusing on education and the development of virtue.[8] This strategy is perhaps most prominently represented by conservative writer and blogger Rod Dreher in his book *The Benedict Option: A Strategy for Christians in a Post-Christian Age.* Other Christians with this thinking attempt to "hold on to the historic mind-set of Christendom . . . or simply to continue doing what we've been doing without any reference to the significantly changed cultural context of Western societies."[9]

Fear

Our world is caught up in fear, and Christians are not immune to this. A recent Barna study of younger Christians states,

> Young adults today are, well, a little tense. *Anxiety about important decisions, uncertainty about the future and fear of failure are among respondents' most commonly reported emotions.* These worries are often tied up in vocation, relationship status or financial means—all things that tend to be unsettled for this age group. Near-constant connection to and emotional investment in what's going on around the world is a defining trait of my generation, but more personal, supportive connections aren't quite so common; *only one in three young adults feels someone deeply cares for or believes in them.*[10]

Of course, fear is not limited to younger Christians. We don't need to have many conversations before we see it evidenced in older Christians as well.

Seeking Power

For those of us who have the opportunity to elect our government officials, we should engage in that process seeking those who best support our values. There are several words of caution here. Not all Christians agree on the best way to embody these values in the laws and regulations of the land. In the United States, for example, there are Christians on both sides of the reversal of *Roe v. Wade* and Christians on both sides of the push for more "green" energy.

Beyond these differences, James Davison Hunter made clear the limits of legislation more than a decade ago. Just because the legislature passes a law or the Supreme Court makes a ruling, that does not in and of itself change the culture:

At best, the state's role addressing human problems is partial and limited. It is not nearly as influential as the expectations most people have of it. It is true that laws are not neutral. They do reflect values. But laws cannot generate values, or instill values, or settle the conflict over values. The belief that the state could help us care more for the poor and the elderly, slow the disintegration of traditional values, generate respect among different groups, or create civic pride, is mostly illusory. It imputes far too much capacity to the state and to the political process.[11]

John Stott,[12] the noteworthy late theologian and pastor, commented on power in a lecture he gave in 2000: "I'm scared of the contemporary Evangelical hunger for power. Even the quest for the power of the Holy Spirit. Be honest. Why do we want power? . . . Is it really a mask for personal ambition? . . . To dominate. To manipulate."[13]

Anger

A fifth strategy might be called—with apologies to H. Richard Niebuhr—"Christ against culture *on steroids*." This approach sees the dominant culture as one that is altogether without redeeming value and should therefore be *actively opposed* rather than simply engaged. Often using military images as it makes its case, this strategy argues that to try to appeal to the dominant culture through a "gentle," "loving," or "winsome" attitude is a waste of time. These Christians argue that the church should be "on offense" rather than "on defense" when it comes to dealing with the dominant culture.

When we see white Christian nationalists screaming in the face of authority on the nightly news, we know that posture does not represent Christian behavior. When we see left-leaning Christians angrily demanding their position in the argument, we know that posture does not represent Christian behavior. And yet, these conflicts are often the way Christianity is perceived by the watching world.

Another Way

There is, however, another approach that doesn't get as much attention as the other five. It's a strategy that, to paraphrase G. K. Chesterton, has not been tried and found wanting but rather has not often been tried because it seems to be more difficult than the others: Dedicating our lives to seeking the world's good and *cooperating with God* in the work of redemption and restoration that he is doing. Using Jeremiah 29:7—"Seek the peace and prosperity of the city to which I have carried you into exile. Pray to the Lord for it, because if it prospers, you too will prosper"—this strategy seeks to "partner" with God in the work he is already doing across every aspect of society. In Micah 6:7–8, God gives us a summary of what faithful living looked like then and still looks like now: "What does the Lord require of you, but to seek justice, love mercy, and walk humbly with your God."

Jeremiah wrote to Jewish exiles who had been taken into captivity in Babylon, a nation that had destroyed Jerusalem, brutally killed many Jews, and carried "the best and brightest" into exile. No doubt these survivors missed their homeland and longed to return. Apparently "some of these refugees believed that their stay in Babylon would be short-lived,"[14] and some false prophets were encouraging this way of thinking. Jeremiah's message to these exiles must have been shockingly counterintuitive. Nevertheless, seeking the peace and prosperity of Babylon and praying for it were God's instructions to them through Jeremiah, and we believe we can learn from these instructions: that our own well-being is tied to the well-being of the cities and countries we live in.

Although Micah wrote before the exile of the Jews from both Israel and Judah, he wrote in the context of a society in which "leaders . . . used their positions of power and privilege to take advantage of the poor, mislead the people, compromise God's Word, and persecute the prophets."[15] God, speaking through Micah, offered a summary of the specific behaviors that could be said to spell out what it means to "seek the peace and prosperity of the city"—regardless of where that city is and how we may feel toward its citizens or and leaders: "seek justice, love mercy, walk humbly with God." We believe that summary applies to Christians wherever we may live, regardless of whether the city we live in is predominantly "conservative" or "liberal," highly educated or educationally struggling, rich or poor, ethnically diverse or largely of one ethnicity.

As we consider these things, we might ask the question: Have we ever been promised, as followers of Jesus, a simple path in a supportive culture? If we look at Scripture, we see that those who walked with God have always faced opposition to one degree or another. None of them was promised an easy path, and much of biblical instruction is there to help us navigate these waters—not in a way that protects us from all harm, but in a way that represents our faith before a watching world.

Jesus said, "You are the salt of the earth. You are the light of the world. Let your light so shine before others that they may see your good deeds and glorify your father who is in heaven" (Matt. 5:13–16). To do this, we must first acknowledge the truth of the brokenness of the world and the brokenness within ourselves. We are in an increasingly secular world, one that is even growing in its hostility toward our faith. We can't ignore the reality of our times, but we also can't give in to that reality or seek to stamp it out through utilizing paths to power as the world defines power. Neither can we believe we are able to put it all right in this life. As Steve Garber reminds us, "We should seek to live proximately"[16]—that is, making a difference where we can in a broken world. We can't fix everything now, but we can make a difference.

All of this calls us to a new kind of respectful, humble engagement with our culture, including our engagement with those in our workplaces as well as our engagement with other Christians. None of this should be taken as a statement that we should never leave the position we're in or even that we should never move to another city. There are a multitude of reasons to do these things, and we need to seek God's wisdom in these choices. Sometimes a family situation may call us to move out of danger, as Mary and Joseph were called to take Jesus to Egypt with the threat from Herod (see Matt. 2). Yet the desire to leave a difficult situation simply for our own personal peace and affluence should not go unexamined. Jesus said, "In this world you will have trouble. But take heart! I have overcome the world" (John 16:33).

What does it look like to live faithfully where God has placed us? We will look for guidance and inspiration from those who have walked faithfully with God throughout the stories that flood the Scriptures.

———

Both of us love stories, and as children, we were taught Bible stories as a part of our experience growing up in church: David and Goliath, Daniel in the lion's den, Jonah and the great fish, and so on. But as we became adults, we began to study the *stories themselves* from either the Old Testament or the New Testament.[17] We began to think about how the different characters in those stories learned to live as people who followed God in cultures that were at best indifferent to God or, at worst, hostile to God and his people. As N. T. Wright reminds us,

The Bible tells a multitude of stories, but in its final form it tells an overarching story, a single great narrative, which offers itself as the true story of the world. This is so, incidentally, whether you take the Jewish form of the Bible, what Christians call the Old Testament, or the Christian form, including both testaments.[18]

We recognize that great care must be taken not to project our assumptions of what is culturally "appropriate" onto a culture separated in time—and geography—by a great distance. Nevertheless, we subscribe to the principle set out by Paul to Timothy: "Every part of Scripture is God-breathed and useful one way or another—showing us truth, exposing our rebellion, correcting our mistakes, training us to live God's way. Through the Word we are put together and shaped up for the tasks God has for us." (2 Tim. 3:16–17 MSG). We can watch, taking notes as it were, how men and women in the Bible followed God in the culture *they* lived in, and then try to carefully and honestly *apply* what they learned to our lives as we attempt to follow Jesus in *our* culture.

Scripture itself offers an important point about the use of the stories it contains. Immediately following the descriptions of faith in Hebrews 11, chapter 12 opens:

> Therefore, since we are surrounded by such a great cloud of witnesses, let us throw off everything that hinders and the sin that so easily entangles. And let us run with perseverance the race marked out for us, fixing our eyes on Jesus, the pioneer and perfecter of faith. For the joy set before him he endured the cross, scorning its shame, and sat down at the right hand of the throne of God.
> (Heb. 12:1–2)

In a very real sense, this is the theme of this book. We have been given an assignment (the race marked out for us) that we are to carry out with perseverance just as others did whose stories are a part of the biblical record (the great cloud of witnesses). To do this, we need to set aside those things that hinder us and keep our eyes on the race course so that we can carry out this work in the power of Jesus. He not only gives us the power to do this, but he also models this life of focus and perseverance.

We are not promised an easy path. Jesus said, "I have told you these things, so that in me you may have peace. In this world you will have trouble. But take heart! I have overcome the world" (John 16:33).

We therefore need to look for guidance in our challenging situations from those we find in Scripture. We will look at those who were highly educated leaders in government and business, such as Moses and Daniel, and we will also look at those with far less formal education who started at the bottom—like Joseph as a slave and a prisoner, Ruth as an immigrant doing manual labor, and Esther as a member of a harem who becomes queen to a Persian king. We will also examine warriors like Joshua and government leaders like David, farmers like Job, and tradesmen and entrepreneurs like Abraham. In addition, we will consider the New Testament stories of Paul, the educator and tent maker, and Peter the fisherman. And, of course, Jesus, the cultural navigator par excellence.

For them, as for us, the primary test came in the marketplace where they were part of the broader cultural mix. They each had different professions, lived at different times and in different cultural contexts, and they each experienced different levels of hostility from their dominant cultures. Their challenges came not only from outside but also from within their faith communities. In each case, their work was integral to their stories. Many of their conflicts and challenges played out in their places of work where they interacted with the broader society. Except for Jesus, none of them were perfect, so we can learn from their failures as well as their triumphs.

Our goal is not to say everything that could be said about these people. Whole books have already been written about most of them. Rather, we want to focus on the ways they navigated their culture, made choices, and represented God to those around them. As we do so, we will see themes emerge. Broadly, those themes represent what Micah said about seeking justice, loving mercy, and walking humbly before God. They represent what Jeremiah said about seeking the good of the city. And they represent what Jesus said about being salt and light in our world. They come to places where they might have been tempted to assimilate with culture, to withdraw, to seek power, or to be angry, but they chose to seek another way.

In the conclusion, we will pull together the lessons we learned. And in the afterword, we will acknowledge a bit of the tension we experienced in writing this because of our vastly different backgrounds. We intentionally used "polarizing" rather than "polarized" in the title and often in the text, recognizing that the issues that divide us will change, but the guidance for dealing with the issues will remain.

Somewhere among the examples, each of us can identify with circumstances, learn from choices, and gain courage and hope for our own paths.

Together—because the Christian life is not a solo flight—we can "spur each other on toward love and good works" (Heb. 10:24).

———

In the introduction to *Reflections on the Psalms*, C. S. Lewis, professionally a tutor in Medieval and Renaissance Literature at the University of Oxford, said that he decided to write as "one amateur to another . . . about difficulties [he] had met, or lights [he] had gained, when reading the Psalms, with the hope that this might at any rate interest, and sometimes even help, other inexpert readers."[19] Lewis's decision to write on the Psalms as an "amateur" resonates with us: Al is a mathematician and Randy is a lawyer. We are not pastors, missionaries, or seminary-trained theologians. Al worked as a researcher and R&D director of a large company and then as a university faculty member. Before becoming city attorney in 2017, Randy practiced law for almost forty years, drafting wills and contracts, closing real estate transactions, advising individual and corporate clients, and arguing cases before juries and judges.

As Lewis said in his *Reflections on the Psalms*, our goal in writing is not so much to instruct but to "compare notes"[20] with biblical characters who, in their "ordinary" lives, tried to walk faithfully with God in the cultures they lived in *as well as* men and women who seek to walk faithfully with God today in the post-Christian twenty-first century.

1 | Abraham

"Aslan," said Lucy, "you're bigger."
"That is because you are older, little one," answered he.
"Not because you are?"
"I am not. But every year you grow, you will find me bigger."

    — C. S. Lewis, *Prince Caspian*

Abraham's story begins at the end of Genesis 11, where we learn that he was the oldest son of a man named Terah who lived in a region located in modern-day Iraq. Abraham's story ends in Genesis 25 when he dies at the age of a hundred and seventy-five. Early in the story, we learn that he was married to a beautiful woman named Sarah who was unable to conceive and bear children. This was a crucial issue in a culture that saw children as not only providers and care-takers for elderly parents and the way to maintain the family's property, but also as the way the family "name" would be carried on after the parents' death, since in Abraham's time there was no widely held concept of resurrection as Christians know it today.

Terah's family, including Abraham, were probably moon worshipers, but Genesis 12 opens with God telling Abraham to leave his homeland, his people, and his father's household to go "to the land I will show you." Professionally, Abraham was what we might today call a "rancher." When God called him to leave his homeland, he took with him both property and people, including two people who become prominent in Abraham's story: his nephew, Lot, and his wife's maidservant, Hagar. He was wealthy when he left his homeland, and he eventually became even more wealthy "in livestock and in silver and gold" (Gen. 13:2).

—

If we have been followers of Jesus for a while, then we know that Abraham is the man who was willing to sacrifice his long-awaited son, Isaac, in obedience to God's command. Of course, every time we hear or read that part of the story, we breathe a sigh of relief when, at the last minute, a substitute—a ram caught in the thicket—is sacrificed instead. In the New Testament, Abraham is commended for his faith in God—and rightly so. But why is he such a pivotal character in this biblical story? To answer that, we need to understand the context into which he was born.

When God created humanity "in his image," he blessed Adam and Eve and then commanded them to "be fruitful and increase in number; fill the earth and subdue it" (Gen. 1:27–28). God repeated this blessing and mandate to Noah after the flood. But instead of filling the earth, Noah's descendants—all the people of the earth at that time, having "one language and a common speech"—apparently chose to settle in a relatively small area and build a city "with a tower that reaches to the heavens, *so that we can make a name for ourselves*; otherwise, we will be scattered over the face of the earth" (Gen. 11:1, 4; italics added). God, however, saw what was happening and concluded that if this is what the people had begun to do, then there was "no telling what they'll come up with next—they'll stop at nothing" (Gen. 11:6 MSG), and so he "confused their language" and made them unable to understand one another, and he then "scattered them from there over the earth, and they stopped building the city" (Gen. 11:5, 7–9).

What was the problem with the city the people were building that caused God to "confuse the language of the whole world" and "scatter them over the face of the earth" (Gen. 11:9)? According to scholars, at least part of the problem was their desire to "make a name for themselves." The idea of "making a name for ourselves" suggests that they wanted to remake themselves and their world through the use of ancient technology; this is, by building a tower that would reach into the heavens, thus "aspiring to transcend the limits of [humankind's] creaturely condition."[1] This is an ambition that certainly sounds familiar to us in the twenty-first century. Both of us see technology—which includes everything from plows and wheels to the printing press to automobiles and airplanes to the cell phones we hold in our hands—as part of the fulfillment of God's "creation mandate" to "take charge" (Gen. 1:28 MSG) of his creation as stewards or trustees, or, as Tolkien describes us, "sub-creators."[2] At the same time, there is the danger of deciding that with our tools we can be *more* than stewards of God's creation: we desire *sole ownership* of a creation that *we* design and build.

After God ends the Babel experiment, the narrator narrows the story's focus to a single family led by Terah who intended to take his family from Ur of the Chaldeans to the land of Canaan but instead "settled down" in Haran, a city several hundred miles to the northeast of Canaan. At this point in the biblical story, the creation project God began in the first few chapters of Genesis seems to be at a dead end: humanity has largely failed in their work as trustees of God's creation, God has to force them to scatter and fill the earth, people seem largely to have forgotten God and now worship creation itself like the moon, and Abraham's wife, Sarah, is unable to conceive, which is "an effective metaphor for hopelessness . . . no human power to invent a future."[3]

But beginning with the first few verses of Genesis 12, the story that seems to have ended in failure for everyone takes an unexpected turn: a "eucatastrophe," as Tolkien calls it, a "good catastrophe."[4] God, we learn, has *not* given up on his creation project, and he takes the initiative to begin a restoration project that will eventually encompass his entire creation. His vehicle for beginning this restoration will be a single individual—the moon-worshiping man with the wife who longs to be a mother: Abraham.

———

Given his family background, it seems unlikely that Abraham knew much, if anything, about God; but the text says that when God said to him "Go from your country, your people and your father's household to the land I will show you" (Gen. 12:1), Abraham does what God tells him. The text doesn't spend any time on *how* God spoke to Abraham or exactly *why* he obeyed God; it seems only interested in his response to God's call to leave the familiar and go somewhere that God will show him later.

In addition to the call to leave the familiar, God makes some promises to Abraham. First, God promises to make Abraham into a great nation and to "bless" him. What Abraham might have thought about this promise at this point, since the couple was childless, we're not told. Second, in contrast to what the Babel builders tried to do for themselves, God also promises that *he, God,* will "make your name great."[5]

Third, God promises to "bless those who bless you, and whoever curses you I will curse," and finally, he promises that "all the peoples of the earth will be blessed through you." Abraham's decision to leave much of his family and homeland behind and accept an assignment from a God he did not know very well (including the promise of being a blessing to others rather than making a name for himself) provides a model for us as we consider what our role is as Christians in the twenty-first century. Will we focus on making a name for ourselves—through technology or otherwise—or will we, like Abraham, choose to focus our energy on blessing not only those who agree with us but also those with whom we profoundly disagree?

Did Abraham even remotely understand what God had in mind for him? We're only told that he went "as the Lord had told him," but that was enough—for the present. Moving away from humanity's failed attempt for greatness at Babel, God is going to *educate* Abraham in an alternative way of life, and Abraham is *willing to learn from God.* As Leon Kass says, "God himself, as it were, will take Abraham by the hand, will serve as his tutor, and will educate him to be a new human being, one who will stand in right relation to his household, to other peoples, and to God."[6]

—

God "called" Abraham to go. Christians today sometimes use the word *called* to suggest some privileged status with God; and while there is truth in that, it is not the only—or even the main—point. God's call to us is, as it was to Abraham, primarily a call to serve. Abraham—and we—are called *for* something, for a task. We are given the same assignment as Abraham: to be a *blessing* to "all peoples on earth"—or more accurately, to be the *instrument of God's blessing* to all peoples.

Early in the story, Abraham and his family travel to Egypt during a severe famine. Just before they enter the country, Abraham tells Sarah to pretend she is his sister rather than his wife, "so that I will be treated well for your sake and my life will be spared because of you" (Gen. 12:10–13).[7] After they arrive, Sarah is taken into the Pharaoh's palace, apparently to be a part of his harem, but God intervened and "inflicted serious diseases on Pharaoh and his household," so Pharaoh tells Abraham to "take [Sarah] and go." In Genesis 20, Abraham repeats this attempt to pass Sarah off as his sister with a different king.

We should be careful about being quick to criticize Abraham's actions here as immoral and demonstrating a lack of trust in God. First, we know very little about the culture Abraham came out of, but it seems apparent that his culture had forgotten how Genesis 1 presents women: made in the image of God as much as men, and that marriage was, in its essence, a man "leaving his father and mother and [being] united to his wife" and becoming "one flesh" with her (Gen. 2:24). Again, we know little about these ancient cultures in Egypt (Gen. 12) and in Gerar (Gen. 20) other than that kings apparently had harems and Sarah would have become one of the king's concubines. As Christians in the twenty-first century, though, we have an advantage that Abraham did not have: we have the Scriptures, including Genesis 1 and 2, readily at hand. So it seems fair to ask ourselves how or when we have forgotten or devalued our marriage partner or sacrificed our family to get ahead in our business or profession? And when we have succumbed to that temptation, what does that say about *our* trust in God?

Second, Abraham was not only Sarah's husband, but he was also the head of a large family including his nephew, Lot, and many others in his "extended family" who traveled with him (Gen. 12:5). What would have happened to everyone else in Abraham's family if he were killed as he feared? While Sarah may not have appreciated being the "sacrificial lamb" in both cases, there is no indication that she refused to go along with Abraham's plan.[8]

Between these two incidents, Sarah becomes discouraged about God's promise to Abraham, and she says to him, "The Lord has kept me from having children. Go, sleep with my maidservant; perhaps I can build a family through her" (Gen. 16:2). Here was a different crisis of faith, and one in which Sarah and Abraham devise a plan to fulfill God's promises in their own way. We can understand their concern. Abraham was eighty-six years old at this time and Sarah was seventy-seven. If God's promises were to come about, perhaps they needed to step in and take control. Abraham agreed to his wife's plan, and the maidservant Hagar bore him a son named Ishmael. The jealousy and drama that follow are predictable.

It might be more reasonable to be critical of the plan Sarah and Abraham had for bearing a child. In this case, they were clearly getting ahead of God and not trusting him. But before we criticize, we should pause and remember how many times we have sought to get ahead of God. We know in our heads that God will accomplish his purposes, yet we often try to "help him" in ways that can be destructive. The result of Abraham and Sarah's choice was the development of a great nation through Ishmael, whose descendants would continuously be in conflict with the descendants of Abraham and Sarah's son, Isaac.

Nevertheless, despite the fact that Abraham tried to pass Sarah off as his sister and their joint decision to use Hagar to "help" fulfill God's promises to them, God did not give up on Abraham and Sarah, and they were still willing to learn from him.

—

When Abraham left his homeland behind, we read that "Lot went with him" (Gen. 12:4). We imagine that Abraham took his nephew under his wing after Lot's father died, and it may well be that Abraham speculated that eventually *Lot* would be his heir, given his and Sarah's inability to conceive a child of their own. Whatever the case, the text suggests that it was Lot's decision to go with Abraham since Abraham's father (and Lot's grandfather), Terah, and some of the rest of the family stayed behind in Haran.

Did Abraham share some of his wealth with Lot? Perhaps, though he may have inherited some from his own deceased father. In any event, we learn that "the land could not support them while they stayed together, for their possessions were so great that they were not able to stay together" (Gen. 13:6). When quarreling broke out between their herders, Abraham took the initiative to defuse the situation and, given that they were in potentially hostile territory, he offered to let Lot have the first choice of land on which to live and graze his flocks. Though he was the patriarch of the family and might reasonably have been expected to take the best land for himself, "he puts the peace between family before individual prosperity."[9] God still has work to do with Abraham in connection with his marriage and his hope for an heir, but Abraham is shown here as a generous person—one who wants the best for his family.

Sadly, it is not uncommon for families in the United States to become estranged over a parent's estate after that parent dies. In one case, three siblings asked Randy to serve as the executor of their deceased mother's estate. The will stated only that the mother's estate would be divided equally among the three children. Randy told the siblings that dividing cash or stocks was easy; all that was needed was a calculator. But when it came to dividing other personal property—furniture, plates, dishes, and books—he would agree to serve as executor on the condition that they agreed in writing that they would accept his decisions as to how their mother's property would be divided. From prior experiences with families and estates and from what he had observed about the siblings' interactions with one another in their initial interview, he suspected there might be problems.

They all agreed to his conditions in writing, and during the estate administration, they continually argued with one another about this item or that piece of furniture ("Mama promised that to me!"). How different the outcome would have been if one or more of the siblings had chosen to be generous and give up what might have been rightfully theirs in favor of one or more of their siblings.

No one (except perhaps Lot) would have thought badly of Abraham if he had taken the best land for himself; nevertheless, Abraham chose to disadvantage himself materially in order to bring about something more important. Are we willing to disadvantage ourselves—to put another person's interest ahead of our own—either to maintain peace in our family or in our workplace or business? We need, however, to be careful here: "maintaining peace" can be a reason for abuse, neglect, or injustice.

———

In Genesis 18, God and two companions arrive unannounced around noon at Abraham's tent, "in the heat of the day." Although at this point, Abraham didn't know who his visitors actually were, he jumped up and issued them an invitation to "wash your feet and rest under this tree. Let me get you something to eat, so you can be refreshed and then go on your way—now that you have come to your servant" (Gen. 18:3–5). They agreed to stay for lunch, and Abraham directed Sarah and a servant to prepare a meal. His titles for them—"my lord"—and himself—"your servant"—make it clear that the humility and grace he demonstrated in giving Lot the first choice of land was not an aberration and reflected his basic character. Abraham is "the consummate host . . . completely at their service."[10]

Hospitality to strangers was, and is, a deeply held cultural value in the Near East, and "hospitality and generosity are often underappreciated in Christian circles. Yet the Bible pictures the kingdom of heaven as a generous, even extravagant banquet."[11] Randy's wife, Kathy, who works as a volunteer with international students who come to study at the University of Southern Mississippi in Hattiesburg, reminds us that the vast majority of international students who come to study in the United States never visit the home of an American family while they are studying here. Inviting international students to a meal in our homes—particularly during holidays like Christmas and Thanksgiving when American students have gone home and the campus is relatively empty—is a great way to follow Abraham's example.

Another kind of hospitality, which includes generosity, is how we compensate those who serve us such as servers in restaurants. Do we generously tip a server who provides good service to us? When we stay in hotels, do we leave a generous tip for those who clean our rooms? Do we ever stop to think about who that person just might be? Jesus himself provides the answer: "Lord, when did we see you?" (Matt. 25:37).

———

After God tells Abraham and Sarah (who is eavesdropping) that Sarah will bear a son in the next year, two of the three visitors head for Sodom, and Abraham is left "standing before the Lord" (Gen. 18:22). As the three strangers walk in the direction of Sodom, we are privileged to hear God's "internal dialogue . . . in order to explain the true nature of the discussion that follows."[12]

> Then the Lord said, "Shall I hide from Abraham what I am about to do? Abraham will surely become a great and powerful nation, and all nations on earth will be blessed through him. For I have chosen him, so that he will direct his children and his household after him to keep the way of the Lord by *doing what is right and just*, so that the Lord will bring about for Abraham what he has promised." (Gen. 18:18–19)

When Randy was in law school almost fifty years ago, his law professors used what is called the "case method" to teach the law. Rather than lecture law students on what the law is, the students would, in preparation for each class, read a series of cases that dealt with a particular aspect of the law that would be covered in class that day, and they would have to be prepared to discuss the cases and the principle of law announced by the court in each case and how that applied to the facts of the particular case: in other words, they would "brief" the case.

The professor would then call on a student to "present" his or her "brief," and the professor would challenge the student to explain how the outcome of the case might be different if certain facts in the case were changed. This daily experience was, not surprisingly, nerve-wracking for law students (particularly in the first year) because no one knew who would be called on to present the case, nor exactly what questions the professor might ask—but woe to the student who was not prepared to discuss the case! This approach might seem harsh, but part of the reason for using this method was to prepare prospective lawyers to answer difficult questions "on their feet" that they would inevitably be asked by judges when presenting their cases to them. In the "case" involving what was taking place at Sodom, God implicitly invites Abraham to learn what is "right and just" through a dialogue about what he should do about Sodom.

In the discussion that follows, Abraham takes the initiative and does most of the talking, and he begins by raising a fundamental issue about justice: is it fair, is it just, that righteous people should suffer in the same way wicked people suffer? Abraham assumes the role of judge himself, challenging God to explain himself: "Will you really sweep [Sodom] away and not spare it for the sake of fifty righteous people in it? Will not the judge of the earth do right?" (Gen. 18:24). This simple question implies that Abraham believes God will, indeed, do the right thing even in a confusing and complex situation.

God certainly could have given Abraham a lecture on what "justice" is all about, but instead he lets him ask questions that are designed to reveal how God views justice in this particular situation.[13] It appears that one thing God is teaching Abraham through this "case method" is that there is often no simple answer to the question of what is fair and just in this or that situation, and that each case must be looked at "on its own merits." What we can be sure of is that God considers *all* the relevant information—as he did here—before deciding on a course of action.

Adjudication—determining what the facts are and what the outcome of the "case" should be—is not just for lawyers and judges. We must be careful not to jump to conclusions about people based on hearsay or incomplete information, whatever our profession.[14] Most of us read or see certain media that reinforce what we already think. It takes effort and care not to prejudge a person or a situation and also to recognize that there is often much more to the story than first appears.

———

God did, indeed, give Abraham and Sarah a son from their own bodies as he had promised. Abraham passed what must have been the hardest test of his life: he was willing to sacrifice that son, Isaac, in obedience to God's command (though God intervened at the last minute by providing a substitute ram). But what about the other promises God had made to Abraham, such as: "I will make you into a great nation. . . . I will make your name great, and you will be a blessing. . . . All peoples on earth will be blessed through you"? As he approached the end of his life, did Abraham wonder about these other—largely unfulfilled—promises God had made to him decades earlier?

The author of the book of Hebrews begins his eleventh chapter with a definition of faith: "confidence in what we hope for and assurance about what we do not see" (Heb. 11:1). After discussing three earlier men of faith, the author asks us to think about Abraham, who "when called to go to a place he would later receive as his inheritance, obeyed and went, even though he did not know where he was going. . . . And so from this one man . . . came descendants as numerous as the stars in the sky and as countless as the sand on the seashore" (Heb. 11:8, 12).

It strikes us—as it did the author of Hebrews—that Abraham was an outstanding example of living faithfully in the present while looking forward in hope to the future God had planned for him. We might say that Abraham had both a short-term view and a long-term view of his life, or that he lived successfully with the tension of the "now" and the "not yet." How about us?

———

Near the end of his life, Abraham needed a place to bury Sarah. He did not own any land, so he went to some Hittites living nearby and asked to buy property for a burial site. One Hittite, Ephron, offered to give it to Abraham, but Abraham insisted on paying him the full price for the property. Though the Hittites recognized that he was a prominent and wealthy person, and though it was customary in that culture for there to be bargaining over the price of property, Abraham did not exploit his position of prominence and insisted on paying for the property.

> Abraham's actions modeled core values of integrity, transparency, and business acumen. He honored his wife by mourning and properly caring for her remains. He understood his status in the land [as a "resident alien"] and treated its long-term residents with respect. He transacted business openly and honestly, doing so in front of witnesses. . . . He swiftly paid the agreed amount. He used the site only for the purpose he stated in the negotiations. He thus maintained good relations with everyone involved.[15]

Abraham seemed to recognize that the handling of money is a vital indicator of integrity. Many of the ethical issues we face stem from the proper use of money since money can become an idol for any of us. This is why Jesus said, "No one can serve two masters. Either you will hate the one and love the other, or you will be devoted to the one and despise the other. You cannot serve both God and money" (Matt. 6:24).

One of the main crops in south Mississippi is pine timber. Pine trees can take twenty or more years to mature depending on the species, so some people in their forties or fifties plant pine seedlings with the intention of harvesting them to help support themselves when they retire. An attorney friend told Randy the story of a man who, in addition to being a general building contractor, also bought and sold timber. His name was John Nelson.

One day, John heard that an elderly woman wanted to sell some timber from her land. John inquired as to what she wanted for the timber, and she told him. Having been in the timber business for many years, John knew that what she was willing to sell the timber for was far less than it was actually worth, and he told her that she needed to have an appraisal of the timber done and that he would pay the appraised value. Randy's attorney friend said that the only way he knew the details of this story is that he handled the closing (for the appraised value), and the elderly woman told him what had happened.

When Abraham left his homeland and much of his family behind, he knew little about the One who had called him to leave. As several commentators have suggested, it is as if Abraham enrolled in elementary school, and we watch as he learns and grows in his understanding of and trust in God. He was a man steeped in his *home culture*, but that was something that God could both work with (in, for example, his longing to be a father) and help him to change (in learning, for example, that a wife was more than someone to produce an heir).

Abraham chose to follow God, to study under him, *for a purpose*: to be blessed *and to bless*. Though our cultures and lives are very different from his, in the end, as followers of Jesus, we have the same call as Abraham—to be blessed and to bless. "Live in me," Jesus said. "Make your home in me just as I do in you. In the same way that a branch can't bear grapes by itself but only by being joined to the vine, you can't bear fruit unless you are joined with me. . . . You didn't choose me, remember; I chose you, and put you in the world to bear fruit, fruit that won't spoil" (John 15:4, 16 MSG).

Abraham lived a hundred and seventy-five years, and he "died at a good old age, an old man and full of years" (Gen. 25:7–8). "The Lord had blessed him in every way" (Gen. 24:1). He arranged the marriage of his son, Isaac, to Rebekah, the daughter of Abraham's brother, and at his death "left everything he owned to Isaac" (Gen. 25:5). While the most obvious meaning of "everything" is Abraham's physical wealth, his livestock, and other personal property, it also suggests that "everything" included an understanding of who God was and what God was capable of.

After Abraham died, Rebekah and Isaac faced the same issue that Abraham and Sarah had faced when they first set out from Ur of the Chaldeans: they were unable to conceive. In the case of Abraham and Sarah, there is no indication in the text that they asked God to provide them with a child. Why would they, since they had little to no knowledge of God prior to Abraham's call? And yet, the first thing we hear in the story of Isaac and Rebekah's barrenness is that Isaac "prayed to the Lord on behalf of his wife, because she was childless." And "the Lord answered his prayer, and his wife Rebekah became pregnant"—with twins! (Gen. 25:21, 24).

Isaac had watched his parents as they matured in their relationship with God, as God taught them what it meant to trust him and follow his direction. At the end of Abraham's life, it can be fairly said that Abraham was spiritually mature. Not "perfect," of course, but mature.[16]

What about us? Do we see our lives as a journey with God, a "walk with God," to use the Bible's language (See, e.g., Mic. 6:8; Ps. 119:1; John 8:12)?[17] Do we learn from the experiences he brings our way, being "educated" by him through those experiences, listening to him through his word and his Spirit, with the goal of becoming "fully mature in Christ" (Col. 1:28)? Will our children and grandchildren "build on" the foundation of trust in God that has developed in our lives? Are we willing, like Abraham and his descendants to not just be blessed, "carrying on as best we can till Jesus returns," but also to *be a blessing* to those we work, live, and "do life" with?

2 | Joseph

[God] sent a man before them—Joseph, sold as a slave. They bruised his feet with shackles, his neck was put in irons, till what he foretold came to pass, till the word of the Lord proved him true.

— Psalm 105:17–19

Joseph was thirty years old, and his life was in the pits, literally.[1]

It hadn't been easy growing up. His mother had died while giving birth to his younger brother, Benjamin. His father regarded him as the favorite of his twelve sons, even providing an ornamental coat for Joseph almost as a symbol of his superiority in the family, creating jealousy with his brothers. Then he had those dreams when he was seventeen years old, starting a series of events that led to his imprisonment in Egypt far from family and friends. It wasn't just his imprisonment that hurt, but the path that led up to that point as well.

He was sure his dreams had come from God: he would become a great leader and even his family would bow down to him. Perhaps he had been a bit self-centered when he eagerly told his brothers about these dreams, because it led to further antagonism with them. His father, Jacob, also reacted negatively but in the end was thoughtful about these dreams. Jacob, like his father Isaac and his grandfather Abraham, also had encounters with God, who promised a blessing to their families that would reach to the whole world. Perhaps he thought Joseph would be a fulfillment of those dreams. Let's give Joseph some grace here since he was only seventeen. But from our vantage point, he may have overestimated his own role and underestimated his own self-centeredness.

His brothers were so upset with his talk of them bowing down to him that they wanted to kill him. Older brother Judah, however, suggested they sell him to a group of traveling merchants who came by. They bought him and took him to Egypt where he became a slave in the house of Potiphar, a senior official to Pharaoh.

Things had been going as well as could be expected as a slave in Potiphar's house. Rather than spending time feeling sorry for himself, however, Joseph got to work. Potiphar soon recognized his talents, and it wasn't long before Joseph was made lord over all of the house where Joseph was able to make all of the key decisions. But then Potiphar's wife tried to seduce Joseph, and when he refused, she falsely accused him of being the instigator, and Joseph was sent to prison. We see two things about Joseph in this incident. His dual argument for resisting Potiphar's wife included not betraying Potiphar and not betraying God: "How could I do such a wicked thing and sin against God?" (Gen. 39:6). Potiphar, though, did not reciprocate the loyalty Joseph had shown to him. Joseph was likely in his early twenties at this point and seems to have been maturing rapidly from the time when he boasted of his dreams to his family.

Again, Joseph demonstrated his hard work ethic, and the head jailer noticed. Soon, Joseph had been assigned as the leader of the jail, responsible for all the other prisoners. Joseph may have thought he was only being rewarded for his good work, but we know "the Lord was with him; he showed him kindness and granted him favor in the eyes of the warden" (Gen. 39:21). We are certain this was not the leadership position Joseph had dreamed of having.

One day he noticed two new prisoners. Pharaoh's chief cupbearer and chief baker had been banished to the prison for some unknown fault, and they were placed under Joseph's supervision. They seemed discouraged, and Joseph noticed and asked them why they seemed so sad. Unlike Joseph at age seventeen, he was clearly aware of the feelings of others.

A similar situation is beautifully portrayed in Alexander Solzhenitsyn's novel *One Day in the Life of Ivan Denisovich*.[2] In 1945, Ivan is sentenced to hard labor under the brutal conditions of a Russian prison camp. In his assignment to build a wall, he suddenly sees a purpose and meaning for the work: "Now Shukov [Ivan] tackled the wall as if it were his own handiwork."[3] Teamed with a less capable fellow prisoner, Kilgas, he works hard to make sure neither of them are punished further, believing Kilgas would not survive on his own.

Like Ivan, Joseph wanted to hear the stories of his fellow prisoners in the midst of his pain. When Joseph heard the two prisoners had suffered distressing dreams, Joseph told them that only God could interpret dreams but that he would listen. He then interpreted the dreams, telling the chief cupbearer that he would be back with Pharaoh in three days but that the chief baker would be hanged in three days. The interpretation of both dreams was indeed fulfilled just as Joseph had said.

Before all this happened, though, Joseph asked the chief cupbearer for a favor: "When all goes well with you, remember me and show me kindness; mention me to Pharaoh and get me out of this prison. I was forcibly carried off from the land of the Hebrews, and even here I have done nothing to deserve being put in a dungeon" (Gen. 40:14–15).

Was there finally hope for Joseph now that he was twenty-eight years old? Sadly, not yet. The last verse of Genesis 40 says, "The chief cupbearer, however, did not remember Joseph; he forgot him." For the next two years, Joseph waited for someone to come and get him out of prison, but no one came. The first few weeks may have been filled with anticipation, but now, at age thirty, the situation seemed hopeless. We wonder if he was ready to settle in for the long term, realizing those early dreams of his would never come to fruition. His life was in the pits, literally.

For those of us in the polarizing world of the twenty-first century, we may look at Joseph and ask why he wasn't angry. He had deep challenges within his family as well as with a culture in Egypt that knew almost nothing about his God. Some in his situation might be tempted to give up and simply withdraw. Somehow, through it all, he seemed to maintain his trust in God and his promises. At this point, he didn't know how the story of his life would play out. We are reminded that for many people a story of challenge is all they see in this life. We wonder what would have happened to Joseph if he never had that next phase of his story in the same way today many are stuck in a difficult position from which they can never escape.

Reflecting on his approach may be helpful for us. For thirteen years, Joseph's life had been on a downward spiral, which included some mistakes he had made, yet he maintained his trust in God! We need to remember that we serve the same God that Joseph served. At least we can take consolation that someone else has gone through a similar level of antagonism and rejection.

In times of discouragement while Al was growing up, his mother would remind him to look around. Many did not have the advantages he had at that moment. It is easy and natural to find someone better off than we are for comparison with our own circumstances, but it takes intentionality to see that we are blessed even in the middle of difficult circumstances.

———

Doors began to open for Joseph after he turned thirty. Pharaoh had some troubling dreams that seemed important, but his wise men were unable to determine what they meant. As Pharaoh was discussing these dreams, the chief cupbearer suddenly remembered Joseph and said, "Today I am reminded of my shortcomings" (Gen. 41:9). He explained to Pharaoh how Joseph had interpreted his dream as well as the dream of the chief baker and that both interpretations proved true. He had meant to tell Pharaoh about Joseph but had forgotten. So Pharaoh called for Joseph.

What would Joseph do when he stood before the king of all Egypt? Would he put on his worst clothes and look downcast to attract sympathy? Would he bargain with Pharaoh to make sure he received the justice he was due? We might be tempted to take such a position, but he did not. Joseph cleaned up and changed his clothes, thereby showing respect to Pharaoh. He then gave credit to God, not himself, when he said, "I cannot do it, but God will give Pharaoh the answer to his dreams." He listens to Pharaoh and does not raise any complaint about his own situation. He then interprets both dreams (there were going to be seven years of plentiful harvest followed by seven years of famine) and develops a strategy for dealing with the coming famine that would be crucial for Egypt.

It is difficult to overestimate what Joseph did here. With all of Pharaoh's staff present, Joseph not only told Pharaoh the meaning but laid out a plan for what to do about it. He ran the risk of someone else leading the project while he went back to prison. Yet he did what he felt was right in spite of that personal risk.

Pete Fox had a senior position at a large software company and was determined to represent his faith in his work. Those around him were playing the political game of seeking personal advantage, while Pete tried to keep his eye on a higher goal of helping the company be successful. For example, when he believed the company would function better if a portion of a colleague's organization were a part of his, he went to his colleague first with the idea. Standard practice would have been to go to the boss and blindside the colleague. He tried in all circumstances to live transparently, seeking the best end result. "Especially as a Christian, I know that how I live, the legacy I leave, how I teach and lead others, these are the ways I will be judged one day. . . . But it is not easy."[4]

Joseph's actions here stand in significant contrast with the Joseph we met in Genesis 37, where his attention seemed to be focused on himself and not others.

In a day where many Christians feel sorry for themselves and demand their rights, Joseph shows us another way that is centered on respect, service, and influence. God told Abraham that he would be a blessing to the nations; Joseph gets the opportunity to become part of that promise by seeking to bring a blessing to his world and beyond. Jesus became the ultimate fulfillment of this promise.

Al lives in the Seattle area of Washington state, one of the most unchurched areas of the country. Changes in culture are dramatic there, as the people advocate for new forms of sexual identity, abortion, and lawlessness. The question is: What should be done about this? Some, for the sake of family, choose to leave to find a better environment for their families. Some, like Abraham and Joseph, are called to continue to live in witness to the gospel in the midst of the challenge.

The idea of living to bring a blessing to the place where you are is in fact happening in many places. In Seattle, Centered is an organization that gathers Christians on a weekly basis to spend time in the heart of the city praying for its welfare. Likewise, through their ministry, Urban Impact, Harvey Drake and Steve Bury are developing programs of racial justice and economic development in the inner city. Centered and Urban Impact illustrate what Joseph was doing in "seeking the good of the city."

—

Joseph laid out the meaning of Pharaoh's dreams and a strategy to deal with the coming famine. For the seven years of plentiful harvests, Joseph proposed taxing the harvest and storing it regionally. Then when the famine came, the food would be distributed and save the nation from disaster. Pharaoh took a bold step and not only put Joseph in charge of the whole project for the coming fourteen years, but he also expanded Joseph's job description: "You shall be in charge of my palace, and all my people are to submit to your orders. Only with respect to the throne will I be greater than you. I hereby put you in charge of the whole land of Egypt" (Gen. 41:40–41). And then

Pharoah rolled out the compensation package: chariots, a wardrobe, access to wealth, and even a new name (Zaphenathaoh) and a wife, Asenath. It also included instructions for the people of the land to say as Joseph approached, "Make way!" He was a true celebrity. And if this weren't enough, Pharaoh added, "I am Pharaoh, but without you no one will lift a hand or foot in all of Egypt without your permission" (Gen. 41:44). Pharaoh invited Joseph into the good life with a new identity.

It may seem that while earlier his life was in the pits, he was on top of the world. But was he?

We often think negatively about the challenges of pain and hardship, but these are the places where we often seek God, where we are at the end of our ropes and cannot make it on our own. Joseph must have felt this way in exile, slavery, and in prison. Perhaps more so when he had a bit of hope sending a message out to Pharaoh and then was forgotten. But too often in a position of great success, we begin to believe that we are self-made. We can look down on others who can't make it, even if they were much like we had been.

Al recalls listening to an interview that Henry Kissinger gave more than fifty years ago. In that interview, Kissinger said,

> Before I went into government, I was very critical of decisions that were being made. "Why do they make the bad choices they make? How can they be so ignorant?" I would often ask. But then I went into government and for a while I thought, "Now that I understand things I never knew before, how I could have made such ignorant comments?" But that lasted only a short time. Then I found myself asking, "How can they be so ignorant to criticize what they do not understand?"[5]

The path between arrogance, humility, and the return to arrogance can be very short indeed!

Many have noted the challenges we face at times of success. Marshall Carter, retired chair of Cleveland Street Bank and the New York Stock Exchange, said, "When you are the CEO, it is really hard to keep your feet on the ground."[6]

In 2009, Tiger Woods' marriage, family, and career collapsed when he was at the peak of his career and started having an affair. In retrospect, he said, "I knew my actions were wrong, but I convinced myself that normal rules did not apply. . . . I felt I had worked hard my entire life and deserved to enjoy all the temptations around me. I felt entitled."[7]

In 1 Corinthians 4:7, Paul reminds us, "What do you have that you did not receive? And if you did receive it, why do you boast as though you did not?" The people of God are called to walk humbly.

Would Joseph succumb to his new identity and assimilate into culture, forgetting what he was called to do? And what would he do to avoid the trappings of the power he had been given? Joseph seemed to have survived his good fortune, and there are several things we note that may have had an influence on him.

First, he had a relationship with someone much greater than himself. Primarily, this was his relationship with God. Before God, none of us are great or powerful. Walking in his presence is a regular reminder of who we are. Joseph, in addition, had a powerful human boss. According to his whim, Pharaoh could send people to prison or have them hanged. He had even changed Joseph's name. This may have also served as a reminder to Joseph that he was not the greatest person in the world.

Second, Joseph had relationships with people who did not know about his greatness; in his case, he had two sons. No matter who he dealt with at work or what was said about him on the streets, when he came home, he was Dad. His kids saw him as a real person, not someone on a pedestal. Al experienced this with his children as they grew up. They were unaware of those differences, particularly at a young age. Al was reminded that whatever position, accomplishment, or failure had happened at work, none of this registered with the children. At home, he was simply Dad.

Marshall Carter, who we met earlier, had another way to be reminded of his identity:

> Because I have been a pilot for almost 25 years now, I keep my plane down at a little airport. They do not really know who I am, just another guy with an airplane. I talk with the guys in the hanger, the guys pumping gas, and you can connect with real people. A lot of these CEOs are isolated. They only see other CEOs. I have never once gone to one of these CEO things over the weekend because I want to avoid that isolation factor.[8]

Third, Joseph had an important fourteen-year project where the lives of many people, including his own, depended on him paying attention and doing the work of saving food. Sometimes leaders in the position of privilege see the perks of the job as being about them rather than as the platform for carrying out what needs to be done.

During the 1980s and 1990s, the ServiceMaster Company was responsible for janitorial and housecleaning work at hospitals across the country and in other parts of the world. The work is often seen as tedious and mundane. Too often, workers are ignored, seen as part of the landscape rather than as real people. To address this, the company did two unusual things that changed the lives of their workers. The executives took periods where they did the janitorial work themselves to be able to understand the life of the worker—both the hard work and their invisibility. The leaders also had doctors and nurses address these laborers, showing them that the work they did was vital to the mission of the hospital. The meaning was bigger than the task.[9]

Whether Joseph did this with his workers, we don't know. But we do know that purpose is vital to staying the course over a long period, and we believe this helped keep Joseph on track.

We can celebrate with Joseph that the painful part of his life was over and that he had opportunity to exercise the gifts and dreams that God had given him. But we all need a strong focus on the purpose God has given us, changing our perspectives from ourselves to others.

Strategy is often done quickly, laying out a plan as Joseph did before Pharaoh. But then he needed to deliver on the promise of that strategy, which meant keeping focused day after day for more than five thousand days. The excitement of the plan can easily give way to the drudgery of carrying it out, especially as unforeseen obstacles arise. In the language of Eugene Peterson, it requires "a long obedience in the same direction."[10] Over this period, there were changes of direction requiring adaptation, including the method of record keeping and the ultimate need to serve customers beyond Egypt. We wonder if there were times when Joseph questioned whether his interpretation was correct. Would the famine start in seven years, six years, or not at all? Scripture doesn't tell us if he had questions.

—

Back in Canaan, Joseph's family was starting to feel the effects of the famine. They had heard there was food available in Egypt, so Jacob called his sons together and told them to go to Egypt to buy food—all but Benjamin, that is. Jacob's favorite wife was Rachel who was the mother of Joseph and Benjamin. Since Jacob had already lost Joseph and then Rachel, he was overly protective of Benjamin and kept him home where he would be safe.

Joseph was overseeing operations of food distribution after the famine began when he recognized his brothers there in Egypt. It was now more than twenty years since they had sold him into slavery. How did he feel about them now? Joseph had reflected both the pain of their actions and the call for his current work in the names of his sons: "Joseph named his firstborn Manasseh and said, 'It is because God has made me forget all my trouble and all my father's household.' The second son he named Ephraim and said, 'It is because God has made me fruitful in the land of my suffering'" (Gen. 41:51–53).

By all appearances, these mixed emotions guided his response to his brothers. When they approached him, they didn't recognize him. The seventeen-year-old was now almost forty, dressed like Egyptian royalty, and spoke to them through an interpreter. Joseph then went through a series of steps with his brothers that may look to us like well-deserved revenge. After accusing them of being spies, he used the opportunity to inquire about their family and learned that both Jacob and Benjamin were well. He sold them the food they wanted but said one of them must remain in prison in Egypt, and Simeon was chosen. He told them that if they wanted to come back for more food and to free Simeon, they had to bring Benjamin with them to prove they were not lying. Then he instructed his servant to put the money they used for the purchase back in their bags.

When they returned to Jacob, they were all concerned when they found the money in their sacks. When Jacob and his sons ran out of food again, he told them to return to Egypt, but the brothers reminded their father that they could not go back without Benjamin. Judah promised his father that he would protect Benjamin with his own life. With great reluctance, Jacob agreed. When they arrived back in Egypt, they brought gifts for "the great man" and returned the money they had found.

Joseph, however, was not finished with what may look like mind games. He let Simeon out of prison and held a banquet for his family and, to their astonishment, seated them in birth order.

Remember, these were all adult men most in their forties and fifties. Joseph saw to it that Benjamin received five times more food than any of the others. When he sent them on their way, he had his steward again put their money in their sacks, but he also planted his silver cup in Benjamin's sack. Not long after they left, he sent his steward after the brothers to charge them with stealing that cup. Though they denied this, the steward searched their sacks and found the cup in Benjamin's sack. They all returned again to

Egypt, bowed down to Joseph, and offered to be slaves. But Joseph said that they were free to go and that only Benjamin would be retained.

Finally, Judah stood and offered a stirring defense of what this would do to their father, culminating in this important statement:

> "Now then, please let your servant remain here as my lord's slave in place of the boy, and let the boy return with his brothers. How can I go back to my father if the boy is not with me? No! Do not let me see the misery that would come on my father." (Gen. 44:33–34)

At this point, Joseph sent his servants out of the room, which left only the brothers with him. Weeping, he revealed his identity and forgave them: "And now, do not be distressed and do not be angry with yourselves for selling me here, because it was to save lives that God sent me ahead of you" (Gen. 45:5). The timing of this statement makes the previous actions seem clear. Joseph had seen his brothers as those who cared only for themselves. Now Judah was prepared to sacrifice his own life for Benjamin's for the sake of their father. This seemed to be the transformation Joseph had been waiting for, which allowed him to then forgive them. Joseph clearly saw the bigger picture of why he was in Egypt.

Joseph provides an important picture of two challenges we face in our own lives. The first is how to deal with those who act destructively against us. Does our goal become one of revenge or justice accompanied by forgiveness?

The second is Joseph's realization that he had been called to Egypt for important work that God had prepared for him. The process of getting him to Egypt and preparing him for his work was painful, but some of the pain faded with the realization that this journey brought him to his present position of influence and blessing.

> For leaders living in an imperfect, broken world, work turns out to be a kind of crucible. A place where they experience the heat, pressure, and corrosion of elevated responsibility. For most of us, the crucible of work is unavoidable. So the question becomes, how do we endure the crucible without being hopelessly deformed by it? Or how can we use the crucible to form us into a more valuable and authentic leader?[11]

Joseph had been shaped by his work at the bottom and at the top of an organization, and he seemed to recognize in the naming of his second son that these experiences were not just the fault of his brothers but also the means God that used in their transformation. Do we ever think about our own painful experiences in this way?

The resolution of Joseph's relationship with his family ended in having all of the rest of the family (Jacob and the families of his brothers) move to Egypt. His brothers were gifted at taking care of livestock, and they went to work for Pharaoh while his father lived out his days there as they endured the famine.

———

As the famine continued, the people who needed food from Joseph's storage ran out of money and were no longer able to purchase it. What would Joseph do? Here, his actions raise questions for the modern person. First, he acquired their livestock in exchange for food, then he acquired their land, and finally he made them all slaves. Could there have been another way to handle this situation in light of the fact that the food had come into the storehouse in the first place through a tax that had been levied on them during the time of plenty?

We could argue the case for Joseph's decision by recognizing that during the time of abundance, people could have set aside some of their own food for later. As they watched the growing storehouses during this period, didn't they recognize what was happening? Too often during times of plenty people relax, raise their standards of living, and continue to spend beyond their means. They do not think of a time when the world could change, yet all the activity of this time pointed to that future.

Bev Bothel, a real estate leader in the Seattle area, drew a parallel to this behavior during the time of the great economic downturn in the United States in 2010 following a boom time that led to this recession. During a period of growth, the housing market had gone crazy. "As the frenzy built," she says, "lots of people saw gold in this market and hopped on board. But they continued to raise their level of living, spending beyond their means during the time of plenty. And when the downtime came, former real estate agents filed for bankruptcy, and some took their own lives."[12]

We could further justify what Joseph did by recognizing that these people were indentured servants within the context of the ancient world, which is something different from how we think of slavery in today's world. They lost ownership of their property, but at a tax rate of twenty percent, they had the opportunity to rebuild with control over eighty percent of their work creation. This stands in contrast to the total ownership and complete lack of autonomy associated with other forms of slavery.

On the other hand, we see no evidence that Joseph consulted others in making this decision. Was there another way to handle this situation? We simply don't have enough information to say for certain. But we are reminded that all of the narratives we are examining are the choices and lives of imperfect people, and we seek to learn from their good insights, not blindly follow them anywhere they might take us.

—

There is a great deal we do not know about other parts of this story. Why didn't Jacob and his family go back to Canaan after the famine? The fact that they stayed led to the challenge we will explore in the chapter on Moses and Israel's exodus from Egypt. Did Joseph encounter Potiphar, or his wife, after he was appointed deputy to Pharaoh? How did he lead those who worked for him? We don't know. But what we do know from the end of the narrative, after Jacob dies, points to another important lesson for us. When Joseph's brothers saw that their father was dead, they said,

> "What if Joseph holds a grudge against us and pays us back for all the wrongs we did to him?" So they sent word to Joseph, saying, "Your father left these instructions before he died: 'This is what you are to say to Joseph: I ask you to forgive your brothers the sins and the wrongs they committed in treating you so badly.' Now please forgive the sins of the servants of the God of your father." (Gen. 50:15–17)

In all likelihood, Joseph's brothers invented this directive from their father. Regardless, Joseph responded to them by weeping. He had already forgiven them, and they hadn't accepted that forgiveness. We also may find that it takes a while for forgiveness to take hold. Perhaps this is what Jesus meant when he answered a question from Peter about how many times he should forgive his brother: "Not seven times but seventy-seven times" (Matt. 18:22).[13]

What Joseph was able to do, and we can learn from, is captured in his answer to his brothers: "You intended to harm me, but God intended it for good, for the saving of many people" (Gen. 50:20). In spite of the pain, he was able to keep the bigger picture, and purpose, in mind. Can we?

3 | Moses

Meekness can be regarded as strength under control.
— Dictionary of Biblical Imagery

Now the man Moses was very meek, more than all people who were on the face of the earth.
— Numbers 12:3 (ESV)

The story of Moses begins in the first chapter of Exodus and continues through the books of Leviticus, Numbers, and Deuteronomy. He is best known as the man who led the Israelites out of Egypt, where they had been enslaved.

Moses was born in Egypt to a Hebrew couple who were both descendants of Joseph's brother Levi. The Pharaoh whom Joseph had served had died, and some years later a new Pharaoh came to power. That Pharaoh enslaved the Hebrew people and eventually decreed that all male Hebrew babies should be killed at birth. In Moses' case, his mother hid him for three months, but when she could no longer hide him, she put him in a papyrus basket, coated it with tar and pitch, and placed it in the Nile River where it was discovered by Pharaoh's daughter. She took the baby into the palace and eventually adopted him as her own son. Ironically, Pharaoh's daughter ended up paying Moses' birth mother to nurse the baby for her.

———

When we last saw Joseph, he was growing old in Egypt, having taken his father's body back to be buried in the cave Abraham had bought years before from Ephron the Hittite (Gen. 50:12–14). As Joseph was nearing his own death some years later, he told his brothers that though he was about to die. "God will surely come to your aid and take you up out of this land to the land he promised on oath to Abraham, Isaac and Jacob" (Gen. 50:24–25). Eventually, Joseph and all his brothers died in Egypt.

Years—perhaps hundreds of years—pass.[1] The Israelites had been living in the best part of Egypt in an area called Goshen. They had prospered, acquiring significant wealth, and they were prolific when it came to having children (see Gen. 47:27–28; Exod. 1:7). But there was trouble on the horizon, as God had told Abraham when he appeared to him in a vision: "Know for certain that for four hundred years your descendants will be strangers in a country not their own and that *they will be enslaved and mistreated there*" (Gen. 15:13; italics added).

That promise came to pass in the form of a "new king, to whom Joseph meant nothing" (Exod. 1:8). When the Israelites continued to "multiply and spread" despite being made slaves, this new king ordered the midwives to kill the male babies they deliver, but to let the female babies live. We are not told whether the king's infanticide order was actually carried out, but at least two midwives refused to kill the babies. The text tells us their names— Shiphrah and Puah[2]—and that they "feared God and did not do what the king of Egypt had told them to do; they let the boys live" (Exod. 1:17).

Apparently stymied by the midwives, Pharaoh turns to "all his people," presumably the Egyptian people themselves, and orders them to throw "every Hebrew boy that is born . . . into the Nile, but let every girl live" (Exod. 1:22). Into this hostile and violent culture, Moses is born.

One of the most underappreciated kinds of work we do as Christians is the work of parenting. While we may recognize that it is indeed hard work to be a parent, we do not always put the work that parents do raising their children in the same category as work "in the marketplace."

> Too often the work of bearing and raising children is overlooked. Mothers, especially, often get the message that childbearing is not as important or praiseworthy as other work. Yet when Exodus tells the story of how to follow God, the first thing it has to tell us is the incomparable importance of bearing, raising, protecting, and helping children.[3]

While we don't know exactly how long Moses remained with his natural parents, the time that he spent there before going to live with his adopted mother in Pharaoh's palace seems to have been a key factor in his decision *not* to wholly assimilate into Egyptian culture as he grew to manhood with his adopted mother in Pharaoh's palace and to identify with the Hebrew people rather than with the Egyptians.

The text is silent with regard to the years Moses spent growing up in Pharaoh's palace. But in Stephen's defense before the Sanhedrin in Acts 7, he tells us that "Moses was educated in all the wisdom of the Egyptians and was powerful in speech and action" (Acts 7:22). It seems reasonable to assume that "as a rising prince [of Egypt] . . . he likely . . . studied mathematics, astronomy, cosmology, metaphysics, and theology,"[4] and, crucially, leadership.

———

One day, after Moses had grown up, he went out to where his own people were and watched them at their hard labor. He saw an Egyptian beating a Hebrew, one of his own people. Looking this way and that and seeing no one, he killed the Egyptian and hid him in the sand. The next day he went out and saw two Hebrews fighting. He asked the one in the wrong, "Why are you hitting your fellow Hebrew?"

The man said, "Who made you ruler and judge over us? Are you thinking of killing me as you killed the Egyptian?" Then Moses was afraid and thought, "What I did must have become known."

When Pharaoh heard of this, he tried to kill Moses, but Moses fled from Pharaoh and went to live in Midian, where he sat down by a well. (Exod. 2:11–15)

There are several points worth noting from this story. First, though Moses had been well educated in Pharaoh's palace on many subjects, his education apparently did not include much in the way of tact or what we might call practical wisdom. Moses' first recorded venture outside Pharaoh's palace was, for all intents and purposes, a disaster. Yes, the Hebrew who was being beaten was saved from further beating, but at what price? Could the beating have been stopped simply by a strong word from Moses, Pharaoh's (adopted) grandson? By hiding the body in the sand, it looks as if Moses realized he had overreacted, but it was worse than that: the other Hebrews (who soon learned about it) resented what he had done—likely because they were jealous of Moses' privileged position as a "prince of Egypt," but also perhaps because they feared that his action—as a Hebrew—would only make things worse for them.

Despite his rocky beginning in "the world of men," it seems clear from this episode—and from the next episode when Moses drives off some shepherds who were harassing a group of women at a well—that Moses tends to take the side of the underdog. This is generally a positive characteristic and is something he will have to do on a much bigger stage later in his life when he returns to Egypt to tell Pharaoh to let the Israelites leave.

But while Moses may be a man of action committed to defending the underdog, the way he goes about it, particularly in the incident with the Egyptian, suggests that at this point he had a lot to learn before he was ready to stand before Pharaoh. Nevertheless, *all* of Moses' background—his "elementary education" with his mother, his education in Pharaoh's palace, and the practical education he is about to experience in Midian—will be used by God.

———

When Moses arrived in Midian, Scripture tells us that he sat down by a well. Shortly thereafter, seven young women, the daughters of a priest of Midian named Jethro, came to draw water to "fill the troughs to water their flocks." Some shepherds attempted to drive off the young women, "but Moses got up and came to their rescue and watered their flock" (Exod. 2:16–17). The girls told their father that "an Egyptian" rescued them from the shepherd bullies, and he told his daughters to invite him to supper. Moses agreed not only to stay for supper but also to stay much longer with Jethro, "who gave his daughter Zipporah to Moses in marriage." Zipporah and Moses have a son, whom Moses names Gershom (which means "a foreigner there") saying, "I have become a foreigner in a foreign land" (Exod. 2:22). Moses then goes to work in the family business as a shepherd.

We've noted how important women were in shaping Moses' life to this point, particularly his natural mother, a Hebrew, and his adopted mother, an Egyptian; but we haven't heard about Moses' Hebrew father, and there is no mention in the text of any man in Pharaoh's palace who might have provided guidance to Moses up to this point.[5] It appears then that there was no one, at least since his childhood, who was what we might call a father-figure for Moses prior to marrying Jethro's daughter. But it also appears that Jethro will become that person for him. He will provide Moses with what he needs at this point in his life: an older man who can give him a stable home life and an opportunity to work at what we might call manual labor.

There are plenty of studies that show how important it is to a child (particularly to boys and young men) to have a father or at least a father-figure, such as a sports coach, as they grow up. We realize how blessed we both have been to have had fathers who (along with our mothers) provided stable, loving homes to grow up in, and who encouraged us along the way. We also know men who have not had those kinds of fathers, but who have found their need for a father met in a father figure either by a kind stepfather or an older man who took the younger man under his wing.

Jethro had seven daughters; there is no mention of any sons. So, Moses settled into a relationship not only with his wife and his own son but with his father-in-law (and presumably, his mother-in-law and his wife's sisters). Jethro is an important figure in Moses' development as a leader. After his encounter with God in the burning bush in Exodus 3, Moses returns to Jethro and asks him to be allowed to "return to my own people in Egypt to see if any of them are still alive" (Exod. 4:18). Rather than trying to get him to stay with questions like: "Who will tend the sheep if you leave?" "Who will take care of the rest of the family when I die?" "How could you take my daughter and grandson away from me!" Jethro simply says, "Go, and I wish you well."

Later, after Moses has led the Israelites out of Egypt, Jethro reappears and recognizes that Moses' attempt to decide all the disputes among the Israelites would not only wear out Moses but would also wear out the people who have the disputes. Moses agrees to Jethro's suggestion that he appoint "lower court judges" to judge routine disputes, leaving the most difficult cases for himself.

Given where he had grown up, it seems unlikely that Moses came into his sheep-tending job already knowing what was involved in being a good shepherd, so Jethro (and perhaps his wife and her sisters?) taught him the details of that kind of work, eventually delegating much of the shepherding responsibilities to Moses. Moses doesn't hesitate when Jethro suggests that he delegate some of the responsibilities of leadership when he was leading the Israelites. He trusted the wisdom of this older man who, after seeing Moses accept his recommendation for a basic judicial system among the Hebrew people, simply left and "returned to his own country" (Exod. 18:27), apparently confident that Moses would be fine without him.

Randy had the privilege of practicing law with his father for some thirty years. In the first few years of law practice, he mostly did work for his father's clients, learning to practice law from the ground up. One day early in his law practice, his father told him that before too many years passed he would have his own clients and that soon enough *he* would be doing work for *Randy's* clients. At the time he said this, Randy could not imagine that would come to pass but, as you might guess, it did. Though Randy has been practicing law now for over forty-five years, he still draws on much of what he learned while apprenticing with his father for those thirty years—as we suspect Moses did from apprenticing with Jethro.

———

While at work tending the sheep one day before he returned to Egypt, Moses sees a bush that is on fire but does not burn up. He decides to go over "and see this strange sight," and "when the Lord saw that he had gone over to look," he calls Moses *by name* "from within the bush." Moses answers, "Here I am," and he is instructed to take off his sandals, "for the place where you are standing is holy ground." The voice identifies itself as "the God of your father, the God of Abraham, the God of Isaac, and the God of Jacob." Moses responds by hiding his face, "because he was afraid to look at God."

God tells him that he has seen the misery of his people in Egypt," and that he "has come down to help them, pry them loose from the grip of Egypt, get them out of that country and bring them to a good land with wide-open spaces, a land lush with milk and honey" (Exod. 3:8 MSG). God then gives Moses an assignment: "So now, go. I am sending you to Pharaoh to bring my people the Israelites out of Egypt" (Exod. 3:10).

In response to this news, Moses offers a list of reasons why he is not the right person for the job and that the assignment is more than he is capable of accomplishing. For each objection Moses raises, God responds with facts about God's own character and promises of his faithfulness (Exod. 3:12, 14–15; 4:3–4, 6–7, 11, 14–15). Moses finally agrees and heads back home to tell his father-in-law about what he must do.

Moses initial objection of "Why me?" suggests that he has serious doubts about his qualifications to undertake such an incredible assignment and that perhaps, at this point, he thinks of his time in Pharaoh's palace as a waste of time (similar to how a young student might say, "I took a lot of courses I've never used!") and his time as a shepherd, alone for long periods of time in the wilderness, as being useless in preparing him for the task God has for him. But obviously, God doesn't see it that way: Moses has exactly the knowledge (both "academic" and "experiential") and the character he is looking for.

As he did with Moses, God is able to use every part of *our story*—the failures and weaknesses as well as the successes and strengths—to accomplish his purposes. In Moses' case, for example, his training in Pharaoh's palace allowed him to read and teach God's law to the Israelites when it was given to him; it allowed him to write the first five books of the Bible, the Pentateuch! His time working for Jethro gave him the experience of leading a flock, which is good training for leading the people of Israel through the wilderness for forty years.

It is worth noting as well that Moses' call from God came *while he was at work*. One of the most pernicious heresies still present in the minds of many Christians is the ancient Greek idea of dualism when it comes to our work (e.g., the work of a stockbroker or rancher is "secular," while the work of a pastor or missionary is "spiritual"). Moses' life wasn't dualistic: "Moses himself was not a priest or religious leader (those were [Moses' brother] Aaron's and [Aaron's sister] Miriam's roles), but a shepherd, statesman, and governor."[6] We might add "Supreme Court justice" to that list. Do we see *our* work—whatever it is—as work in God's kingdom?[7]

Before we move to how Moses engaged with Pharaoh, it is worth considering another question Moses may have had as he and God dialogued (argued?) about God's desire for Moses to return to Egypt. "Why does God need me? If *God*, as he says, has come down to deliver *his* people out of Egypt, then why does he need to send *me* to Pharaoh?"

The obvious answer is that God doesn't "need" Moses, in the sense of God being incapable of delivering the Israelites without Moses, but it appears, as C. S. Lewis says, that God "seems to do nothing of himself which he can possibly delegate to his creatures. He commands us to do slowly and blunderingly what he could do perfectly and in the twinkling of an eye. He allows us to neglect what he would have us do, or to fail."[8]

The reality of Moses' call was that God was inviting Moses *into a partnership*: "I am sending *you* to Pharaoh to bring *my* people out of Egypt." After Moses questions God's choice of him as the one to do that, God responds by saying, "*I* will be with you."

Do we see *our work*—whatever it might be—as a partnership between God and us? Do we believe that, inadequate though we may sometimes feel to do our work well, God is with us and that he will use our efforts—even when we fail—to accomplish his purposes and make us into people who more and more reflect the image of the One who made us?

So Moses returns to Egypt accompanied by his brother Aaron. They get off to a good start with the Israelites who, after hearing that "the LORD was concerned about them and had seen their misery, they bowed down and worshiped" (Exod. 4:31). Pharaoh, however, has no intention of letting the Israelites go into the wilderness to hold a festival to God (whom he says he does not know) as Moses requests. After that initial interview, Pharaoh ordered that the Israelite slaves be required to gather their own straw for making bricks (previously it had been provided to them) but that the quota of bricks for each person is not to be reduced.

In response to Pharaoh's order, the Israelite foremen turn on Moses and Aaron, telling them, "May the Lord look on you and judge you!" (Exod. 5:21). In response to this double rejection, Moses "returned to the Lord and asked him, 'Why, Lord, why have you brought trouble on this people? Is this why you sent me?'" (Exod. 5:22). Clearly, Moses believed he had failed in his assignment—and he did, at least to some degree.

Before we get to God's response to Moses' plea, let's pause to note a couple of things about his first meeting with Pharaoh. It seems apparent that despite what God had told Moses about his being with him, Moses failed to follow God's specific instructions in this first meeting with a man who believed that *he* was a god.

When Pharaoh responds to Moses' opening demand with utter contempt—"Who is the Lord, that I should obey him and let Israel go?"—Moses slightly revises his earlier statement by saying that God had met with him, but then he adds something that was completely different from what God had said to him in the wilderness: Let us take this three-day journey "or he may strike us with plagues or with the sword" (Exod. 5:3). Where in the world did this come from? We aren't told, but perhaps Moses is so intimidated by Pharaoh's initial response that he thinks he needs to add some drama to what he was instructed to say. In addition to apparently forgetting why God had appeared to him in the first place, "because he had seen the misery of his people in Egypt," Moses has also forgotten that God told him that Pharaoh "will not let you go unless a mighty hand compels him."

Though Moses experienced a double failure—both with Pharaoh and with his own people—he returned and essentially blamed God for his failure. God does not take offense at Moses' complaining, nor does he bring up the fact that Moses had garbled and incorrectly stated to Pharaoh what God had told him to say. Instead, God simply says, "Now you will see what I will do to Pharaoh. Because of *my* mighty hand he will let them go" (Exod. 6:1).

Later, after God directs Moses to return to Pharaoh and tell him "*everything I tell you*," Moses again expresses doubts about his ability to speak convincingly. God explains to him that Moses will have *human* help in accomplishing this assignment: Moses' brother, Aaron, will be his spokesman.

None of us wants to fail in our work (or in any aspect of our lives), but we all have and will again because we are human. What do we do with that failure? We wouldn't call Moses' complaining to God a model of acknowledging failure, but it was apparently enough for God. In our experience—and we have all had many such experiences—it is far better to admit our mistakes than to try to cover them up or push off the responsibility to someone else (perhaps a clerk or administrative assistant who didn't catch a mistake in a letter we failed to proof-read before it was mailed).

After God told Moses that he had made Moses "like God to Pharaoh," Moses and Aaron did just as God commanded them (Exod. 7:6, 10, 20). Then after a series of demonstrations of God's power, Pharaoh finally relented and agreed to allow the Israelites to leave Egypt. In his meetings with Pharaoh, Moses was respectful of Pharaoh's position, even allowing him on one occasion to "save face" by setting the time that he, Moses, would pray for an end to the plague of frogs (Exod. 8:9), but he also is clear and firm that he was speaking for God and that, in the end, Pharaoh must yield to God.

When we believe someone is wrong on an issue, can we speak both clearly and respectfully to that person—or will we "cancel" them through the use of personal insults? Moses teaches us that we don't have to sacrifice our beliefs to speak respectfully to a person we strongly disagree with. It does not have to be either/or, one way or the other; we can talk with those we disagree with honesty and, at the same time, with respect.

———

After the Israelites left Egypt, Pharaoh had second thoughts about letting them go, and he sent his army after them. When the Israelites saw the approaching Egyptian army, they were terrified and cried to Moses, "Was it because there were no graves in Egypt that you brought us to the desert to die? What have you done to us by bringing us out of Egypt? Didn't we say to you in Egypt, 'Leave us alone; let us serve the Egyptians'? It would have been better for us to serve the Egyptians than to die in the desert" (Exod. 14:11–12).

God then rescues them at the Red Sea, but the people continue complaining to Moses at various points in their journey, and Moses, in turn, continues asking the Lord for help in dealing with the problem. This becomes a pattern. Each time the people complain, God provides for them, but the constant grumbling must have worn Moses down emotionally. This could explain Moses' decision *not* to follow God's direction to "speak to that rock before their eyes and it will pour out its water." Instead, Moses and Aaron gathered the people together in front of the rock and say to them (we can hear the frustration and exasperation in their words), "Listen, you rebels, must we bring water out of this rock?" (Num. 20:10). And instead of speaking to the rock as God had directed, Moses *strikes* the rock, and water gushes out of it.

Being a leader is not easy, and one of the most difficult parts of the job is the criticism that people—who often have little knowledge of what the facts actually are—level against the decisions that leaders make. In our day, social media has exacerbated this issue many times over. While we do not believe that leaders should be immune to criticism, as Christians, we need to exercise caution and wisdom, not always assuming the worst about a leader's decision.

Toby Barker, the mayor of Hattiesburg with whom Randy works as city attorney, was first elected to that position in 2017 at the age of thirty-five. When COVID-19 arrived in earnest in the spring of 2020, Barker had to make decisions about dealing with it: mask mandates, which businesses were "essential" and which were not, how to enforce the city's and the governor of Mississippi's orders, and many more. In all, during the pandemic, he issued over twenty executive orders himself. He appeared live on Facebook regularly to update Hattiesburg area residents (after consulting with doctors at hospitals and clinics who were spearheading the health-care efforts to deal with the pandemic) about the number of people who were in the hospital and those who had died from the disease as well as his response to the situation.

As Randy read the comments on the city's Facebook page following the mayor's updates, the vast majority of people praised his decisions as wise, given what we knew at the time. But invariably there were people who would second-guess his decisions: some argued that his decisions were too restrictive on personal freedoms; others argued that they were not restrictive enough to protect public health. Randy remembers an occasion when, in the midst of the pandemic, a television reporter asked the mayor whether he read the comments on Facebook about his decisions. He said that he did, but he went on to say that he could not responsibly govern on the basis of social media comments. In the next election, in June 2021, Barker was reelected mayor with 85 percent of the vote.

———

Eventually, of course, Moses led the Israelites to Mount Sinai (where he had first encountered God in the burning bush) where God had him give to the people not only the Ten Commandments but also a lengthy series of laws dealing with virtually every aspect of community life. He wrote down everything God said and led the Israelites in a covenant ceremony in which the people pledged to obey what God said. He gave the Israelites God's instructions for the construction of the tabernacle and then oversaw its construction.

After Moses died, Deuteronomy ends with this epitaph:

> Since then, no prophet has risen in Israel like Moses, whom the Lord knew face to face, who did all those signs and wonders the Lord sent him to do in Egypt—to Pharaoh and to all his officials and to his whole land. For no one has ever shown the mighty power or performed the awesome deeds that Moses did in the sight of all Israel. (Deut. 34:10–12)

Even after he had walked with God for years and spoken to God "as one friend to another," he was not perfect and occasionally struggled with his temper. His striking the rock in exasperation over the Israelites continuous whining led to God's decision not to allow him to enter the Promised Land with the rest of the Israelites. But without question, Moses had matured into an extraordinary leader.

To his credit, as Moses approached the end of his life, he did not try to hold on to power. Once God had made it clear to Moses that he would not be going into the Promised Land himself, Moses told the Israelites that Joshua, who had been Moses' aide, would be his successor. Moses blessed the people one last time and reminded them to follow all the commands God had given them.

Both of us have seen leaders of all kinds try to hold on to power when they need to step aside and assume the roles of encouragers and "consultants," while letting younger leaders step into roles of leadership: pastors and leaders of churches, corporate and business leaders, elected public officials, and even parents. Trying to hold on to leadership too long is sad and unhealthy. It is not always clear when the time is right, but perhaps the constitutional amendment limiting anyone serving as president of the United States to two terms provides a good model for those in positions of authority: periodically refreshing the office with new ideas is healthy.

The superscript for Psalm 90 says that it is a "prayer of Moses the man of God." It seems likely that Moses wrote this near the end of his life, perhaps as he contemplated turning over his leadership responsibilities to Joshua. In verse 12 of that psalm, Moses prays that God would "teach us to number our days, that we would gain a heart of wisdom." It appears that God had indeed taught Moses—and the Israelites who may have been tempted to resist Joshua's succession to leadership—that we are ultimately only responsible for the days and responsibilities that are given to us, that God will provide what is needed for the next generation, and that there is wisdom in resting in that assurance.

———

In Numbers 12, Miriam and Aaron "began to talk against Moses because of his Cushite wife, for he had married a Cushite." Though Miriam and Aaron used this reason as the starting point for their criticism of Moses, it is obvious that the real issue was that they were *jealous* of Moses. Rhetorically, they asked, "Has the Lord spoken only through Moses? Hasn't he also spoken through us?" (Num. 12:1–2).

We're not sure if Moses overheard what they were saying, but God heard and told the three of them to "come out of the tent of meeting," and he confronts Miriam and Aaron regarding their criticism of Moses. After God departs, Miriam's skin becomes leprous. Horrified, Aaron begs Moses "not to hold against us the sin we have so foolishly committed," and Moses "cried out to the Lord" to heal her—which he does, but he requires that she be confined outside the camp for seven days. After that, the people of Israel move on (Num. 12:4–16). It is in the context of this incident that the narrator says, "Now the man Moses was very meek (or humble),[9] more than all the people who were on the face of the earth" (Num. 12:3). Rather than paying back Miriam and Aaron for their rebellion, Moses immediately begged God to heal his sister and there is nothing in the text that suggests he held a grudge against either of them. If we contrast Moses' response to Miriam and Aaron with what he did to the Egyptian who was beating Moses' fellow

Hebrew, we can see that, by this point in the story, what the narrator said about Moses being "very meek, more than all the people who were living on the face of the earth" was true. He had power, but it was under control.

In the Bible, meekness and humility are presented as "robustly positive virtues, not a display of passive timidity," and "in classical Greek the word from which we derive *meekness* was used to describe tame animals, soothing medicine and a gentle breeze."[10] As Christians engage the world, we believe that we have the power of the Holy Spirit within us. Are we willing to use that power as Moses did, not to get payback on people who have unjustly criticized or embarrassed us, but to intercede with God for those people? How might a regular demonstration of meekness and humility by Christians be a "soothing medicine and a gentle breeze" to our divided culture?

4 | Joshua

I felt as if I were walking with destiny, and that all my past life had been but a preparation for this hour and for this trial.

— Winston Churchill on becoming
prime minister of Great Britain (1940)

Looking back on it, Joshua thought, *leaving Egypt was the easy part!* After God brought a series of plagues on Egypt, Pharaoh and the Egyptians were so anxious for the Israelites to leave that they gave them silver, gold, and clothing for their journey. God moved ahead of them in a pillar of cloud to guide them during the daylight hours and in a pillar of fire by night. At that point, it seemed to be all downhill to the Promised Land.

But when Pharaoh changed his mind and came after the Israelites with his army, the people, not surprisingly, were terrified and began blaming Moses for leading them out to die in the desert. God protected them, though, and they marched across the dry bed of the Red Sea, which God through Moses divided into "walls of water on their right and their left" (Exod. 14:22). After they were safely on the other side, they watched as the Egyptians were swept into the sea after Moses, at God's direction, directed the waters to cover the seabed once again. The entire Egyptian army was drowned.

Naturally, the Israelites celebrated this incredible deliverance; but, as we saw in Moses' story, they almost immediately began to complain to Moses about one thing after another. Moses asked Joshua to be his aide, and he quickly agreed, but it was hard for him to watch this great man deal with all the whining. Finally, though, the Israelites reached the outskirts of the Promised Land and Joshua was asked, along with eleven other men, to explore the land and report back what they had found there.

From Joshua's perspective, the Promised Land was just as God had said: a land flowing with milk and honey. Yes, there were strong tribes of people living in the land, but so what? This was the land that God had promised to the people of Israel. But now, at the doorstep to this place, the majority of the people balked at going forward. They even said it would be better to go back to Egypt, and they should get someone other than Moses to lead them. Incredible! Was this how the story of the Israelite people was to end—here at the entrance to the Promised Land?

—

Joshua appears in the story for the first time in Exodus 17 as a military recruiter and commander to whom Moses turns when the Israelites are attacked by the Amalekites not long after the people have left their Egyptian slave masters behind. In response to Moses' direction, Joshua chose some Israelites to fight with him while Moses said he would stand on top of the hill with his staff in his hands. "As long as Moses held up his hands, the Israelites were winning, but whenever he lowered his hands, the Amalekites were winning" (Exod. 17:8–12). Not surprisingly, Moses' "hands grew tired and Aaron and a man named Hur took a stone and put it under him and he sat on it. Aaron and Hur held his hands up—one on one side, one on the other—so his hands remained steady till sunset." By the end of the day, "Joshua overcame the Amalekite army with the sword." After the battle, God told Moses to write down on a scroll what had happened with the Amalekites "as something to be remembered, and make sure Joshua hears it" because God intended to "completely blot out the name of Amalek" (Exod. 17:14). Even though the Israelites had just begun their journey to the Promised Land, God was already preparing Joshua for his eventual work as the man who would lead them into the Promised Land and conquer the people they found there. But we are getting ahead of ourselves.

While Moses was acting as commander-in-chief of the Israelite army in the battle with the Amalekites, the text is clear that the outcome of the battle was dependent on Moses' keeping his arms raised, but he needed help. It is easy to overlook Aaron and Hur's role in this victory, but they were crucial to the outcome. Wise leaders recognize that even if they are the commander-in-chief of a business or department, they recognize and praise the crucial role of those who are in essence holding up their hands.

Before we focus on Joshua's experience in this battle, let's note that the attack by the Amalekites was unprovoked and that Moses had no choice but to take steps to defend the Israelites. The fact that Moses directed Joshua to recruit some of their men to fight suggests that self-defense was not something he had spent a lot of time thinking about prior to this point: his mind had been occupied by getting the Israelites safely out of Egypt, and then dealing with practical issues such as getting food and water for them.

Christians today are not immune from "unprovoked attacks," but thankfully, in the West at least, these attacks are not usually physical in nature, nor do they require actually going into physical combat. But at the same time, that does not mean that such attacks must simply be accepted. Though Christians should not "repay anyone evil for evil," and "if it is possible, as far as it depends on you, live at peace with everyone" (Rom. 12:17–18), there will be times when engaging the culture means defending ourselves through the judicial system and seeking to pass legislation that guarantees Christians (and others) equal opportunity to have their voices heard in the marketplace. Going to court to seek to overturn a state university rule that bars certain religious groups on campus because these groups do not allow non-Christian members to serve as officers of the organizations is one recent example of legitimate self-defense.[1]

When it's functioning as it should, the judicial system in the United States, including the adversarial nature of the work of lawyers who try cases, is designed to resolve disputes by an agreed-on alternative to a duel or a war: judges or juries—disinterested third parties—decide who is right and who is wrong. When a person or an organization is attacked unjustly, there are often financial penalties placed on the attacker. When a crime is committed, more often than not the perpetrator of a crime is caught, tried, and punished if found guilty. There can be no doubt that our judicial system is a far better way of dealing with disputes—including disputes growing out of family issues as was perhaps the case with the Israelites and the Amalekites[2]—than actual physical combat.

So what do we say about Joshua at this point?

Apparently, he was already functioning as a trusted aide to Moses, and it seems reasonable to assume that he had already demonstrated some skill with his sword. His name means "God saves," and it certainly fits here, but perhaps it also serves as a reminder of who actually won the battle against the Amalekites.

———

If he was not already Moses' aide before the battle with the Amalekites, then Joshua now clearly becomes his understudy. After leaving Egypt behind, Joshua had numerous opportunities to watch and learn from Moses during the forty years that his mentor led the Israelites. The text mentions several incidents, but there were probably many more that went unrecorded.

The morning after God gave Moses the law, Moses built an altar at the foot of Mount Sinai and set up "twelve stone pillars representing the twelve tribes of Israel," took the blood of some young bulls that had been sacrificed and splashed it against the altar, and he then "took the Book of the Covenant and read it to the people." The people responded, "We will do everything the Lord has said; we will obey." Moses then "took the blood [of the bulls], sprinkled it on the people and said, 'This is the blood of the covenant that the Lord has made with you in accordance with these words'" (Exod. 24:4–8).

Shortly after the ceremony, God told Moses to climb back up the mountain to him, where God would give him the tablets of stone with the law and the commandments he wrote for their instruction (Exod. 24:12). Moses then set out with Joshua, leaving the rest of the elders of Israel to wait (Exod. 24:13–14). Eventually, Moses left Joshua (perhaps halfway up) and made the final part of the journey to meet God alone.

We are not told what Moses and Joshua talked about on their way up Mount Sinai, but we can imagine that they discussed the covenant-ratification ceremony that had just occurred, as well as what God said about how he would send an angel ahead of the Israelites to bring them to the place he had prepared (Exod. 23:20). We are reading with the benefit of hindsight, of course, but we may wonder if they also discussed what God had said about the fact that he would not "drive out [the people of Caanan] in a single year, because the land would become desolate and the wild animals too numerous for you." Instead, God had said, "Little by little I will drive them out before you, until you have increased enough to take possession of the land" (Exod. 23:29–30).

It is one thing to learn the technical aspects of your work, but the opportunity to learn from those willing to take you under their wing and help you develop as a skilled worker and a mature disciple of Jesus is a great gift. It is not always the case that the person doing the mentoring anticipates that the person they are mentoring may someday take their place, but at some point God revealed that to Moses.

Becoming an apprentice like Joshua did with Moses involves a long-term commitment to learn skills from a master of the work we do, so that one day we will be able to teach others those same skills. Apprenticing is not twelve easy steps to success, nor should we want it to be. Gradually becoming good at our work—whether parenting, carpentry, plumbing, practicing law, repairing automobiles, teaching at a university, or serving in law enforcement—is deeply satisfying.

Peggy Sealy began her career in law enforcement as a meter maid in 1988, and she advanced through the ranks to become the first female chief of police in the history of the City of Hattiesburg, Mississippi, in 2021. When she was appointed chief, she recognized the role other women police officers had in helping her reach that position:

> "I don't think I could have done this alone," she said. "Other female officers have paved the way for me. Jackie Dole Sherrill in 1974 . . . became the first female officer for the department and the first female supervisor for the police department and later died in the line of duty. [The] first African American female, Captain Annie McGee . . . went all the way to captain before her retirement. These ladies set the foundation for other females such as myself."[3]

Jesus told the Jewish leaders who "began to persecute him," that "the Son . . . can do only what he sees his Father doing, because whatever the Father does the Son also does" (John 5:19). When he calls us to be his disciples, he is calling us to be his apprentices. Becoming an apprentice—to a human mentor in the workplace as well as to a divine mentor in every aspect of our lives—is not a sign of weakness; it is a mark of wisdom.

There is no indication in the text that Joshua ever had issues with his role as an apprentice to Moses. In fact, Joshua may have grown to be almost *too loyal* to Moses personally and confused loyalty to Moses with loyalty to God and his purposes. In Numbers 11:16–17, God told Moses to bring "seventy of Israel's elders who are known to you as leaders and officials" to the "tent of meeting, that they may stand there with you. I will come down and speak with you there, and I will take some of the power of the Spirit that is on you and put it on them. They will share the burden of the people with you so that you will not have to carry it alone."

God does as he said he would after the elders are assembled around the tent of meeting, and "when the Spirit rested on them, they prophesied—

but did not do so again" (Num. 11:24–25). Two of the elders, Eldad and Medad, however, "remained in the camp" for some reason, "yet the Spirit also rested on them, and they prophesied in the camp" (Num. 11:26). Joshua heard about this, and he "spoke up and said, 'Moses, my lord, stop them!'" Moses wisely asked Joshua, "Are you jealous for my sake? I wish that all the Lord's people were prophets and that the Lord would put his Spirit on them!" (Num. 11:29).[4]

There is nothing wrong with loyalty to a leader—be it a pastor, president, or corporate executive—but there is danger in *blind* loyalty. We must be loyal to God and his purposes when those purposes conflict with a beloved leader's behavior. It seems to be built into us as humans to want a Messiah. Christians are not immune from putting a leader on a pedestal and defending that person even in the face of overwhelming evidence that they have abused trust. The ripple effects of such blind loyalty can be deep and wide. Unfortunately, when faced with such evidence, many Christians close ranks and even quote passages from Scripture to justify their defense of a leader who has clearly demonstrated that they have feet of clay. The tortured defenses of the followers of well-known religious and political leaders who have repeatedly committed serious misbehavior may be obvious examples on the national stage, but it can and does happen among people in any organization and on the local political and church level as well as the national. It says a great deal about Moses' own character that he saw in Joshua's comments a dangerous tendency to put Moses above God; no wonder Moses was described in the text a few verses later as "a quietly humble (or meek) man, more so than anyone living on earth" (Num. 12:3).[5]

———

There is one more incident involving Joshua's apprenticeship with Moses that needs to be mentioned. In Exodus 32:8, after Moses dealt with the Israelites' great sin of worshiping an "idol cast in the shape of a calf," the narrator seems to pause in order to explain the tent of meeting that has been mentioned several times before in the narrative.

> Now Moses used to take a tent and pitch it outside the camp some distance away, calling it the "tent of meeting." Anyone inquiring of the Lord would go to the tent of meeting outside the camp. And whenever Moses went out to the tent, all the people rose and stood at the entrance to their tents, watching Moses until he entered the tent. As Moses went into the tent, the pillar of cloud

would come down and stay at the entrance, while the Lord spoke with Moses. Whenever the people saw the pillar of cloud standing at the entrance to the tent, they all stood and worshiped, each at the entrance to their tent. The Lord would speak to Moses face to face, as one speaks to a friend. Then Moses would return to the camp, but his young aide Joshua did not leave the tent.

(Exod. 33:7–11)

Joshua, of course, did not accompany Moses into the tent, but he surely must have gained some deeper understanding of the relationship of these two "friends" so that when God told him that *he* would be leading the people of Israel into the Promised Land, and that "As I was with Moses, so I will be with you; I will never leave you nor forsake you" (Josh. 1:5), he had good reason to believe that God would keep that promise—because he had seen the way God and Moses had "operated" as friends.

How do leaders—whether corporate executives, middle management, solo entrepreneurs, or professionals—continue to move their organization forward in the face of the daily stresses of making payroll, dealing with difficult employees (or employers), and finding and retaining good employees? How does anyone in the workplace avoid burnout?

The key to Moses' ability to continue to move the Israelites forward—despite many setbacks and his own exhaustion from having to deal with these difficult people—was his intimate relationship with God, described in Exodus 33:11: "The Lord would speak to Moses face to face, as one speaks to a friend."[6] We sometimes imagine that only pastors or missionaries can have this kind of relationship with God, but Moses was not, as we would define it, a traditional pastor or a missionary. He was a leader, a judge, and a lawgiver. Whatever our work may be, God is deeply interested and *invested* in it, by virtue of his decision to let humans do much of the work of developing his creation. If we intentionally develop our relationship with him through Bible study, prayer, worship, and a regular Sabbath, he will provide us with *spiritual and emotional refreshment* we need to have the stamina to deal with whatever we may face in our workplaces. Joshua witnessed this pattern in Moses, and it no doubt gave him confidence in God's provision when his turn to lead came.

———

In addition to being an army recruiter, a commander, and an aide to Moses, Joshua was also an *explorer* who went, at Moses' direction, with eleven other men to gather information about the Promised Land and its inhabitants. The twelve men explored the entire area, returning after forty days with evidence of the fertility of the land in the form of "a branch bearing a single cluster of grapes" and "some pomegranates and figs" (Num. 13:23). Showing Moses, Aaron, and "the whole assembly" of Israel the "fruit of the land," the report of the explorers began positively: "We went to the land to which you sent us and, oh! It *does* flow with milk and honey. Just look at this fruit!" But then ten of the explorers changed their tune dramatically: "The only thing is that the people who live there are fierce, their cities are huge and well-fortified. Worse yet, we saw descendants of the giant Anak" (Num. 13:27–29 MSG).[7]

Caleb, one of the twelve, "interrupted, called for silence before Moses and said, 'Let's go up and take the land—now. We can do it'" (Num. 13:30 MSG).[8] But the ten again focused their report on how much stronger the people residing in Canaan were than the Israelites: "We can't attack these people; they are way stronger than we are."

> Then Moses and Aaron fell face down in front of the whole Israelite assembly gathered there. Joshua . . . and Caleb . . . , who were among those who had explored the land, tore their clothes and said to the entire Israelite assembly, "The land we passed through and explored is exceedingly good. If the Lord is pleased with us, he will lead us into that land, a land flowing with milk and honey, and he will give it to us. Only do not rebel against the Lord. And do not be afraid of the people of the land, because we will devour them. The protection is gone, but the Lord is with us. Do not be afraid of them."
>
> (Num. 14:5–9)

All twelve men who explored Canaan *saw* the same things: a land flowing with milk and honey and large and powerful people and fortified cities that would have to be overcome if the Israelites were to take possession of the land. How then did they reach such different conclusions about the Israelites' prospects in Canaan?

Randy's father used to describe some people as "nut-grass people": people who, when looking at a beautiful garden of flowers, focused on the weeds that were inevitably growing in the garden among the flowers rather than on the flowers themselves. The ten explorers who saw only obstacles in Canaan saw what they expected to see; they had no *vision* of what God was able to do as their "senior partner" in the Canaan "project." They were essentially near-sighted, focusing only on the weakness of the

Israelite people compared to the people living in Canaan: they were "nut-grass people."

Caleb and Joshua, on the other hand, were confident of success because they clearly understood that with God leading the way, the Canaanites had no protection. As *The Message* colorfully renders Caleb and Joshua's conviction, "Why, we'll have them for lunch!" In contrast to the other ten, Joshua and Caleb were *far-sighted*. They took God at his word, believing they could trust him to bring Israel successfully into the Promised Land, despite any obstacles that lay before them.

What about us? Do we focus on the nut-grass or on the flowers? It is interesting that the dictionary defines the word *vision* in several ways. "Vision" can mean "the faculty or state of being able to see," and the *New Oxford American Dictionary* illustrates that meaning with an example apropos for the majority of the explorers: " [the person] had defective vision." The dictionary also defines "vision" as "the ability to think about or plan for the future with imagination," and it also illustrates that meaning: "the organization had lost its vision and direction." Finally, it defines "vision" as "a mental image of what the future will or could be like."[9] Joshua and Caleb embody the latter two definitions.

Harvard professor Clayton Christensen's book *The Innovator's Dilemma*[10] captures the challenge a company faces dealing with new technology. Simply stated, he notes that new technology creates opportunity to do things differently, but often companies have a difficult time disrupting their tried-and-true way of doing things. They stay with what they know produces revenue and profit, not wanting to risk a disruptive new approach. In the end, companies fail because a new competitor develops an edge by taking advantage of a new way of doing things. His message to companies is, "You can't stay where you are!"

Our world is rapidly changing around us, and the latest technology can intimidate us. For example, "doing church" looks far different from the way it did even five years ago. We worry about the polarization we see in our politics and even in our own families. We recognize that God has led us this far in our lives, but we are reluctant to take the next step into that changing world.

What do we see ahead of us as we follow Jesus into the future: opportunity and adventure as we are led by God, or "giants in the land"? Can we go forward by faith—as Joshua and Caleb encouraged the Israelites to do—or do we stay where we are?

—

After forty years of wandering, a new generation of Israelites reached the border of the Promised Land and prepared to enter it. At that point, however, God tells Moses, who is now an old man, that he would not be going into the land with them; he would only be able to take a look from a distance (Num. 27:12–13). Hearing this, Moses asks God to "appoint someone over this community, to go out and come in before them, one who will lead them out and bring them in, so the Lord's people will not be like sheep without a shepherd" (Num. 27:16–17). God then tells Moses that Joshua, "a man in whom is the spirit of leadership," (Num. 27:18) is to be that person, and he directs Moses to have Joshua "stand before Eleazar the priest and the entire assembly and commission him in their presence. Give him some of your authority so the whole Israelite community will obey him" (Num. 27:20). Moses follows God's directions to the "T."

Though it is almost time for Moses to leave the stage of history, he knows better than anyone the tendency of the people of Israel not to follow God's directions, and so he sets before them—and their leader-to-be Joshua—two straightforward alternatives as they contemplate entering the Promised Land:

> "If you fully obey the Lord your God and carefully follow all his commands I give you today, the Lord your God will set you high above all the nations on earth." (Deut. 28:1)

> "However, if you do not obey the Lord your God and do not carefully follow all his commands and decrees I am giving you today . . . the Lord will send on you curses, confusion and rebuke in everything you put your hand to, until you are destroyed and come to sudden ruin because of the evil you have done in forsaking him." (Deut. 28:15, 20)

Years later, after Joshua had led the Israelites to partially drive out the Canaanites from the land and as he prepared to leave the stage of history, he told the Israelites they have the same choice as they did before they entered the Promised Land: they must choose who they are going to serve: the "gods of the Amorites, in whose land you are living," or the Lord. Joshua clearly laid out the dangers they would face if they did not fully carry out God's command to drive out all the Canaanite people:

> "Do not associate with those nations that remain among you; do not invoke the names of their gods or swear by them. You must not serve them or bow down

before them. But you are to hold fast to the LORD your God, as you have until now.... If you turn away and ally yourselves with the survivors of these nations that remain among you..., then you may be sure that the LORD your God will no longer drive out these nations before you. Instead, they will become snares and traps for you." (Josh. 23:7–8, 12–13)

What Joshua was talking about here is a problem God's people have faced almost from the beginning: how to remain faithful to God *in the midst* of a culture that worships other gods and not become fully *assimilated* into that other culture. Most thinking Christians are aware of the dangers of assimilation. But as we think about where Christians today have improperly assimilated into the dominant culture, it is easier to see this negative assimilation in someone else than it is to see it in ourselves. Perhaps we recognize churches and individuals who have drifted away from orthodox Christian belief into what C. S. Lewis called "Christianity And." As Screwtape explained to his nephew, Wormwood,

> What we want, if men become Christians at all, is to keep them in the state of mind I call "Christianity And." You know—Christianity and the Crisis, Christianity and the New Psychology . . . Christianity and Faith Healing, . . . Christianity and Vegetarianism. . . . If they must be Christians, let them be Christians with a difference. Substitute for the faith itself some Fashion with a Christian coloring.[11]

But in identifying this danger and tendency among many so-called Christians, do we fail "to see the log in our own eye" (Matt. 7:3)? Are we unaware of a tendency to, perhaps, elevate a political party or leader or a philosophy to the status of a messiah or allow material success to define our self-worth? Assimilation into the dominant culture is dangerous, as Joshua made clear to the Israelites. But in our evaluation of that issue today, we need to begin with evaluating ourselves: Have *we*, perhaps unknowingly and with the best of intentions, allowed ourselves to "become so well-adjusted to [our] culture that [we] fit into it without thinking" (Rom. 12:2 MSG)?

After Canaan was at least partially subdued, Joshua participated in dividing the land among the various Israelite tribes. During this process, Joshua's old friend, Caleb, reappears for the first time in the story since he and Joshua had stood together in opposition to the other ten men who gave a negative report about the prospects for subduing Canaan. Caleb reminds Joshua of what had happened that day, and that he "brought [Moses] back a report according to my convictions," while "my fellow Israelites who went up with me made the hearts of the people melt in fear. I, however, followed the LORD my God wholeheartedly" (Josh. 14:7–8). He also reminds Joshua of Moses' promise to give Caleb a certain portion of hill country within the territory designated for Judah, because Caleb had "followed the LORD [his] God wholeheartedly." Caleb says that although he was now eighty-five years old, "I am still as strong as the day Moses sent me out; I'm just as vigorous to go out into battle now as I was then" (Josh. 14:10–11). Apparently, the rest of the tribe of Judah concurred with Caleb's request since they came with Caleb to see Joshua. In response, "Joshua blessed Caleb, son of Jephunneh and gave him Hebron as his inheritance. So Hebron has belonged to Caleb . . . ever since, because he followed the LORD, the God of Israel wholeheartedly" (Josh. 14:13–14).

It had been more than forty years since Caleb and Joshua made their minority report about Canaan and, given the inherent difficulty of dividing land fairly and equally among twelve tribes, Joshua could have reasonably suggested that Caleb work out his "land issues" with his fellow Judahites, but he didn't. He could have said, "Well, that was Moses; he's not here now, and I've got to make what I think is the best decision for everyone." Instead, he blessed Caleb and gave him just what Moses had promised him. Although Joshua—not Caleb—was Moses' successor, he recognized that it was actually Caleb who first interrupted the ten explorers who gave a negative report (Num. 13:30).

There is nothing wrong with feeling good when we are recognized for some accomplishment, but when something is accomplished through *collaboration*, there is a temptation to play down the role of that other person or people who contributed to the success of an invention or policy. The two men who believed God's promises at the border of Canaan were Joshua *and* Caleb.

Many people know that C. S. Lewis and J. R. R. Tolkien were close friends and that Tolkien played a significant role in Lewis's decision to become a Christian. What may be less well known is how they influenced each other's writing. While they did not co-author any books, their collaboration took the form of mutual encouragement. As Alister McGrath notes, "It is no exaggeration to say that Lewis would become the chief midwife to one of the great works of twentieth-century literature—Tolkien's *Lord of the Rings*."[12]

Joshua's story ends with another renewal of the covenant between God and the people of Israel in which the people promise that they, too, "will serve the Lord, because he is our God." Ever the realist, Joshua tells them, "You are not able to serve the *Lord*. He is a holy God; he is a jealous God," and "if you forsake the Lord and serve foreign gods, he will turn and bring disaster on you and make an end of you, after he has been good to you." After he "took a large stone and set it up under the oak near the holy place of the Lord at Shechem as a witness," Joshua "dismissed the people, each to their own inheritance" (Josh. 24:1–28). After this, Joshua died at the age of one hundred and ten, and the narrator of the book of Joshua records that "Israel served the Lord throughout the lifetime of Joshua and of the elders who outlived him and who had experienced everything the Lord had done for Israel" (Josh. 24:29–31; Judg. 2:7–8).

Unlike Moses, God did not designate a successor for Joshua, though there seems to have been for a period of time some "elders" who remembered and directed the people to follow what they had promised to Moses and Joshua: serve the Lord and him only. But time doesn't stand still, and after Joshua's generation had passed from the scene, "another generation grew up who knew neither the Lord nor what he had done for Israel" (Judg. 2:10). Israel descended into a chaotic period in which the "people did whatever they felt like doing" (Judg. 21:25 MSG).

As Christians, we are responsible to God for living faithfully during the time he has given us, and that includes passing on to our children (and grandchildren, if we have the opportunity) a knowledge of God and what he has done in our lives. In the end, we do not and cannot *control* the future, but we can *influence* the future—through our example of following Jesus as best as we can and praying for those who come after us to follow him as well.

5 | Ruth

We came to believe that God was calling us not only to grow apples, but also to use that work as a context in which people who were being overlooked or ignored could grow as well.

— Cheryl Broetje, co-owner, Broetje Orchards

Ruth was at a decision point. She was a Moabite woman whose Jewish husband had died, and her mother-in-law Naomi was leaving the land of Moab to return to her homeland of Judah. The case for going to Judah with her mother-in-law was not compelling. She would be a foreign woman among a people who treated both foreigners and women poorly. If she went, she would start at the bottom as a laborer and her prospects for a husband were not good. Alternatively, she could stay in Moab with her own people and try to start her life over. Naomi urged her to stay with her sister-in-law and to find a husband among her people, but Ruth was determined to go with Naomi and responded with the words that have been memorialized in song:[1]

> "Don't urge me to leave you or to turn back from you. Where you go I will go, and where you stay I will stay. Your people will be my people and your God my God. Where you die I will die, and there I will be buried. May the LORD deal with me, be it ever so severely, if even death separates you and me."
>
> (Ruth 1:16–17)

How did she come to this predicament?

Ten years earlier, Elimelech and his wife, Naomi, with their two sons Mahlon and Chilion, had left their homeland in Judah during a famine because they had heard that food was available in Moab. Going to Moab in the first place was a challenging decision. Though a neighboring country, Moab and Judah were not on the best of terms. On the positive side, the Moabites were descendants of Abraham's nephew, Lot, albeit through an incestuous relationship. God had protected the Moabite people because of Abraham, not allowing the children of Israel to have any of their land. On the negative side, the Moabite people had tried to stop the children of Israel as they passed through the wilderness on their way to the Promised Land. They were also idolatrous people and sought to bring others into their ways. Nehemiah said of them,

> On that day the Book of Moses was read aloud in the hearing of the people and there it was found written that no Ammonite or Moabite should ever be admitted into the assembly of God, because they had not met the Israelites with food and water but had hired Balaam to call a curse down on them. (Our God, however, turned the curse into a blessing.) When the people heard this law, they excluded from Israel all who were of foreign descent. (Neh. 13:1–3)

The situation was made even more challenging for Elimelech and Naomi as they decided to settle down there. While living in Moab, Elimelech and Naomi's two sons married Moabite women, Orpah and Ruth. Then Elimelech, Mahlon, and Chilion all died. We don't know the circumstances or even the order of their death, but Naomi found herself in Moab as a childless widow with two daughters-in-law. The *Theology of Work Bible Commentary* on Ruth sets up this dilemma:

> Along with aliens and the fatherless, widows received a great deal of attention in the Law of Israel. Because they [Naomi, Ruth, and Orpah] had lost the protection and support of their husbands, they were easy targets for economic and social abuse and exploitation. Many resorted to prostitution simply to survive, a situation all too common for vulnerable women in our day as well. Naomi had not only become a widow, but was also an alien in Moab. Yet, if she returned to Bethlehem with her daughters-in-law, the younger women would be widows and aliens in Israel. Perhaps in response to the vulnerability they faced no matter where they might live, Naomi urged them to return to their maternal homes, and prayed that the God of Israel would grant each of them security within the household of a (Moabite) husband.[2]

Orpah finally agreed to stay, but Ruth persisted.

Why did Ruth want to go with Naomi, knowing that she faced abuse as an immigrant with few prospects? We don't know, but something about

Naomi's God must have attracted her. She must have seen this through Naomi in spite of the fact that her mother-in-law was a defeated woman. This is evident from her statement to those who recognized her when she returned to Bethlehem:

> "Don't call me Naomi [meaning pleasant]," she told them. "Call me Mara [meaning bitter], because the Almighty has made my life very bitter. I went away full, but the LORD has brought me back empty. Why call me Naomi? The LORD has afflicted me; the Almighty has brought misfortune upon me."
>
> (Ruth 1:20–21)

We see no evidence that Naomi took any ownership for her situation, though perhaps she had little choice. In that time, women often had to do what their husbands decided. While she did blame God for her plight, somehow Ruth saw something of her God through the relationship with her mother-in-law. There is a reminder here for each of us. Even at our lowest point, when we feel we don't represent God very well, God can use us in the lives of others.

As this story unfolds, we will see application to many of the topics that divide our world today: the roles of capitalism and socialism, immigration policies, women in society, and relationships across ethnic backgrounds. These are not new topics!

—

When Naomi and Ruth arrived in Judah, it was the time of the barley harvest, which created an opportunity for Ruth. God had laid out an economic plan for Israel that was different from other cultures around them in that day and from the way many businesses are run today. Here were God's instructions for harvesting:

> "When you reap the harvest of your land, do not reap to the very edges of your field or gather the gleanings of your harvest. Do not go over your vineyard a second time or pick up the grapes that have fallen. Leave them for the poor and the foreigner. I am the LORD your God." (Lev. 19:9–10)

We must remember that Boaz and Ruth lived in the time of the judges, when "everyone did as they saw fit" (Ruth 1:1, Judg. 21:25). Given this cultural situation, Boaz was faithfully seeking God's way by following the pattern set out in Leviticus 19 and allowing Ruth (and others) to glean in his fields. As Christopher Wright comments,

Those who possessed land, and had done all the hard work of clearing, plough-ing, sowing and harvesting might feel entitled to 100 percent of the produce of their own (or their employees') labor. But these instructions counteract such an attitude to remind the Israelite landholder that the Lord is the ultimate landlord and reserves the right the right to insist that all Israelites should "eat and be satisfied." . . . Human need is brought to the forefront as a moral priority that relativizes the personal benefits of landownership.[3]

Now Ruth steps into that opportunity by going into the fields to glean, though it was not easy. She says to Naomi, "Let me go to the fields and pick up the leftover grain behind anyone in whose eyes I find favor." Tim Keller observes that "she was taking her very life in her hands in doing so, not just because she was a woman, but because she was a Moabitess, 'a racially marginalized woman.'"[4]

Today, some of our polarization comes from the challenges of wage disparity and opportunity for those on the margins. Looking carefully at Ruth's situation, we see three factors that allowed her to thrive. First, she was working in an economic system that was given by God and that provided opportunity for those on the margins. Second, she was working for a leader who was committed in his whole life to serve God, and thus he cared for those under his charge, both faithfully following the economic system and going beyond to a level of empathy with his workers. Third, Ruth was com-mitted to working hard with a purpose. We don't have the same economic system and we don't all have bosses who are committed to carry out God's leading. Let's look at these in turn.

The economic system she became a part of allowed the owner to do well and also allowed opportunity, at the expense of the owner, for the marginalized in the community. Today, in much of the West, we have some form of free-market capitalism as our economic system, and this system has taken many out of poverty. But free-market capitalism has no fundamental principle to allow for the marginalized, particularly as defined by Milton Friedman, with its goal to maximize profit within the constraints of the law, reducing people to a utility.[5] We face choices here at this point. Some take the view that this is the system of choice among God's people today because it is the most consistent (when compared with other economic systems) with Judeo-Christian values.[6] Perhaps a better choice is to ask how we might adapt the economic system in which we work to one more closely aligned with God's call on us. It is not hard to find examples of such refocusing, including the leaders of the Mars Company and the adapted economic system of mutuality they have developed.[7] But it is not enough to strictly work within a system.

Second, Ruth had a godly leader, Boaz, who was willing to faithfully adhere to the system that God had ordained. But he also went beyond the requirements of the system. We will see that he demonstrated servant leadership by engaging with his workers and seeking their best interests. It appears that Boaz sought to do what Paul would later call us to do when in a position of leadership:

> Masters, provide your [workers] with what is right and fair, because you know that you also have a Master in heaven. (Col. 4:1)

Third, Ruth herself needed to commit to do the hard work of gleaning. While this may seem obvious, it is the call from Scripture for us as well. As Paul wrote,

> Whatever you do, work at it with all your heart, as working for the Lord, not for human masters, since you know that you will receive an inheritance from the Lord as a reward. It is the Lord Christ you are serving. (Col. 3:23–24)

There are many today who work hard like Ruth did but without the adaptation of the economic system or a godly or benevolent boss. Each of us is called to work as well as we can before the Lord, but the disparity contributes significantly to today's polarization. There are also some who are unwilling to work hard, believing the world owes them a living. Even with committed leadership and a recognition of the needs of the marginalized, the person is unable to thrive.

—

As it turned out, Ruth went to the fields of Boaz, a relative of Naomi's on her husband's side. When she told Naomi about this, Naomi recognized another possibility. When Naomi and her husband had left the country, they sold their land, which added to her poverty when she returned. Jewish law, however, was established to create barriers to poverty by allowing a "kinsman redeemer" to buy back the land. Boaz fit that category.[8]

When Boaz saw a new worker in his fields, he asked his foreman who it was and received this report: "The overseer replied, 'She is the Moabite who came back from Moab with Naomi. She said, "Please let me glean and gather among the sheaves behind the harvesters." She came into the field and has remained here from morning till now, except for a short rest in the shelter'" (Ruth 2:6–7). Ruth had shown respect as she approached the opportunity to glean, humbly asking permission, rather than approaching this as an entitlement. By being engaged with his workers, Boaz was able to recognize the opportunity to serve them, which he might have missed had he remained in the enclosed bubble of his success.

Al recalls a time from college in DeKalb, Illinois, when he realized his world was too small. He was talking with an African American student and learned he was going to travel sixty miles into Chicago to visit a barber. When Al innocently asked why he would travel so far for a haircut, Al was surprised at the response: "There's no barber in DeKalb who will give a haircut to a Black person." This lit a fire under Al to do something about it. Since he was editor of the college newspaper, he began discussions with barbers and ran an editorial campaign. A couple of months later, the biggest barber shop in the town opened, ready to serve anyone who wanted to come in.

We all live in our own bubbles, often unaware of problems that constrain others because we don't face those same limitations. A key step is to broaden our engagements beyond the familiar and the comfortable. Boaz seemed to make a habit of this, engaging with the workers in his fields, recognizing them as human rather than simply units of production.

Ruth also needed an advocate. As a young immigrant woman in a patriarchal society, Ruth faced risks, and Boaz came forward as an advocate for her. After encouraging this good worker to stay in his fields, he told her, "Watch the field where the men are harvesting, and follow along after the girls. I have told the men not to touch you. And whenever you are thirsty, go and get a drink from the water jars the men have filled" (Ruth 2:9).

Both then and now, women are subject to harassment and marginalization in the workplace. The situation was even worse for Ruth because of her minority status, but Boaz provided protection. Naomi was also pleased with this arrangement: "It will be good for you, my daughter, to go with his girls, because in someone else's field you might be harmed" (Ruth 2:22). Keller points out that Boaz provided this extra protection (having her glean with his workers rather than being on the edge of the fields) out of concern for potential harassment from other gleaners.[9]

———

Ruth not only worked hard but had results to show her work paid off. We read that after her first day, "she gleaned in the field until evening. Then she threshed the barley she had gathered, and it amounted to about an ephah [half bushel]." Her mother-in-law was impressed. Ruth came home with enough for the two of them to eat and have grain left over. Her work was not just for herself, but also for her family.

Boaz was also impressed, and he invited her to stay with the work not only through the barley harvest but through the wheat harvest as well. We don't know how Ruth learned to do all this work but learn she did. One of the signs of a great worker is one who is always learning, ever aware of the need to prepare for a new situation that could arise at any time.

In the movie *Hidden Figures*, we see this initiative displayed brilliantly by the "computers," the women who carried out complex calculations for NASA early in the space program.[10] Dorothy Vaughan, the oldest of the three African American women working there, saw that they would soon lose their jobs with the arrival of electronic computers. Rather than dreading this, she took the initiative to learn how to use the new equipment herself. She became one of the first programmers to work on NASA's IBM computer, but it was no simple transition.

Beyond her initiative, another part of Ruth's success was the quality of leadership Boaz displayed. In many ways, he has the qualities one would desire in a manager. Here is the way the *Theology of Work Commentary* on Ruth puts it:

> As Ruth 2:2 relates, Boaz was "a prominent rich man." Whatever connotations that might have today, in Boaz's case that meant he was one of the best bosses in the Bible. His leadership style began with respect. When we first encounter him, he is greeting his workers with "The Lord be with you!" "The Lord bless you!" they called back" (Ruth 2:4–5).

This is not a common practice among employer/employee relations!

> Boaz put his respect for his workers into practice by providing them with water as they worked (Ruth 2:9), by eating with them, and most of all by sharing his food with the person regarded as the lowest among them (Ruth 2:14). Later we learn that at harvest time, Boaz the landowner winnowed with his harvesters and slept with them out in the field (Ruth 3:2–4, 14).[11]

In these actions, Boaz went beyond faithfully executing the gleaning laws. As a servant leader, he extended grace to those under his responsibility. Perhaps he was motivated by the grace God had extended to him. Whatever the reason, we can learn from these actions for our own calls in leadership.

———

Cheryl Broetje faced a similar challenge when she and her husband, Ralph, started Broetje Orchards in the 1970s in eastern Washington. The two of them worked closely together, though Cheryl was often the spokesperson for the business. From a small beginning, they grew to a major business with eighteen hundred workers (swelling to roughly twenty-five hundred during harvest for about four months per year), dealing with the produce from about six thousand acres of fruit trees. Here are some key features of how they managed the farm and its workers:

> They came to believe that God was calling them not only to grow apples, but also to use that work as a context in which people who were being overlooked or ignored could grow as well. In the early days, the workforce was made up of white migrant workers who started in Texas, moved to California, and then came up the coast to Washington, following the harvest. Almost overnight this group stopped coming and was replaced by people with brown faces who spoke Spanish and were primarily young males.[12]

Having a special eye for the vulnerable is important in the agricultural business, and they quickly learned that these values must guide the way they operated. They committed to pay more than minimum wage and provide opportunities for education and development. But harvesting an orchard is hard work and people who have other ways to earn money don't come. "We hire any local person who applies, and it amounts to two or three people a year," she said. Unlike Ruth, there were many in that community who were not prepared to do the hard work of harvesting.

After they built a warehouse in 1987, Broetje Orchards became a grower, packer, and shipper organization. They hired a hundred women to work in the warehouses and soon began to hear some disturbing stories about their families. Because both parents needed to help contribute to the household economy, many children were left locked in apartments so their parents could work, while other kids were pulled out of school to take care of their younger siblings. When they discovered there were serious health issues among these children, they set up an on-site day care/preschool.

The challenge only grew from there. "One family started to ask us about housing," Cheryl said. "Their boy was being bitten by rats as he slept at night. In this country! We knew we had to do something more. Our people needed decent, affordable housing." So they built some housing next to the warehouse.

> We had achieved the "American dream." But our employees were excluded from that. So we took all of our savings and built 100 two-, three-, and four-bedroom homes along with a gym that doubled as a community center, chapel, store, and laundry. The first residents held a contest and named the new community Vista Hermosa (beautiful view).[13]

Of those first residents, about a third had children with some prior gang involvement. They soon realized they needed to become social workers as well as apple growers or face the possibility of serious trouble with their neighbors. Over the years, they started numerous programs as a response to the needs of their people. These programs included an on-site bilingual library, a Christian elementary school, a residential program for at-risk teen boys (Jubilee Youth Ranch), after-school tutoring, college scholarships, ESL classes, parenting and job training, and so on. "We kept discovering new needs that, if not addressed, will become barriers to the health, stability, and development of our families."[14]

This work by the Broetjes remained hard and challenging, not just in dealing with the workers but also in dealing with the law. They estimated that upwards of half of their employees did not have legal documents. Cheryl said,

> We require proper I.D., and they give us I.D., but we aren't detectives to determine which I.D. is real. When the government calls us or sends out those nice little papers saying please advise this person that something's not right with their card, we do our "due diligence," of course. We do everything that we're required to do by law.[15]

But the Broetjes also came to believe that those showing up in the orchard were economic refugees, desperate to work toward a better future. In a statement made in his 1967 pastoral letter, Pope Paul VI said, "The human right to feed the family supersedes the right of a nation to establish borders and control entrance to and from that nation."

Some years after this interview, Al talked with Cheryl again about how they walked the line between creating opportunity and creating dependency. Cheryl related this story:

> It was Christmas time, and a local Rotary Club had collected toys to give to the poor in their community. They had more than they could distribute, and contacted Broetje Orchards to see if they had some poor children who could benefit from Christmas gifts. Rather than make the decision herself, Cheryl brought together Vista Hermosa Community engagement team to make the decision. They concluded that about 50 of the children could benefit from the gifts, but they didn't want them to just be delivered to the children. Rather, they set up a program where the parents of the needy children could do some community service and then receive the gifts. In doing this, the parents could provide the gifts to the children, preserving dignity in the home and valuing their work. An Agriculture Jobs Bill was created so that workers could become legal in three years, but it was voted down. [16]
>
> Now we are concerned about [the Department of] Homeland Security. For any number of reasons, we could be forced out of business by the government's treatment of our employee group. [17]

In 2019, the Broetjes sold their orchard to an outside company. The Broetjes set up a family trust, chaired by Cheryl, with this statement,

> With this transition, we took the lessons learned from living as one community in that place as guiding principles for how to more heavily invest in multiplying this work around the world. The Broetje Family Trust was established in 2019 to steward the legacy of Broetje Orchards and the mission to *"go and bear fruit, fruit that will last."*

The challenge of work and charity, the requirements of the law, and the need for advocacy were present realities for Boaz and Ruth just as they were for Cheryl Broetje and the immigrant workers on her farm.

———

The story of Ruth then takes a fascinating turn. Naomi and Ruth work out a plan for Ruth to build a deeper relationship with Boaz. In Ruth 3:2–4, Naomi instructs Ruth,

> "Tonight he will be winnowing barley on the threshing floor. Wash, put on perfume, and get dressed in your best clothes. Then go down to the threshing

floor, but don't let him know you are there until he has finished eating and drinking. When he lies down, note the place where he is lying. Then go and uncover his feet and lie down. He will tell you what to do."

After Boaz had finished eating and drinking, and was in good spirits, he went to lie down by the grain pile. Ruth went over to him and lay at his feet. "In the middle of the night, something startled the man and he turned and discovered a woman lying at his feet" (3:8). Ruth identified herself and said, "Spread the corner of your garment over me for you are my kinsman redeemer" (3:9). Boaz then asked Ruth to stay the rest of the night, because there was another kinsman-redeemer who was a closer relative than he. He committed to resolve the whole matter honorably the next day.

In our modern world, many read seduction and sexual intrigue into this passage, but Jewish scholar Robert Alter offers a different view:

> Naomi certainly appears to leave open the possibility that Boaz will ask Ruth to have sex with him, but she is counting that he will instead virtuously devise a plan to do social and matrimonial justice to his kinswoman by marriage. . . . There is both a practical and symbolic reason for Boaz's urging Ruth to spend the night with him on the threshing floor. He is concerned that it might be dangerous for her to make her way back through the town in the dark of night. . . . But the night spent together is also an adumbration of marital union, though here, in the most likely reading, still unconsummated.[18]

As was the custom, the next day Boaz went to the relative most closely related to Naomi and Elimelech, offering the opportunity to this unnamed person to redeem the family: to marry Ruth, acquire the family property, and carry on the family name of Ruth's deceased husband. "If that relative chooses to do so," Alter says, "Boaz can only lend his assent and approval."[19] The relative quickly agrees to do so, causing Boaz to remind him of his legal obligation: "On the day you buy the land from Naomi and from Ruth the Moabitess, you acquire the dead husband's widow, in order to maintain the name of the dead with his property" (4:5). Alter notes the care of the phrasing used by Boaz:

> Boaz makes a point of identifying Ruth as a Moabite, calculating that this will trouble the kinsman, for the Moabites were not merely foreigners but traditional enemies with whom contact has been proscribed. . . . While the reason is left unstated, many commentators believe that he does not want to contaminate his family by introducing a Moabite woman.[20]

Alter also notes that since Ruth had been childless in her first marriage, it might be a signal that she would never have children. This proves too much for the would-be redeemer. In front of the elders, he declines the offer, leaving the opportunity for Boaz to step in. Boaz commits to marrying Ruth and all this entailed and does so with this intriguing blessing of the elders:

> "We are witnesses. May the LORD make the woman who is coming into your home like Rachel and Leah, who together built up the family of Israel. May you have standing in Ephrathah and be famous in Bethlehem. Through the offspring the LORD gives you by this young woman, may your family be like that of Perez, whom Tamar[21] bore to Judah." (4:1–12)

Indeed, God did bless this marriage, and Ruth and Boaz had a son named Obed who became the grandfather of King David. Ultimately, this was the family of Jesus.

—

The story of Ruth (with Naomi and Boaz) and the parallel story of Ralph and Cheryl Broetje raise helpful insight for us as our world polarizes around issues of immigration, economic systems, good leadership, and hard work. Ruth reminds us that God's ways of defining economic systems, servant leadership, and the call to good work can come together as a picture of what it might look like if we leaned into God's wisdom and let God's purposes guide us. The Broetjes demonstrate adapting the economic system and trusting God for wisdom and insight about his call for leadership. They did this with a particular emphasis on the marginalized of their society.

While we cannot impose these solutions on the world, we can demonstrate what God through Jesus has called us to do: "Let your light so shine before others that they may see your good deeds and glorify your Father in heaven" (Matt. 5:16).

6 | David

But if privilege is not bad, it is still dangerous. . . . And privilege is danger-
ous because of how easily it becomes invisible. . . . How many times have
I been put in the front of the line without even knowing there was a line?
How many times have I walked through a door that opened, silently, for
me, but slammed shut for others? How many lines have I cut in a life of
privilege?

— Andy Crouch, *Playing God: Redeeming the Gift of Power*

With great power comes great responsibility.

— Uncle Ben to Peter Parker, *Spider Man*

"Who am I, Sovereign Lord, and what is my family, that you have brought
me this far?" The promise God had made must have taken David's breath
away. At long last, after years and years of Israel fighting one enemy after another and then surviving a civil war against King Saul and his family, David
hears from God that he "will provide a place for my people Israel and will
plant them so that they could have a home of their own and no longer be
disturbed," that he will give King David and the people of Israel "rest from
all your enemies" (2 Sam. 7:10–11). And God says that he had appointed
David, whom he says he "took . . . from the pasture, from tending the flock"
to shepherd God's people, Israel, as their king.

This promise from God is clearly the high point of David's life, but we
wonder if there is more to David's response than simply an expression of
amazement at how far God had brought him in his life. Was he also won-
dering, "Who am I, really? Will I continue to be worthy of God's trust in

me or will I wind up, in the end, like my predecessor, Saul? Can I continue to keep my priorities straight? Can I continue to be that 'man after God's own heart?'" (1 Sam. 13:14).

———

After the death of Joshua and his generation, "another generation grew up who knew neither the Lord nor what he had done for Israel." (Judg. 2:10). The Israelites began to serve the "gods" of the native Canaanites, which "aroused the Lord's anger." Consequently, "the hand of the Lord was against them" whenever they were attacked, and the people "were in great distress." So the Lord "raised up judges, who saved them" from these enemies, "Yet [the Israelites] would not listen to their judges but prostituted themselves to other gods and worshiped them" (Judg. 2:14–17).

Eventually, there was chaos and corruption—morally and politically— among the Israelites, and "everyone did as they saw fit" (Judg. 21:25). There were exceptions to this pattern, of course, like Ruth and Boaz. But the cultural climate and the weariness of fighting one war after another while being led by one temporary leader after another grew so great that, in desperation, the elders of Israel went to the last of these leaders, Samuel, and demanded a king "to lead us, such as all the other nations have" (1 Sam. 8:5). Not surprisingly, Samuel was not happy with this demand.[1] But after consulting with God and warning the people of what having such a king would mean in practice,[2] he grudgingly anointed Saul, a tall, handsome thirty-year-old from the tribe of Benjamin as Israel's first king.[3]

It soon became apparent, however, that Saul was not up to the job, and God directs Samuel to anoint another man to take Saul's place as king of Israel. Saul nevertheless remained king for a long time, but from this point on, "the Spirit of God left Saul and in its place a black mood sent by God settled on him" (1 Sam. 16:14 MSG). Saul increasingly suffered from what we would call chronic depression.

———

Though Samuel knew that Saul proved to be the wrong person to be king, he almost made the same mistake in choosing Saul's successor as he did with Saul: he focused on what a person looks like on the outside rather than what the person was on the inside. When God told Samuel to visit Jesse in Bethlehem because he had "chosen one of his sons to be king," apparently Samuel did not ask God how he would know *which* son of Jesse was "the one." Instead, when he arrived in Bethlehem, he assumed that the first of Jesse's sons that he saw must the right one, but God corrected him:

> "Looks aren't everything. Don't be impressed with his looks and stature. I've already eliminated him. God judges persons differently than humans do. Men and women look at the face; God looks into the heart." (1 Sam. 16:7 MSG)

After interviewing seven of Jesse's sons, Samuel tells Jesse that "God hasn't chosen any of these." Then he asks him, "Is this it? Are there no more sons?" Jesse replies, "Well, yes, there's the runt. But he's out tending the sheep." Samuel tells Jesse to "go get him." and when David is brought in, God tells Samuel, "Up on your feet! Anoint him! This is the one!" After Samuel anoints David with his brothers standing around watching, "the Spirit of God entered David like a rush of wind, God vitally empowering him for the rest of his life" (1 Sam. 16:8–13 MSG).[4]

It is easy to criticize Samuel for wanting to find a king who "looked the part," but we also live in a culture that often pays far more attention to the way someone looks—the "image" they project—rather than what is inside the person. We don't have the ability, as God has, to look into a person's heart, but we can—and should—be careful about reaching a conclusion about someone we may meet or work with based solely on first impressions.

Randy's friend Ann Jones, the chief administrative officer for the City of Hattiesburg, has conducted dozens of interviews to fill positions with the city since she was appointed to that position in 2017. In a typical interview, she says, the initial focus is on the particulars of the job and whether, based on the person's training and experience, he or she seems to be a good "fit" for the position. But about half way through the interview, she asks the applicant: "Tell me about yourself." That open-ended question almost always prompts the person to talk about what they consider important in their lives in addition to their work: their families, their hobbies, their outside interests. Ann doesn't dismiss the importance of being well-dressed, being on time for the interview, looking her in the eyes, and the experience the person has. But she also wants to get a good sense of how well the applicant will work with a wide range of people, what fiduciary experience he or she may have had if dealing with money is involved, and that person's work ethic. She often asks, "What does 'a lot of work' look like to you?" But as she interviews, she is most interested in understanding, as best she can, what that person is like and whether he or she is likely to be successful in that position.

———

Though depression may be the "common cold" of mental illness, as a counselor once told Randy, Saul's advisors say to him, "This awful torment-ing depression from God is making your life miserable," and they urge him to enlist a musician to serve as, what we would call, a "music therapist."

> "I have seen a son of Jesse of Bethlehem who knows how to play the lyre. He is a brave man and a warrior. He speaks well and is a fine-looking man. And the Lord is with him." (1 Sam. 16:18)

So Saul sends for David, and he enters Saul's service as an armor-bearer and music therapist. Whenever Saul had an episode of serious depression, David would "take up his lyre and play. Then relief would come to Saul; he would feel better; and the evil spirit would leave him" (1 Sam. 16:23).

Thus far in the narrative, we have not heard David speak, so we don't know exactly what he is thinking or whether he understood all the implica-tions of what had happened to him when Samuel anointed him and "the Spirit of the Lord came powerfully on him" (1 Sam. 16:13). Nevertheless, he is willing to serve the current king, bringing his skills as a musician to help soothe Saul's depressed spirit. This attitude of service to the man whose place he will eventually take is a confirmation that David is, indeed, the right man to be king.

People who serve in positions of leadership are human, and they some-times suffer from depression and other maladies caused by the burdens of responsibilities they cannot imagine. As many have observed, it is instruc-tive to compare how much those who are elected president of the United States age in appearance during the time they serve in that office, and the same can often be said of leaders of companies, businesses, and churches—large and small. If we see ourselves as someone who may succeed such a leader, will we provide support and encouragement to that leader during the time he or she is leading—as David did with Saul—or will we undermine the leader and speed the process of aging and deterioration of the leader's health along so that our time to lead will come more quickly? Or if we are a member of the senior management team and conclude that the leader of the organization is hurting the organization because he or she has stayed too long, what is our responsibility to both the leader and the organization?[5]

The ServiceMaster Company had a practice for many years of using a concept they called "shingles on a roof" to carry out leadership transitions.

They would actively develop a new leader while at the same time recognize that they wanted the new person to work collaboratively with the one stepping aside. When Ken Hansen became CEO of the company in 1957, Marion Wade became the company chairman. But Ken saw that Marion had better sales skills and brought him into customer visits. Marion knew Ken had better business skills, so he would close the deal. Working together meant both leaders needed to set aside their personal egos.[6]

David made the decision, based on what he knew, to try to help Saul by using his musical abilities. He knew he would take Saul's place one day, but he did not let that knowledge stop him from providing Saul with help and support through musical therapy. David simply saw a man in a position of leadership who needed help, and he was willing to provide that help.

———

Though David "entered Saul's service" as a musical therapist and armor-bearer, he only worked part time for him. He "went back and forth from Saul to tend his father's sheep at Bethlehem." When David heard that the Philistine giant, Goliath, had challenged the Israelite army—and King Saul—to put forth a champion to do battle with him, David volunteered despite his youth and size in comparison to Goliath, and despite Goliath's threat to "give [his] flesh to the birds and the wild animals." David expressed confidence that he would kill Goliath not because he was a mighty warrior, but because of who he represented in this fight:

> "You come against me with sword and spear and javelin, but I come against you in the name of the LORD Almighty, the God of the armies of Israel, whom you have defied. This day the LORD will deliver you into my hands, and I'll strike you down and cut off your head. . . . All those gathered here will know that it is not by sword or spear that the LORD saves; for the battle is the LORD's, and he will give you into our hands." (1 Sam. 17:45–47)

David was not afraid to fight, but rather than fight with conventional weapons—a coat of armor, a bronze helmet, and a sword—he told King Saul, "I can't even move with all this stuff on me. I'm not used to this" (1 Sam. 17:39)—he understood that "the battle belongs to God" and that he "doesn't save by means of sword or spear" (1 Sam. 17:47 MSG).

We do not believe that Christians should be cultural pacifists, simply going along with the cultural flavor of the month, but we need to learn to be creative in how we respond. We need to learn from David's fight with Goliath to think about the *best* way, *situation by situation*, to be salt and light in a culture that is increasingly hostile to Christianity. There is no one-size-fits-all response to an attack by non-Christians on Christianity and its values.

Sometimes it involves graciously but clearly confronting those who attack Christianity and its values, defending Christianity *intellectually*, pointing out the defects and inconsistencies in the alternative view of life and the world, as people like G. K. Chesterton, C. S. Lewis, and Dorothy Sayers did in their generation and Alister McGrath, Tim Keller, and Andy Crouch have been doing in our generation. Sometimes it involves learning to present Christianity as a more beautiful story than the one offered by the general culture.

In the fall of 2022, Randy's daughter Valerie began serving as a campus staff worker for InterVarsity Christian Fellowship/Canada in Vancouver, British Columbia, where her husband Clay was in graduate school at Regent College. We recently received a newsletter from Valerie that described Vancouver and how she and her family—and the students she works with at the University of British Columbia—are learning to engage with what she has called Vancouver's "post-post-Christian culture." She writes,

> Vancouver is a very interesting place. On the one hand, people are generally friendly and conflict-avoidant. All the streets have bike lanes, and almost everywhere you look you can see snow-capped mountains in the distance. Most of it is beautiful and affluent. . . .
>
> [And yet] it's a secular place. Even with the amazing Christian spaces our family has been gifted to inhabit in our work and church community here, the general belief all around us is that this life is all there is. And the pressure to make the most of every minute, confident in every aspect of one's identity and purpose, can be paralyzing, especially for young people.
>
> The good news is that our children and [the] students [we minister to] are intentionally working to figure out how to live in the world but according to a different story. And these conversations are starting to shape and strengthen our family and the InterVarsity community in some new and important ways.
>
> A dominant theme among Jesus's followers here (which I think applies in the U.S.) is learning to live "in exile," as the Israelites did in Babylon. How can we have integrity and faithfulness as God's people, while seeking the good of the city He has placed us in (Jer. 29:7)? How can we allow our identity to be shaped by the Story of God as his image-bearers in the world, letting Jesus show us what it means to be human instead of [simply accepting the dominant culture's] narratives?

When David tells Saul he is going out to fight Goliath, Saul tells him, "Go, and God help you!" (1 Sam. 17:37 MSG). He clearly believes David will be quickly killed by Goliath, but David is confident, as he shouts to Goliath in response to the giant's taunts, that "the battle belongs to God—he's handing you [Goliath] to us on a platter!" (1 Sam. 17:47 MSG). Which is, of course, exactly what happened. From Saul's standpoint—and the standpoint of the rest of the Israelite army—David is foolish to take such a risk in fighting Goliath. But David is prepared because of his past experience in fighting wild animals and, most importantly, because he knows God is with him.

Not long after the Goliath incident, Saul became jealous of David's popularity and tried to kill him. David fled and became a fugitive with a price on his head. One day, Saul, who was pursuing David, stepped into a cave to relieve himself. David's men encouraged him to kill Saul while he was "incapacitated," and David sneaked into the cave, cut off a corner of Saul's robe, and then yelled to Saul that the fact that he cut off only a corner of his robe rather than kill him was evidence he was not guilty of rebellion. The fact that David did this *himself* seems almost foolishly risky and, in addition, David is "conscience stricken" when he realizes that he has reached out against God's anointed. There are risks worth taking and risks not worth taking, as David realizes.

Later in the story, after David becomes king and has defeated the Philistines, he brings the long-lost ark of God back to Jerusalem. Not content to simply walk alongside the precious ark on the way to Jerusalem, David leads a joyful parade, "dancing before the Lord with all his might, while he and all Israel were bringing up the ark of the Lord with shouts and the sounds of trumpets" (2 Sam. 6:14–15). David's wife, Saul's daughter Michal, is deeply offended by the spectacle that David, now king, has made of himself, "going around half-naked in full view of the slave girls of his servants as any vulgar fellow would!" (2 Sam. 6:20). He has, Michal believes, degraded the office he now holds: a king should act more dignified than exposing "himself to the eyes of the servants' maids like some burlesque street dancer!" (2 Sam. 6:20 MSG).

This time, David correctly believes the risk to his reputation is worth it: "In God's presence I'll dance all I want! . . . Oh yes, I'll dance to God's glory—more recklessly even than this. And as far as I'm concerned . . . I'll gladly look like a fool . . . but among these maids you're so worried about,

I'll be honored no end" (2 Sam. 6:21–22 MSG). David understood better than Michal what it meant to be a king of Israel: giving God glory with his body—even at the risk of some people thinking it unseemly—was more important than looking dignified to her or the crowd. Hundreds of years later, Jesus takes the "risk" of eating with sinners, tax collectors, and prostitutes, but he considered it a risk well worth taking to make clear what kind of kingdom he was inaugurating.

Whatever our work, we will often be faced with the choice of whether to take a risk or not. Is the risk we're considering taking an *appropriate* one? Is the end goal a *worthwhile* one? We are not guaranteed success when we take a risk, even if the risk is taken for a worthy goal, but that should not cause us to hold back when an opportunity to advance some good goal in our organization—or in our family—presents itself. And we should be careful about criticizing those who take worthwhile risks, as Michal did of her husband, David, when she saw him "leaping and dancing before God" (2 Sam. 6:16 MSG).

In 1910, President Theodore Roosevelt gave a speech called "Citizenship in a Republic," but the part of the speech that is remembered is known as "The Man in the Arena." It beautifully expresses the importance of a leader of any organization taking risks to advance a good goal:

> It is not the critic who counts, not the one who points out how the strong man stumbled or how the doer of deeds might have done them better. The credit belongs to the man who is actually in the arena, whose face is marred with sweat and dust and blood; who strives valiantly; who errs and comes short again and again; who knows the great enthusiasms, the great devotions, and spends himself in a worthy cause; who, if he wins, knows the triumph of high achievement; and who, if he fails, at least fails while daring greatly, so that his place shall never be with those cold and timid souls who know neither victory nor defeat.[7]

———

After fighting and eventually winning a defensive war against Saul and his family, David finally becomes king over all Israel. He conquered Jerusalem and took up residence there, calling it "the City of David" (2 Sam. 5:9). "And he became more and more powerful, because the Lord God Almighty was with him" (2 Sam. 5:10). He understood that "the Lord had established him as king over Israel and had exalted his kingdom for the sake of his people Israel" (2 Sam. 5:12). With God's help, David defeats the Philistines and returns the ark to Jerusalem. He builds a palace for himself and, after he settled in the palace, God gives him rest from all his enemies. It was at this point that Nathan came to David and told him that God had said that he was going to establish David's kingdom and throne forever.

Because God was with him, David achieved tremendous success. His people were finally united after years of civil war and, as king, he was "doing what was just and right for all his people" (2 Sam. 8:15). In a sense, he had no worlds left to conquer; he had accomplished all he had ever dreamed of or imagined and was ready to take some well-deserved time off. But then: "In the spring, at the time when kings go off to war, David sent [General] Joab out with the king's men and the whole Israelite army. They destroyed the Ammonites and besieged Rabah. But David remained in Jerusalem" (2 Sam. 11:1). What happened next is perhaps, besides the Goliath episode, the most well-known part of David's story.

One evening, David got out of bed and took a walk on the roof of his palace. From there, he saw a beautiful woman bathing, and he sent messengers to bring the woman, Bathsheba, to him. He slept with her, and she became pregnant. In a panic, David brought Bathsheba's husband, Uriah, back from the war and encouraged him to spend some time with his wife in hopes that they would have sexual relations and that the father of the child Bathsheba was carrying would be assumed to be Uriah's. Uriah, however, told David that it wouldn't be fair to the other soldiers for him to spend time with his wife while they were "living in tents," and he spent that night with David's servants and did not go home to his wife.

Frustrated, David then directed General Joab to put Uriah in the front lines where he was certain to be killed—which is what happened. Believing the cover-up to be successful, and after an appropriate time for mourning Uriah's death, David again has Bathsheba brought to him, "and she became his wife and bore him a son" (2 Sam. 11:2ff.).

Nathan the prophet now reappears, but this time he confronts David with his evil deeds of adultery and murder—but he does not do so directly. Instead, he tells David a story of a rich man and a poor man, with the rich man taking the poor man's beloved lamb for a meal he was hosting for a wealthy guest instead of using one of his own sheep or cattle as the meat dish. Outraged at this obvious injustice, David proclaims, "As surely as the LORD lives, the man who did this must die!" (2 Sam. 12:5). At this point, Nathan springs the trap:

Then Nathan said to David, "You are the man! This is what the LORD, the God of Israel, says: 'I anointed you king over Israel, and I delivered you from the hands of Saul. I gave your master's house to you, and your master's wives into your arms. I gave you all Israel and Judah. And if this had been too little, I would have given you even more. Why did you despise the word of the LORD by doing evil in his eyes?'" (2 Sam. 12:7–9)

Nathan's use of a story to help David see the reality of what he had done provides a good example for us. Unlike Nathan with David, we aren't seeking to trap someone into admitting they're wrong. Rather, like Jesus did with his frequent use of parables, by using stories to convey truth, we are seeking to help people—and ourselves—see *reality* rather than the world as we wish it was.

C. S. Lewis understood the power of stories and how it was often a better form of communication than simply telling someone the truth directly. Writing about his decision to use the form of a "fairy story," the *Chronicles of Narnia*, Lewis asked:

> Why did one find it so hard to feel as one was told one ought to feel about God or about the sufferings of Christ? I thought the chief reason was that one was told one ought to. . . . The whole subject was associated with lowered voices, almost as if it were something medical. But supposing that by casting all these things into an imaginary world, stripping them of their stained-glass and Sunday school associations, one could make them for the first time appear in their real potency? Could one not thus steal past those watchful dragons? I thought one could.[8]

Once David realized Nathan was talking about *him*, he immediately admits his wrongdoing, saying, "I have sinned against the Lord" (2 Sam. 12:13). Nathan tells him that God has forgiven him and that he, David, is not going to die, but that God has decided that there will be different consequences for what he has done:

> "Out of your own household I am going to bring calamity on you. Before your very eyes I will take your wives and give them to one who is close to you, and he will sleep with your wives in broad daylight. You did it in secret, but I will do this thing in broad daylight before Israel." (2 Sam. 12:11–12)

As Christians, we rightly pray for those we know are in difficult or distressing situations: someone is struggling with a health issue or an addiction or the loss of a job. While we should not stop being concerned about and praying for these sorts of things, we would do well to recognize that those who have had *success* in their lives—a promotion or a raise at work, a new job with a large salary, or acceptance into a well-respected university or graduate school—need prayers just as much as those who have suffered loss, since success brings all sorts of unanticipated temptations, as David learned.

One of the temptations that success can bring is that we feel the rules don't apply to us. People may not use those words, but that is what's in their minds when they engage in behavior that, before becoming successful, they would have recognized as wrong. Leona Hemsley may have famously said out loud that "the rules are for the little people," but, unfortunately, examples of this attitude are not uncommon among many leaders in business, government, and the church.

It takes *intentionality* for a person who has experienced success not to let it go to their head. Being accountable to another person or group of friends—as our friend David Gill says, having a "posse" to help us look honestly at ourselves—is an effective way of helping us keep our feet on the ground when we are successful.[9] David apparently did not have anyone to help hold him accountable—until Nathan appeared after the fact.

In his actions with Bathsheba and Uriah, perhaps David believed that he was acting not as king of Israel—he was, after all, taking some time off from going to war himself—but simply as David, a man. If that was what he thought, then he made the same mistake that many people—including many Christians—make today: he was attempting to compartmentalize his life into "public" and "private" spheres. There is nothing wrong with trying to achieve what is commonly called a "work-life balance," though that term is misleading and exposes the very compartmentalization mistake we make: *Our work is part of our life.* When Christians buy into the idea that their lives can be compartmentalized into public and private spheres, they are following the thinking that religion is "private," and it has nothing to do with how we think and act in public.

———

The Bible doesn't tell us whether Nathan's confrontation of David was done in public or in a private meeting, but the text's language seems to suggest that it was done privately—though the consequences, God told David through Nathan, would be painfully public (2 Sam. 12:11–12). Regardless, David was still the king and, especially if it was a private confrontation, he could have had Nathan killed or banished from his kingdom without much trouble. But he did not do that; instead, he simply said to Nathan, "I have sinned against the LORD" (2 Sam. 12:13). He basically threw himself on the mercy of Nathan—and God. At some point afterward, David wrote Psalm 51, which expresses his deep desire to be forgiven by God for his sin and to be restored in his relationship with God. The psalm is incredibly poignant and, not surprisingly, it is a model for us to pray when we have done something wrong and want God's forgiveness.

To admit we have made a mistake—even a serious mistake—that affects others is a difficult thing to do, but accepting responsibility for our mistakes is always preferable to attempting to cover them up or trying to shift the blame to someone else—as David's predecessor, Saul, did. We don't know exactly when Psalm 51 was written, but it seems to have been shortly after Nathan confronted David with his sins of adultery and murder. David begins, "Have mercy on me, O God, according to your unfailing love; according to your great compassion blot out my transgressions. Wash away all my iniquity and cleanse me from my sin" (vv. 1–2).

God indeed forgave David (2 Sam. 12:13), and while it may have taken some time for David to accept God's forgiveness, he eventually did. Sometime later, David seems to have been reflecting on all that had happened—perhaps particularly his decision to come clean about what he had done—when he wrote Psalm 32, which begins, "Blessed is the one whose transgressions are forgiven, whose sins are covered."

———

Unlike Moses, who was explicitly said to be "a very humble man, more humble than anyone else on the face of the earth" (Num. 12:3), David is not referred to that way in the biblical narrative. Yet if humility is defined as understanding, accepting, and playing the role one is assigned[10]—whether that role is one of leadership or not—David is portrayed in the narrative as consistently humble, despite having serious flaws. In fact, this characteristic may be key to understanding God's judgment that David was a "man after his own heart" (1 Sam. 13:14; Acts 13:22).

When considered only from the outside, Saul and David both had the physical attributes often associated with being a leader. But as the narrative unfolded, Saul's story was "a downward spiral into fear, jealousy, hatred, spiritual rebellion and even the occult."[11] David, on the other hand, is presented, with a few exceptions, as a person who understands and accepts his role. He was anointed by Samuel as the "future king" while Saul was still reigning, but the narrator makes it clear that even though from that day on "the Spirit of the Lord came powerfully upon David" (1 Sam. 16:13), he did not try to usurp Saul's authority. Instead, he willingly entered Saul's service, first as a musical therapist (1 Sam. 16:21–23) and then as a warrior (1 Sam. 17).

When Saul hunts for David in a jealous rage in order to kill him, David has several opportunities to kill Saul, but he refuses to harm Saul and even becomes "conscience-stricken" when he cuts off a corner of Saul's robe.

After David "was settled in his palace and the Lord had given him rest from all his enemies" (2 Sam. 7:1), David says that it was not right for him to be "living in a house of cedar, while the ark of God remains in a tent" (2 Sam. 7:2), and he decides to build God a "house" (i.e., a temple) for the ark. God, however, has plans for something far greater than a physical temple for himself, as he tells Nathan who then reports this to David (2 Sam. 7:4–17). God has decided to establish a dynasty—a "house"—through David (2 Sam. 11–13), and David is awestruck: "Who am I . . . that you have brought me this far?"

Perhaps the most famous example of David's essential humility before God is his reaction, expressed Psalm 51, to Nathan's confrontation. Though he had committed adultery with the wife of a man he subsequently murdered, David saw what he had done primarily as sinning against God himself: "Against you, you only, have I sinned and done what is evil in your sight" (Ps. 51:3), and he prayed for restoration of the relationship he had with God before his actions—a relationship that recognized who the actual king of Israel was.

It is rare to find leaders who can resist the temptation to try to become larger than life. David was not perfect, but we believe that, more than any other quality, it was this characteristic of humility—this willingness to accept the roles he had been given at different points in his life—that caused God to say that David was a man after his own heart. Are we willing to play the part(s) we have been "assigned" in the story we find ourselves in?

7 | Esther

By almost any outside measure, it appeared that Esther had it made. Once, she had been an orphaned Jewish girl raised by her uncle Mordecai while living in captivity in faraway Persia. Now she was queen of all the land. A fairy tale come true. But deep within, Esther knew that appearances were deceptive. Three things must have gnawed at her in her quiet moments.

First, she knew the reason the position of queen had become an opportunity for her. The prior queen, Vashti, had refused to respond to King Xerxes' request to show off her beauty at the conclusion of his seven-day drunken party. The king and all of his leaders got together to discuss what to do about her. What might happen to their position as men if the queen could get by with refusing the king? How might the wives of other men in the country respond to such a stand? So, Queen Vashti was banished from the land and the king started his search for a replacement queen. Queen Esther would need to keep her opinions to herself. It was a difficult time to be a woman in Persia.

Second, she knew the role that deception had played in allowing her to be queen. At the advice of her uncle, she had hidden her Jewish identity. The contest for the new queen required the candidates to spend a year in beauty treatments and other training before being invited in to spend a night with the king. She knew the moral guidelines from her Jewish heritage that prohibited her from sleeping with someone before she was married. That the king was not a Jew made matters much worse. It is unlikely she sought out the position by her own choice; the king had sent his men throughout the land looking for beautiful young virgins, and Esther had been swept up in the process.

Nonetheless, once she had been chosen as queen, she must have felt some level of guilt or victimhood for being there. Recent headlines involving entertainment and political leaders have been focusing on the sexual demands of men in powerful positions, which puts women in a terrible situation. These encounters often left these women voiceless and marginalized through no fault of their own.

Finally, the reality of Esther's position underscored her powerlessness. When Mordecai sent a message to her asking that she go to the king, she sent back a message saying that only those who were called to see the king could go in, and unless the king extended his scepter to a visitor, that person was put to death. "And it has been thirty days since I was called to go to the king" (Esther 4:11), she explained. She was truly marginalized.

It would have been easy for Esther to assume, because of her morally compromised position and the severity of the environment, that she no longer had a voice. God could no longer use her. Perhaps it was time to sit back, enjoy the pleasures of being queen, and assimilate into the life of Persian royalty.

For ourselves, our careers may look great from an outside view. We may have a title and compensation package that is truly impressive. But did we cut a few corners to get there? Are there pressures to walk the organizational line? Do we sit back and enjoy the position, not making any waves? For many, fear and guilt may keep our voices silent, as was the case with Esther. Can we recover our voice, and can we still live out God's kingdom in such a position and a time as this?

When Al was working at the Boeing Company, he encountered a person in a senior position who had replaced a retired colleague. The former leader had a significant impact on the company and had been a major supporter of the technology R&D center that Al led. The new person seemed to do very little in this significant position. One day he called Al into his office and opened their meeting in a surprising way by saying, "You must be disappointed in me. I was given this position with the stipulation that I not make any waves. I can't do what the previous leader did. I am sorry." Indeed, he had no voice and needed to stay that way to keep his position. In Esther's case and in our own, can we still be used by God if we feel we have been marginalized in this way?

Tim Keller and Kathryn Alsdorf came to this conclusion in their discussion of Esther: "In such morally, culturally, and spiritually ambiguous situations, does God still work with us and through us? The answer of the book [of Esther] is yes."[1] This is truly good news for those who find themselves in such a position. But we can learn even more from Esther by seeing how she found her voice and how she used it.

—

Mordecai had a serious reason for contacting Esther: he had learned that Haman, the chief counsel to the king, had convinced the king that the Jewish people were a problem in the land and should be put to death. Haman's motivation for this was, unfortunately, purely personal. When Haman had encountered Mordecai outside the palace, Mordecai had not bowed down to him, which infuriated him. This led to Haman immediately making plans for revenge. The king listened to Haman and signed a bill authorizing this action for a future date.

Mordecai wanted Esther, from her position within the palace, to do something about it. While Esther felt powerless to act, Mordecai challenged her with this argument:

> "Do not think to yourself that in the king's palace you will escape any more than all the other Jews. For if you keep silent at this time, relief and deliverance will rise for the Jews from another place, but you and your father's house will perish. And who knows whether you have not come to the kingdom for such a time as this?" (4:12–14)

The words of Mordecai echo down to us through the ages. Are we on assignment for God in our current position? Are we here for such a time as this?

We, like Esther, can get wrapped up in our own worlds where our perspective narrows. Particularly in the individualistic West, we may believe we are self-sufficient and can make decisions by ourselves. These words from Mordecai disrupted her small world, opening a perspective she had missed.

Do we have someone who can speak into our lives, someone who will be honest with us and shatter the small world we live in?

In considering this question, perhaps our minds go to "reluctant" heroes from history: George Washington had a strong preference *not* to be the first president of the United States but instead preferred to retire to his beloved Mount Vernon and live out his days there. Or William Wilberforce who, after being converted to Christianity, preferred to give up his seat in Parliament and go into the ministry. In both cases, these men reluctantly answered the call to continue in public service and, as a result, changed the course of history.

At this point, however, there is no indication that Esther had any idea her actions would be "heroic" and "change the course of history." She was just an ordinary young woman living, if not "the dream," at least more or less secure where she was.

In C. S. Lewis's novel *Perelandra*, Ransom, the protagonist, was just an ordinary professor teaching at a college in England who was faced with a decision not unlike Esther's. He realized that the reason he had been brought to the planet Perelandra (what we call Venus) is to be God's representative on the planet and to engage in physical combat with a man named Weston, Satan's representative, whose mission was to corrupt Perelandra by leading a woman like Eve (whom Lewis calls "the Lady") to disobey Maledil's (God's) instructions about a specific matter. Ransom's mental attempts to avoid the mission reminds us of what Esther must have wrestled with:

> "Oh, this is nonsense," said the voluble self. He, Ransom, with his ridiculous piebald body and his ten times defeated arguments—what sort of miracle was that? His mind darted hopefully down a side-alley that seemed to promise escape. Very well then. He *had* been brought here miraculously. He was in God's hands. As long as he did his best—God would see to the final issue. . . .
>
> Relentlessly, unmistakably, the Darkness pressed down upon him the knowledge that this picture of the situation was utterly false. His journey to Perelandra was not a moral exercise, nor a sham fight. If the issue lay in Maledil's hands, Ransom and the Lady *were* those hands. The fate of the world really depended on how they behaved in the next few hours. The thing was irreducibly, nakedly real. They could, if they chose, decline to save the innocence of this new race, and if they declined its innocence would not be saved. It rested with no other creature in all time or all space . . . .
>
> The voluble self protested. . . . Did Maledil *want* to lose worlds? What was the sense of so arranging things that anything really important should finally

and absolutely depend on such a man as himself? . . . He writhed and ground his teeth, but could not help seeing. Thus, and not otherwise, the world was made. Either something or nothing must depend on individual choices. And if something, who could set bounds to it? A stone may determine the course of a river. He was that stone at this horrible moment which had become the center of the whole universe. The [angels] of all worlds, the sinless organisms of everlasting light, were silent in Deep Heaven to see what Elwin Ransom of Cambridge would do.[2]

For Esther, she had someone to help her in the decision she needed to make. We need this as well. The writer of Ecclesiastes put it this way,

Two are better than one, because they have a good return for their labor: If either of them falls down, one can help the other up. But pity anyone who falls and has no one to help them up. (Eccl. 4:9–10)

Esther pondered Mordecai's words. Perhaps it was at this point, after hiding in her culture, that she was able to conclude what Tish Harrison Warren challenges all of us to do in our age:

The future orientation of Christian time reminds us that we are people on the way. It allows us to live in the present as an alternative people, waiting for what is to come, but never giving up on our *telos*. We are never quite comfortable. We seek justice, practice mercy, and herald the kingdom come.[3]

Esther was now ready to act, but how? Sometimes once we get past our fears and accept a call to action, we simply just do it. It would be tempting to boldly leap to action with this new perspective, but Esther chose a different path. She sent a message to Mordecai that read:

"Go, gather all the Jews to be found in Susa, and hold a fast on my behalf, and do not eat or drink for three days, night or day. I and my young women will also fast as you do. Then I will go to the king, though it is against the law, and if I perish, I perish." (4:16)

She was willing to do what she knew she needed to do, but not in her own strength. She challenged Mordecai to gather the Jews for a three-day fast, and she committed to bring the women in her charge together to do the same.

In our call to action, it is easy to jump right in and get started. It is too easy to think that this kind of action is just a matter of courage and motivation. But we serve a great and powerful God who can go before us—Esther's step reminds us of this. Ironically, Esther is the only book of the Bible where the name of God is not explicitly mentioned. Some suggest this is the case because of the exile of the Israelites where God had seemingly withdrawn from the lives of his people. In our modern, secularized world, we may believe that God has withdrawn from our everyday lives and cares only about spiritual matters. But once again, we are reminded that all of life is under his reign, and we go to him for guidance and direction while participating with him in his solution.

Now the preparation had passed, and it was time for her to act. At great risk to herself, she must go to see Xerxes.

—

When she approached the king after the three-day fast, it is easy to imagine the pit in her stomach. Would she be received, or was this the end of the line? We wonder if she anticipated what she would say if her request to see the king was granted? To her great joy, and perhaps astonishment, the king received her with these wonderful words, "What is it, Queen Esther? What is your request? Even up to half the kingdom, it will be given to you" (5:3). The door was now wide open.

The wisdom she had asked for is demonstrated in her response. Instead of stating her case, she invites King Xerxes and his chief counsel Haman to a dinner party later that day. She must have concluded that a discussion over a meal would be a more conducive environment for this difficult conversation. The king readily accepted, and so did Haman, and that afternoon they arrived for a banquet.

During the feast, King Xerxes once again raised his question to Esther: "Now what is your petition? It will be given to you. And what is your request? Even up to half the kingdom, it will be granted."

Is this the time for Esther to lay out her case? She delays once again, stating, "If it please the king to grant my wish and fulfill my request, let the king and Haman come to the feast that I will prepare for them, and tomorrow I will do as the king has said." This request was again granted by the king. The invitations delighted Haman who went home and boasted to his family that he was now in exclusive company: "I'm the only person Queen Esther invited to accompany the king to the banquet she gave. And she has invited me along with the king tomorrow" (5:12).

From our modern perspective, it might seem that she is stalling, trying to work up the courage to lay out her case before the king. Many leadership books laud the leader who is able to make quick, decisive suggestions. In *Contrarian's Guide to Leadership*, however, Stephen Sample offers a different way to look at decision making: "Never make a decision today that can reasonably be put off until tomorrow."[4] Sample is making the case that better decisions can be made when more information is available, so rushing to a decision is unwise unless the decision must be made immediately.

Esther may not have had any of this insight about decision making, but she did have time. And she had fasted before going to the king. Let's look at what happened between the two banquets to see why the ensuing events made a difference in the outcome. Over the next twenty-four hours, three key events would unfold.

First, as Haman left the palace following the first banquet, he was elated for the invitation but was angered when he passed Mordecai on the way home. Unlike others, Mordecai again refused to bow down to Haman. Haman was still angry when he got home. In spite of his elation at being invited to another exclusive banquet with the king and queen, he said to his family, "But all this gives me no satisfaction as long as I see that Jew Mordecai sitting at the king's gate" (5:13). Haman did not know that Esther was a Jew, nor did he know that Mordecai had raised her. In his wrath, Haman decided to build a gallows on which to hang Mordecai, and he would make his case to King Xerxes before the banquet the next morning.

Second, and seemingly unrelated, King Xerxes could not sleep that night and called for one of his men to read to him from the annals of the king's reign. The passage read told the story of how Mordecai had overheard some of the king's eunuchs plotting to kill the king. He had sent a warning to the king through Esther, the case had been investigated, and the eunuchs were hanged. This caused the king to ask, "What honor or distinction has been bestowed on Mordecai for this?" The king's young men who attended him said, "Nothing has been done for him" (6:3). So the king, not knowing what Haman was plotting, decided to consult with Haman the next morning regarding how he should honor Mordecai.

Third, that next morning when Haman arrived for work, two competing agendas were on the table: Haman wanted to tell of his plans to hang Mordecai, and the king wanted to develop a plan to honor Mordecai!

Since Xerxes was the king, he first asked Haman how they could honor someone who had done great things for the kingdom. Haman, believing the king was talking about him, proposed an elaborate honor that would have this person led through the city center on the king's horse with someone declaring, "This is what the king does for those he delights to honor" (6:9). Before he could say anything about hanging Mordecai, Haman found himself assigned to the job! He was the one chosen to lead Mordecai through the city on the king's horse, proclaiming Mordecai's worth. Haman was totally humiliated. To his credit, he didn't raise his own plan to the king.

After carrying out this task, he had to hurry home to change clothes for the great banquet. Haman's family and advisors, on hearing what had happened, offered a dire forecast: "Since Mordecai, before whom your downfall has started, is of Jewish origin, you cannot stand against him—you will surely come to ruin!" (6:13).

When Xerxes, Haman, and Esther gathered for the second banquet, once again the king said to Esther, "Queen Esther, what is your petition? It will be given to you. What is your request? Even up to half the kingdom, it will be granted" (7:2). Now the situation was different because of the intervening events, and she responded to King Xerxes by stating,

> "If I have found favor with you, Your Majesty, and if it pleases you, grant me my life—this is my petition. And spare my people—this is my request. For I and my people have been sold to be destroyed, killed and annihilated. If we had merely been sold as male and female slaves, I would have kept quiet, because no such distress would justify disturbing the king."
>
> King Xerxes asked Queen Esther, "Who is he? Where is he—the man who has dared to do such a thing?"
>
> Esther said, "An adversary and enemy! This vile Haman!"
>
> Then Haman was terrified before the king and queen. (7:3–6)

Had Esther made this case at her first meeting with the king, or even at the first banquet, there is no telling what may have happened. By allowing time to pass, Esther allowed God time to work. Haman could not deny his plot against Mordecai since the gallows he had built were a testimony to his plans. Further, King Xerxes had established the loyalty and value of Mordecai by hearing about his heroics that had exposed the plot on the king's life. Mordecai was a good person for the king. Acting as only a king could do, Xerxes had Haman hanged on the gallows he had built for Mordecai.

Esther's wisdom in letting some time pass between the first and second meetings with the king must have had the effect of increasing Xerxes' curiosity about what Esther wanted from him. When she finally told him, he was ready to hear it.

Something Randy learned over the years practicing law is that not every problem is best solved by immediate action. Sometimes, the better approach is to let time pass and let the situation mature or ripen. In that case, the solution will be more apparent, and the client will be more prepared to accept his advice because they are able to see more clearly what the outcome should be. That is not to say that immediate action is not sometimes required, but wisdom is knowing when to act and when to wait.

We, too, need to be reminded that situations that are seemingly impossible for us are possible with God. We can certainly learn from Esther that we need to trust God in making a bold stand, and we need to leave room for him to act. It is so easy to run ahead of God, believing we have everything in control.

There is a remarkable story in 1 Samuel 4 where the children of Israel are preparing for a battle with the Philistines and the elders decide they can gain an advantage in the conflict by taking the ark of the covenant into battle with them. It all turns out horribly wrong. The Israelites are defeated, suffering great loss, and the Philistines capture the ark for themselves. This approach to God's guidance is different from Esther but may be more like our own approach. Here is what the *Theology of Work Bible Commentary* says about this passage:

> Eli's sons, alongside the leaders of the army, made the mistake of thinking that because they bore the name of God's people and possessed the symbols of God's presence, they were in command of God's power. Perhaps those in charge believed they could actually control God's power by carrying around the ark. Or maybe they had deceived themselves into thinking that because they were God's people, whatever they wanted for themselves would be what God wanted for them. Ironically, the ark contained the greatest means of God's guidance—the Ten Commandments—but Eli's sons did not bother to seek any kind of guidance from God before attacking the Philistines.
>
> Can it be that we often fall into the same bad habit in our work? When we are faced with opposition or difficulty in our work, do we seek God's guidance in prayer for *what to do* or do we just throw up a quick prayer asking God for help in doing what *we want to do*? Do we consider the possible courses of action in the light of scripture, or do we just keep a Bible on our desk? Is it possible that we are using God as a good luck charm, rather than following him as the master of our work?[5]

———

After all of this, there remained one problem for Esther and her people. The Jews were still vulnerable to attack because a signed order from the king could not be rescinded. Esther told the king about her relationship with Mordecai, and the two of them now approached the king:

> Esther again pleaded with the king, falling at his feet and weeping. She begged him to put an end to the evil plan of Haman the Agagite, which he had devised against the Jews. Then the king extended the gold scepter to Esther and she arose and stood before him.
>
> "If it pleases the king," she said, "and if he regards me with favor and thinks it the right thing to do, and if he is pleased with me, let an order be written overruling the dispatches that Haman son of Hammedatha, the Agagite, devised and wrote to destroy the Jews in all the king's provinces. For how can I bear to see disaster fall on my people? How can I bear to see the destruction of my family?" (8:3–6)

The king went beyond her request. He put Esther in charge of all of Haman's estate and took the signet ring that Haman had worn and gave it to Mordecai, the new second-in-command. Then he assigned his scribes to allow Mordecai to draft a new regulation giving the Jews the authorization to assemble and protect themselves from any armed force of any nationality.

The Jews did indeed defend themselves, triumphing over their destroyers. The holiday of Purim was established to celebrate the victory, and it is celebrated by Jews to this day.

———

We have already discussed the way Esther found counsel to help her see the situation beyond her own thoughts: how she acted with courage, prayed, and made time for God to work, and then how she acted, knowing that she needed to take a risk—even the risk of her life.

Several other general comments might be helpful to the twenty-first-century person hearing this story.

First, we see its relevance even though it took place in ancient Persia more than twenty-five hundred years ago. Christians today may feel the pressure of a post-Christian world. Pressure to be silent, to keep their relationship with God as a personal matter. More and more modern workplaces are demanding this behavior. In this sense, we can look to Esther for insight.

We may not have power, but we have influence. Can we, like Esther, use this influence to advance God's kingdom?

Second, a key theme throughout the story is the way she speaks with respect to the king. We see that in comparison to the way Xerxes disposed of Queen Vashti, readily signed a decree that would have led to the death of all Jews in the land, and exercised the power he had to deal with visitors, the "oppressive government" that some Christians complain about, particularly in the West, is mild compared with her life. Yet she maintained respect for the king.

Note her remarkable statement at the end of the second banquet: "If we had merely been sold as male and female slaves, I would have kept quiet, because no such distress would justify disturbing the king" (7:4). This sounds like an extreme statement to the modern ear. Slavery is okay?! Not at all; rather, this was her way of conveying the urgency and magnitude of the matter. Again, there is a reminder for us. There are lots of things wrong in the world. We could spend our entire lives pointing out failures and problems. Can we instead use our social capital to approach these important things? And can we use discernment to determine which of those things rise to that level of urgency?

She also had a good solution to propose that was not about her. "If it pleases the king, and if he regards me with favor and thinks it the right thing to do, and if he is pleased with me, let an order be written" (8:5). She did not say, "This is how the matter should be handled." Rather, she left room for the king to have a say in the solution. Having seen what Mordecai had done for him and how wise he was Xerxes assigned Mordecai to draft the new ordinance.

It could be argued that she had to be respectful or lose her head, so she approached the king in the best way possible. But the king had extended his scepter to her, inviting her to state her case. Her level of respect seems to mirror what Paul said to the Romans:

> Therefore, it is necessary to submit to the authorities, not only because of possible punishment but also as a matter of conscience. This is also why you pay taxes, for the authorities are God's servants, who give their full time to governing. Give to everyone what you owe them: If you owe taxes, pay taxes; if revenue, then revenue; if respect, then respect; if honor, then honor. (Rom. 13:5–7)

In the Beatitudes, Jesus calls us to humility and meekness and to love our enemies. What are we saying to the watching world when we are only concerned with our own rights and seeking power for ourselves?

We also note the respect shown in the dialogues between Esther and Mordecai. Esther was the one in the palace putting her life on the line. In the end, Mordecai is promoted to second-in-command in the kingdom. Yet they seemed to continue to collaborate and demonstrate oneness of purpose. Together, they influenced power far beyond them.

Today, Christians are too often divided from other Christians, championing ideology above the call of Christ in our world. In John 17:20–21, Jesus says, "My prayer is not for them alone. I pray also for those who will believe in me through their message, that all of them may be one, Father, just as you are in me and I am in you. May they also be in us so that the world may believe that you have sent me." Regarding this prayer, Francis Schaeffer made this comment: "We cannot expect the world to believe that the Father sent the son, that Jesus's claims are true, and that Christianity is true, unless the world sees some reality of the oneness of true Christians. Now that is frightening."[6]

———

Al was discussing the story of Esther with Christian women in government in a country that ranks as "very corrupt" on the Transparency International Corruption Perception Index.[7] The women were interested in how to navigate their own challenging situation, and together they talked through this narrative of Esther and the choices she made. Then one woman asked a question that surprised Al: "Three different times when Esther was welcomed by the king, he made an offer to her with his statement, 'What is your request? Even up to half of the kingdom it will be given you.' Why didn't she take it?"

Indeed, why did she not take advantage of such an amazing offer?

She could have thought, "If I had half the kingdom, look at all the good I could do!" But then she might have thought about her predecessor, Queen Vashti. Would she really have that much power when the king has the final word? Even if she did, seeking power to be able to do good can often be a false bargain. The corruptive nature of power ultimately leads to places we don't want to go.

With careful thought, Esther saw a different choice: satisfy her personal needs by gaining great wealth or address an issue that would have profound impact on her fellow Jews. Remember, she was there to address the problem of the Jews being annihilated, not to make her own life better. On further discussion, these women suggested that many seek a government position in their country not for what they can do for others, but for what they can do for themselves.

In the workplace, do you ever ask yourself why you are there? Jack van Hartesvelt, a hotel developer and a Christian, often reminds people, "It's not about you, and it's not about right now."[8] Likewise, Esther kept a sharp focus on her mission, avoiding the distraction of personal gain in wealth or power.

For too many, particularly in the West where individualism prevails, the workplace is about personal gain and credit. Recognizing God's call in our work must mean that God cares not only about how we do our work but in the work itself. This is a bigger calling than our own gain, and we need to keep our focus on what God wants us to do in our workplaces.

8 | Job

"Son, in years of religious studies I've come up with only two hard, incontrovertible facts: There is a God . . . and I'm not him."

— Fr. John Cavanaugh, former president of
the University of Notre Dame

By almost any measure, Job was a model citizen, one who was revered and respected by all. The opening verse captures our first look at him: "This man was blameless and upright; he feared God and shunned evil" (Job 1:1).

These were not just words said about him, but through his actions he lived them. Job had ten children, seven sons and three daughters. His children used to gather together in one of their homes to have feasts and party together. When the feasting had ended, Job would have them purified and then offer a sacrifice for them saying, "Perhaps they have sinned and cursed God in their hearts" (1:5). This was his regular practice.

Beyond his family, his care extended to the community. His friend Eliphaz speaks of this when he says to Job, "If someone ventures a word with you, will you be impatient? But who can keep from speaking? Think how you have instructed many, how you have strengthened feeble hands. Your words have supported those who stumbled; you have strengthened faltering knees" (4:2–4). Yes, Job's care went far and wide, and he was an encourager to many.

Job was also wealthy. Through the work of his hands and the blessing of God, his flocks and herds "spread throughout the land" (1:10). It seems he had it all. But then disaster struck Job, not just once but in multiple tidal waves.

During one of the feasts at his oldest son's home, Sabeans attacked the farm and carried off all the oxen and donkeys. This seemed totally unexpected, as the Sabeans were a peaceful Middle Eastern group of Semites who lived nearby.[1] The servants were killed, all but one, and he escaped to let Job know what had happened.

Before Job had time to digest this news, his sheep and the servants caring for them were struck by lightning. Again, all but one servant was killed, and he escaped to bring the news to Job.

While Job was still reeling, another servant arrived. He said that Chaldeans had formed three raiding parties and carried off all of the camels, while killing all but one of the servants who escaped to tell Job.

All of Job's wealth was gone in a matter of hours!

—

Steve Bell, a builder and cabinet maker, is someone who knows what it's like to lose his wealth. Laid off from his building job during the recession of the early 1980s, he turned to his entrepreneurial skills to start his own business, making cabinets in his garage. He was a stereotypical entrepreneur.

Steve met a dentist who was opening a series of dental clinics and secured a contract to begin building cabinets for these clinics. It wasn't long before Steve had eight people working for him building cabinets. "I thought I was God's gift to business."[2]

Then one day, he got a call from his lawyer who began by asking, "Are you sitting down? Did you see the newspaper this morning?" His lawyer then told him, "Your dentist buddy is on the front page of the paper. He has been arrested for drug smuggling and money laundering, and all of his assets have been seized."[3] Steve had $100,000 of work in progress, debts to all of his suppliers, and now no customer.

He was told to file for bankruptcy protection and start over. When Steve said his only real asset was his good name, and he wanted to commit to working off all the debt, his lawyer said, "You are naive. You will be sued by everyone, and your wife will be hounded by bill collectors. You have been had and you have no choice."[4] Steve remembers weeping with his wife that evening, knowing there was no good way out, but she told him, "I believe in you." Like Job, he was determined to hold on to his integrity. Steve acknowledged that bankruptcy might be the correct solution in the end, if one of his vendors filed suit, but he wanted to try it his way first. We will see the outcome of this when we discuss the outcome of Job's story: his word was his bond.

—

Unfortunately for Job, his loss of wealth and the death of many of his servants was not the final blow. Another messenger came to report that a hurricane had struck the house where his children had gathered to feast. The report was the worst yet: the house had collapsed on them, and all were killed.

Just like that, his family, wealth, and servants were all gone. Although Job despaired, the Bible text tells us that he kept his integrity: "'Naked I came from my mother's womb, and naked I will depart. The LORD gave, and the LORD has taken away; may the name of the LORD be praised.' In all this, Job did not sin by charging God with wrongdoing" (1:21).

Even now, Job knew he was not at the end of his trials when painful sores broke out all over his body. "He took a piece of broken pottery and scraped himself with it as he sat among the ashes" (2:8). It is difficult to comprehend a fall as great as this. If that weren't enough, Job's wife was not supportive as Steve Bell's was. "His wife said to him, 'Are you still holding on to your integrity? Curse God and die!' Yet in all this, Job did not sin in what he said" (2:9).

In all of these events, we see an extreme of what many people face today. The enemies from outside our sphere (in Job's case, the Sabeans and the Chaldeans) make it difficult to walk with God in a hostile culture. Added to this are natural disasters (in Job's case, the lightning strike and the hurricane) over which Job has no control. Surely, however, those closest to us are there for comfort and support, yet Job didn't have even this. There was his unsupportive wife and, as we will soon see, his friends were not better. We can learn a great deal about walking with God from the story of Job. The reality is that suffering is part of our world because of the disobedience of the first couple, Adam and Eve, and because of our own sin. We are sinners by nature and practice. In addition, as Tim Keller says,

> Another controlling reality is that the creation order—the fabric of this world—is frayed and broken through. Suffering and pain are distributed disproportionately so that often the innocent suffer more and the wicked suffer less. In light of this second reality, we must be very slow to assume that suffering has come upon us or others because of not living right. . . . If we ignore either of these truths, we will be out of touch with the universe as it really is.[5]

Keller wrote these words in 2014, little knowing that less than a decade later they would move from an abstract concept to a present reality. In May 2020, he was diagnosed with Stage 4 pancreatic cancer. Just three years earlier at age sixty-seven, he had stepped down as senior pastor at Redeemer Presbyterian Church with the plans to write and travel. He entered into one of the most productive phases of his life writing books, speaking, and seeking to serve God as a public theologian. Yet he said,

> "[Knowing] you are really going to die changes the way you look at your time, the way you look at God, the way you look at your spouse," he said. "Everything just changes when you actually realize time is limited and I'm mortal."

"This is going to sound like an exaggeration. My wife and I would never want to go back to the kind of prayer life and spiritual life we had before the cancer, never," he said, adding that his cancer journey has made him genuinely experience Psalm 90:14: "Satisfy us in the morning with your unfailing love, that we may sing for joy and be glad all our days."[6]

He died May 19, 2023.

———

Though Job's wife offered no comfort for the pain he was going through, Job had many friends he had previously helped. Three of them (Eliphaz the Temanite, Bildad the Shuhite, and Zophar the Naamathite) heard about Job's troubles and came together to offer him comfort.

They started off well.

When they first approached him, they hardly recognized him and wept. "Then they sat on the ground with him for seven days and seven nights. No one said a word to him because they saw how great his suffering was" (2:13). A suffering person does not need answers, or questions, just empathy. This they provided simply by being there with him, sitting in silence.

———

In 1968, Randy's wife, Kathy, was a sophomore at the University of Southern Mississippi when Martin Luther King Jr. was assassinated. There were only a few Black students who lived on the Southern Miss campus at that time, and the Black women students all lived in a suite on the second floor of a dormitory called Mississippi Hall in the middle of the campus. Kathy lived on the third floor of that same dorm.

The day after King was assassinated, the Black students closed the door to their suite and did not come out the entire day. At the end of that day, a group of white women students, including Kathy, gathered in the two stairwells leading up and down to the second floor and began to softly sing hymns. After some time, the door to the suite opened and some of the girls emerged; it was obvious they had been crying. Several of the white girls climbed the stairs to bring them food. Some hugged them and cried with them. You must remember that this was Mississippi in 1968, and Southern Miss had admitted its first Black students only three years earlier. Kathy's memory from that night is that other than singing hymns, giving food, and weeping with the Black students, none of the white girls said anything.

———

After a week, Job finally speaks, lamenting that he had ever been born: "May the day of my birth perish . . . may it turn to darkness; may God above not care about it" (3:3–4). Then he switches to the why question, though not the one we might expect. He does not ask why these things happened to him, or why God allowed this to happen to someone who had sought to follow him. Rather he asks, "Why did I not perish at birth and die as I came from the womb? . . . Why was I not hidden in the ground like a stillborn child, like an infant who never saw the light of day?" And he concludes with the statement, "I have no peace, no quietness; I have no rest, but only turmoil" (3:11, 16). This is a person in pain, one totally discouraged who does not want to live. Job's friends now lose their good start as comforting friends and push Job down a different path by seeking to tell him why it all happened.

Eliphaz assumes Job's troubles must be because he did something wrong:

> "Who can keep from speaking? Should not your piety be your confidence and your blameless ways your hope? Consider now: Who, being innocent, has ever perished? Where were the upright ever destroyed? As I have observed, those who plow evil and those who sow trouble reap it." (4:5–8)

Bildad suggests that Job may have lost sight of God, that he needs to be better connected with God:

> "If you will seek God and plead with the Almighty for mercy, if you are pure and upright, surely then he will rouse himself for you and restore your rightful habitation. . . . Such are the paths of all who forget God; the hope of the godless

shall perish. . . . Behold, God will not reject a blameless man, nor take the hand of evildoers." (8:5–6, 13, 20)

Zophar echoes the others with similar challenges:

> "If you prepare your heart, you will stretch out your hands toward him. If iniquity is in your hand, put it far away, and let not injustice dwell in your tents. . . . And you will feel secure, because there is hope; you will look around and take your rest in security. You will lie down, and none will make you afraid; many will court your favor. But the eyes of the wicked will fail; all way of escape will be lost to them, and their hope is to breathe their last." (11:13–14, 18–20)

We see no humility in their responses to him, no acknowledgment of their own shortcomings. Everything they say to Job focuses on his shortcomings, where they seek to play the role of God, demonstrating why Job deserved what had happened to him. In playing the role of God, they totally miss the point of what was going on. Their words remind us of the famous saying by H. L. Mencken, "There is always a well-known solution to every human problem—neat, plausible, and wrong."[7]

Job's lengthy responses to his friends can be summarized in two key points. First, he repeats his unwavering commitment to God:

> "Oh that my words were written! Oh that they were inscribed in a book! Oh that with an iron pen and lead they were engraved in the rock forever! For I know that my Redeemer lives, and at the last he will stand upon the earth. And after my skin has been thus destroyed, yet in my flesh I shall see God, whom I shall see for myself, and my eyes shall behold, and not another. My heart faints within me!" (19:23–27)

Second, Job rejects the advice from his friends and seeks a direct audience with God:

> "Behold, my eye has seen all this, my ear has heard and understood it. What you know, I also know; I am not inferior to you. But I would speak to the Almighty, and I desire to argue my case with God. As for you, you whitewash with lies; worthless physicians are you all. Oh that you would keep silent, and it would be your wisdom!" (13:1–5)

But he is also angry with God:

> "God has turned me over to the ungodly and thrown me into the clutches of the wicked. All was well with me, but he shattered me; he seized me by the neck

and crushed me. He has made me his target; his archers surround me. Without pity, he pierces my kidneys and spills my gall on the ground. Again and again he bursts upon me; he rushes at me like a warrior." (16:11–14)

On the death of his wife, Joy, C. S. Lewis offered this lament:

Meanwhile, where is God? This is one of the most disquieting symptoms. When you are happy, so happy that you have no sense of needing Him, so happy that you are tempted to feel His claims upon you as an interruption, if you remember yourself and turn to Him with gratitude and praise, you will be—or so it seems—welcomed with open arms. But go to Him when your need is desperate, when all other help is vain, and what do you find? A door slammed in your face, and a sound of bolting and double bolting on the inside. . . . Why is He so present a commander in our time of prosperity and so very absent a help in time of trouble?[8]

The most precious gift that marriage gave me was this constant impact of some-thing very close and intimate yet all the time unmistakably other, resistant—in a word, real. Is all that work to be undone? . . . Oh God, God, why did you take such trouble to force this creature out of its shell if it is now doomed to crawl back—to be sucked back—into it?[9]

Could Job and Lewis lash out at God in this way and get away with it? Mal-colm Guite suggests yes:

It is good for us to thunder back at God, if we need to. The Psalms and Job are full of it and God is big enough to take it. . . . When we finally release our tension in prayer and let God have the full blast of what we're feeling, all the energy of our prayer runs up the conductor, who is Christ himself, and is "earthed" with him in Heaven.[10]

———

In all this, Job did not lose sight of God and his power:

"From where, then, does wisdom come? And where is the place of understand-ing? It is hidden from the eyes of all living and concealed from the birds of the air. Abaddon and Death say, 'We have heard a rumor of it with our ears.' God understands the way to it, and he knows its place. For he looks to the ends of the earth and sees everything under the heavens. When he gave to the wind its weight and apportioned the waters by measure, when he made a decree for the rain and a way for the lightning of the thunder, then he saw it and declared it;

he established it, and searched it out. And he said to man, 'Behold, the fear of the Lord, that is wisdom, and to turn away from evil is understanding.'"

                (28:20–28)

Perhaps from this insight about God, and perhaps inspired by questions from his friends, Job does some serious reflection on his life, offering a number of places where he thought he had remained faithful to God.

> "If I have walked with falsehood" (31:5)
> "If my heart has been enticed toward a woman" (31:9)
> "If I have rejected the cause of my manservant or my maidservant" (31:13)
> "If I have withheld anything that the poor desired" (31:16)
> "If I have raised my hand against the fatherless" (31:21)
> "If I have made gold my trust" (31:24)
> "If I have rejoiced at the ruin of him who hated me" (31:29)
> "If I have concealed my transgressions as others do" (31:33)
> "If my land has cried out against me" (31:38)

Tim Keller says of this passage, "He calls every failure to help the poor a sin, offensive to God's splendor and deserving of judgment and punishment. To not 'share his bread' and his asset with the poor would be unrighteous, a sin against God and therefore by definition a violation of God's justice."[11] Keller draws on Francis I. Anderson's Job commentary to say, "In Job's conscience, . . . to omit to do good to any fellow human being, or whatever rank or class, would be a grievous offence to God."[12]

If Job was indeed living in a way that honored God, then what were these trials about? With that, his three friends fall silent.

———

Then a younger person, Elihu, who had been watching the dialogue, speaks up. He starts with an acknowledgment of his own youth, a humble posture that proves helpful. He says he had listened carefully to the arguments of his elders, but they had not satisfied him. He had waited because of his youth, unwilling to speak, until now:

> "Therefore I say: Listen to me; I too will tell you what I know. I waited while you spoke, I listened to your reasoning; while you were searching for words, I gave you my full attention. But not one of you has proved Job wrong; none of you has answered his arguments." (32:10–12)

He urges Job to remember who God is rather than seeking to justify himself:

> "No one looks on the light when it is bright in the skies, when the wind has passed and cleared them. Out of the north comes golden splendor; God is clothed with awesome majesty." (37:21–22)

Elihu continues to pound on this theme, not to answer Job's questions but to remind him who God is. In his lengthy speech to Job, he adds,

> "God is mighty, but despises no one; he is mighty, and firm in his purpose. . . . Remember to extol his work, which people have praised in song. All humanity has seen it; mortals gaze on it from afar. How great is God—beyond our understanding! The number of his years is past finding out. . . . Out of the north he comes in golden splendor; God comes in awesome majesty. The Almighty is beyond our reach and exalted in power; in his justice and great righteousness, he does not oppress. Therefore, people revere him, for does he not have regard for all the wise in heart?" (36:5–6, 24–26; 37:22–24)

Throughout Elihu's lengthy dialogue, Job remains silent.

———

Finally, God speaks directly to Job. He does not question the fact that Job was challenging him, but rather invites Job into a discussion:

> Then the LORD spoke to Job out of the storm. He said: "Who is this that obscures my plans with words without knowledge? Brace yourself like a man; I will question you, and you shall answer me." (38:1–3)

Job quietly listens to God, speaking only when God demands he do so:

> The LORD said to Job: "Will the one who contends with the Almighty correct him? Let him who accuses God answer him!" Then Job answered the LORD: "I am unworthy—how can I reply to you? I put my hand over my mouth. I spoke once, but I have no answer—twice, but I will say no more." Then the LORD spoke to Job out of the storm: "Brace yourself like a man; I will question you, and you shall answer me. Would you discredit my justice? Would you condemn me to justify yourself?" (40:6–8)

It is important to notice that God does not condemn Job for trying to understand, for wanting an accounting from God, or even for lashing out. Rather, he makes it clear that if Job wants that kind of audience, then he must deal with God on his own terms. God steps in with his argument, which spreads over four chapters. None of God's statements show Job why these things happened to him. Rather, he carefully explains to Job who he is. As Tripp Parker puts it, "'Who' matters more than 'why.'"[13]

God asks Job where he was when he laid the foundations of the world, when he separated the seas from the land, when he brought rain, when he laid out the heavens, when he nurtured the animals (Job 38–41). God concludes with the statement, "Nothing on earth is his equal—a creature without fear. He looks down on all that are haughty; he is king over all that are proud" (41:33–34).

In the end, Job has heard God and recognized he cannot compete with God's wisdom and knowledge:

"I know that you can do all things, and that no purpose of yours can be thwarted. 'Who is this that hides counsel without knowledge?' Therefore I have uttered what I did not understand, things too wonderful for me, which I did not know. 'Hear, and I will speak; I will question you, and you make it known to me.' I had heard of you by the hearing of the ear, but now my eye sees you; therefore I despise myself, and repent in dust and ashes." (42:1–6)

———

We may look at this ancient story and ask what this has to do with us and the challenges of following Jesus in the twenty-first century. There are several nuggets we can gain from Job. When we encounter challenges in our own lives, it is natural and right to ask why. There are three potential sources of our difficulties:

› Our own bad behavior
› Others seeking to disrupt us
› Circumstances and events that defy explanation

Often the answer is that we just don't know. Job, to his credit, asks himself some hard questions. There were certainly others who were a party to disrupting his life. The Sabeans and Chaldeans were the raiders who stole from him and killed his servants. This is another place where Job could have placed blame. But Job didn't dwell on this since the question remained: Why did this happen at this point?

Job ultimately knew there was something deeper going on, and he wanted God to explain why someone who had followed God so intentionally would be so mistreated. In effect, he was asking the age-old question: Why do bad things happen to good people?

Of all of those listening to Job, Elihu was the most helpful. He pointed Job to a God who is much bigger than any human being. He prepared Job for his discussion with God by describing God as someone whose ways are past finding out. And when Job engaged in listening to God, he heard an answer that was different from what he expected.

God did not tell him why. Like Job, we are incapable of fully understanding God's reasons or plans. God only told him who he is.

Sometimes in our own lives, there is no answer to the "why" question, only the "who" question. Building a trust in God is vital for those times when we don't understand. Bill Pollard, former chairman of ServiceMaster, was going through a hard time when he was in college after his father had died. Dr. V. Raymond Edman, Wheaton College president, told him, "Bill, don't doubt in the dark what you have seen in the light."[14] When we don't have answers, we need to remember the character of God we have come to know.

———

There is a difficult part of this story that we haven't yet mentioned. At the beginning of the book, we are told the source of all of Job's troubles: the accuser. The accuser, or Satan, claimed that Job was faithful to God only because God blessed him. So Satan challenges God, asking for permission to strike Job, and the Lord responds: "Very well then, everything he has is in your hands, but on the man himself do not lay a finger" (1:11).

But Job does not curse God after Satan causes the external attacks that destroyed his family and wealth. So Satan returns to God and says, "Stretch out your hands and strike his flesh and bones, and he will surely curse you to your face." The Lord says, "Very well then, he is in your hands; but you must spare his life" (2:5–6). It was after this that Job became covered in sores and was despondent.

We delayed this part of the story because there is no indication that Job was aware of this dialogue. Scripture reveals it to us and we are left to ask why God would bargain with Satan to attack one of his committed followers? The full answer is that we don't know. One possible answer comes from Isaiah 55:8–9:

> "For my thoughts are not your thoughts, neither are your ways my ways," declares the LORD. "As the heavens are higher than the earth, so are my ways higher than your ways and my thoughts than your thoughts."

We learn from this text what Job learned from his dialogue with God. He is God, and Job and we are not. Scripture offers many insights on this topic, perhaps none more powerful than Philippians 2. In the incarnation, Jesus chose to take on the limitations of human flesh. To live as we do, God had to limit himself.

A second insight comes from God's dialogue with Satan where, in the first instance, he tells Satan not to "lay a finger" on Job. Then in the second instance, he tells him to spare Job's life. God set limits on what Satan could do to his servant Job. Perhaps this is the origin of that overly simplistic statement, "God doesn't give us more than we can handle." Many people need to deal with much more than they can handle, as did Job. But God can and does limit what happens to us in this world, and for that we can be thankful.

Third, some say that God brings pain and suffering on us. This Scripture is clear that it is Satan doing the dirty work, not God. James echoes this thought when he says,

> When tempted, no one should say, "God is tempting me." For God cannot be tempted by evil, nor does he tempt anyone; but each person is tempted when they are dragged away by their own evil desire and enticed. Then, after desire has conceived, it gives birth to sin; and sin, when it is full-grown, gives birth to death. (1:13–15)

Though these words are helpful, we are ultimately called to remember what Father John Kavanaugh said, "There is a God . . . and I'm not him."

Some wrongly conclude from this account that we should never question God. Yet at the conclusion of the story, God commends Job. When the conversation ends, God has some harsh words for Eliphaz, Bildad, and Zophar. Instead of asking questions, they were offering bad opinions. Still, God asks Job to pray for them. In our own challenging situations, we don't believe that God is sitting idly, ignoring our suffering though he has the power to stop it. Rather, like Job, we diligently search for reasons, examine ourselves, and seek truth. But through this account, God reminds us that there may be situations when we never get the answers.

—

The story of Job ends with his restoration. Job is once again a wealthy man with ten children. Since all the things he had lost were later restored to him, we may want to conclude that this will happen to us as well. But we must be careful here. Restoring health and wealth may have happened for Job, but this may never happen for us. We may ask "why?" but God only answers with "who." We need to trust him for things beyond ourselves. In the end, Job was a better man than he was in the beginning.

> The LORD blessed the latter part of Job's life more than the former part. He had fourteen thousand sheep, six thousand camels, a thousand yoke of oxen and a thousand donkeys. And he also had seven sons and three daughters. . . . Nowhere in all the land were there found women as beautiful as Job's daughters, and their father granted them an inheritance along with their brothers. After this, Job lived a hundred and forty years; he saw his children and their children to the fourth generation. And so Job died, an old man and full of years. (42:12–17)

Near the end of Alec Hill's fourteen-year term as president of InterVarsity Christian Fellowship, he was diagnosed with cancer. Now on the other side of that harrowing ordeal, he says,

> The additional time we receive is not borrowed time—that implies something negotiated or loaned. Rather we live in bonus time, a season of grace. How we live in bonus time matters. As survivors, we are stewards of a great trust. Not everyone gets the opportunity that we have—to have our souls reordered, to encounter God's presence in unique ways, and to serve others with remarkable motivation. For the most part, the Lord has felt incredibly close through my various treatments. But to be honest, there have also been stretches of deep confusion, incredible frustration, and intense sadness.[15]

Job must have felt the same: being grateful and knowing he was living in bonus time.

Earlier we introduced Steve Bell, whose business and wealth were lost through an outside force. He wrote to each person to whom he owed money and asked for time, agreeing to pay them back in full with interest. Month after month, he paid what he could. It took seven years, but he paid off all his creditors. Today, he is the owner of Bellmont Cabinets and employs over three hundred people. He continues to work with many of the vendors he owed money to earlier. He has been recognized across the country for his work as an entrepreneur. He too was restored, responding with a foundation that generously seeks to do good.

We must be careful about concluding that everything works out all right in this life for everyone. Though it ultimately happened for Job, and for

Steve Bell, that is not the norm. Remember, Jesus went to the cross. Why do some come through great pain and trial and find a better answer in this life and others do not? We don't know. God ultimately has a promise of restoration for us, but it may not be in this life.

When we have been given grace, we need to offer grace to others in response. Early on, Job caught a glimpse of the truth he learned in the end, and this is certainly at the heart of what we need:

> "From where, then, does wisdom come? And where is the place of understanding? It is hidden from the eyes of all living and concealed from the birds of the air. Abaddon and Death say, 'We have heard a rumor of it with our ears.' God understands the way to it, and he knows its place. For he looks to the ends of the earth and sees everything under the heavens. When he gave to the wind its weight and apportioned the waters by measure, when he made a decree for the rain and a way for the lightning of the thunder, then he saw it and declared it; he established it, and searched it out. And he said to man, 'Behold, the fear of the Lord, that is wisdom, and to turn away from evil is understanding.'"
>
> (Job 28:20–28)

9 | Daniel

In evaluating the state of the world, consider this: God has his people everywhere, in places and positions that most of us would never imagine.
— *The Word in Life Study Bible*

"I believe you are the Lord's servant, and are in the post He has assigned you; and though it appears to me more arduous and requiring more self-denial than my own, I know that he who has called you to it can afford you strength according to your day."
— John Newton to William Wilberforce (1796)

Daniel was a young man, probably fifteen or sixteen years old,[1] when he went away to "graduate school" to prepare for future government service. Up to that point, he was a member of the Jewish royal family or the nobility (Dan. 1:3). In addition, he left with some friends—a group of young Hebrew men who were the "best and brightest" from Jerusalem: "young men without any physical defect, handsome, showing aptitude for every kind of learning, well informed, quick to understand, and qualified to serve in the king's palace" (1:4).

But Daniel was not beginning this training to serve the king of Israel; instead, he had been brought to Babylon after God had delivered Jerusalem into the hands of the Babylonian king, Nebuchadnezzar. Daniel apparently had no choice in the matter, and after three years of training, he was expected to serve as a counselor to the very man who had defeated and humiliated his country and his king.

It seems likely that part of the reason Daniel and his friends were chosen to come to Babylon and serve its king is that they "already have had
diplomatic training and have been proved to be capable of benefiting from
the specialized education designed for them by the Babylonian king."[2] Their
primary, secondary, and undergraduate education in Judah had prepared
them well for what they would face in Babylon.

———

By the time Daniel and his friends arrived in Babylon, they had a strong
foundation in their faith, but the Babylonian culture was not only very
different from their "home culture," they were immediately faced with decisions that tested their commitment to a worldview that placed God at
the center of their lives. They had to decide which parts of the Babylonian
culture were acceptable, or at least not prohibited by God's law, and which
were not acceptable to them as worshipers of God. It seems that Nebuchadnezzar wanted Daniel and his friends, as much as possible and regardless
of their "ethnic" identity, to *become Babylonian*, to fully *assimilate* into the
Babylonian culture. Daniel and his friends faced several assimilation issues right off the bat and for some of those issues, they apparently had no
qualms about integrating into Babylonian culture. For example, they were
given Babylonian names (1:6–7), and they studied and learned "all kinds of
[Babylonian] literature and learning" (1:17).

There was a line, though, that the four friends concluded they could not
cross and still maintain their commitment to God. It had to do with eating
food and drinking wine from the king's table. We are not told exactly what
the problem with the food and wine was, but for them, partaking of it would
amount to defiling themselves.[3]

Interestingly, however, Daniel did not dig his heels in over the issue and
simply refuse the food and wine. Instead, he suggested an alternative to his
Babylonian guard, an experiment to let him and his friends eat vegetables
and drink water for ten days, and then "compare our appearance with that of
the young men who eat the royal food and treat your servants in accordance
with what you see." The guard agrees, and at the end of ten days, Daniel and
his friends "looked healthier and better nourished than any of the young
men who ate royal food" (1:11–16).

It may be easy to focus on the fact that Daniel and his friends drew a
line in the sand and refused to cross it by eating and drinking the rich and
nonkosher food and drink. But there's a lesson for us as well in *how* they

refused to cross the line. They recognized that a simple refusal would put their guard in danger—"The king would then have my head because of you," he says (1:10)—and so Daniel proposed the alternative. The result—good physical health for the young exiles—was the goal the royal official and guard had in mind. The goal was good and one that Daniel and his friends shared. By offering an alternative way to reach the same goal as the Babylonians, Daniel and his friends demonstrated that they were, indeed, wise beyond their years and well qualified to become advisors to the king.

But note that in his discussion with his guard, Daniel is speaking to his supervisor and that he, Daniel, has no real power: he was a captive in exile. Yet what Daniel does is a good illustration of how someone with little or no power (in the traditional sense) can still be a person of influence: *lead without power*.

Psychologists tell us that power is often "positional" in nature: people have power because it comes with the territory when they are chosen to be the director of a company or the principal of a school. Influence, on the other hand, "is more subtle and sometimes invisible. It is the ability to bring others around to your way of thinking, not because you control the situation as you might with power, but because you persuade others to view a situation or thing in a certain way."[4]

We have seen and have worked with a number of people over the years who may not have had much power, at least in the traditional sense, but who nonetheless exercised *influence* for the good of their company or organization. In Daniel's case, it was some time before he would gain power in Babylon, but he already had some influence with his supervisor because "God had caused the official to show favor and compassion to Daniel" (1:8), and he exercised that influence to gain something beneficial to himself and his friends: good physical health, which obviously made an impression on those above him. And approaching the problem as he did—by suggesting an alternative approach to reach the same goal—was also a way of building trust in the Babylonian officials as the story unfolds.

Al had been at Boeing for only a short time when he and seven others were invited to a lunch meeting with the CEO of the company, Frank Shrontz. In his opening comment at this lunch discussion, he offered a life-changing perspective to Al and the group about the difference between power and influence:

> You probably wish you were in my position so you would have more control. You must deal with all the things that come from corporate, and some of these

things don't make much sense to you. You likely think I have total control as CEO, but I don't. I don't control the economy, my customers, my competitors, or even the actions of my staff as they reinterpret what I say to their advantage. I am convinced I actually have about 15 percent control. Yes, there are some things you need to deal with that come from corporate. But you are closer to your colleagues, closer to the detailed knowledge of your work, and closer to the customers than I am. You have some control over how you use this knowledge, and I believe you have about 15 percent control. Don't think of 15 percent as small; know it is large. Use the influence and judgment you have to make a big difference for the company. That is what I try to do with my 15 percent.

———

Our first instinct may be to see the Babylonian king, Nebuchadnezzar, whom Daniel would serve as a cartoon-like despot, a one-dimensional character, and his act of bringing Daniel and his friends back to Babylon as strictly selfish. We could caricature it as a desire to surround himself with the elite of those he conquered—a bit like King Xerxes did rounding up all the beautiful women in his kingdom, including Esther, so that they could "audition" to be his queen. Without denying that Nebuchadnezzar was certainly despotic in many ways, what if the primary reason he brought Daniel and his friends to live in his palace and advise him was because he recognized that he *needed* the counsel of wise men, and that he aspired not only to be recognized as "great" himself, but that his Babylonian Empire would also be recognized as great, and not just militarily?

Daniel and his friends were not, of course, the only Jews who had been forcibly resettled in Babylon, and naturally they would have asked themselves how long this exile might last and to what extent they should "assimilate" into Babylonian culture. There were some Jews, perhaps, who would have seen no great problem in becoming Babylonian in every way: it would be a lot easier just to integrate into the culture rather than try to maintain their religious and ethnic distinctives.

There were others—perhaps a majority—who resisted that idea and could not get their homeland out of their mind:

> By the rivers of Babylon we sat and wept
>   when we remembered Zion.
> There on the poplars
>   we hung our harps,

> For there our captors asked us for songs,
>> our tormentors demanded songs of joy;
>> they said, "Sing us one of the songs of Zion?"
> How can we sing the songs of the LORD
>> while in a foreign land?
> If I forget you, Jerusalem,
>> may my right hand forget its skill
> May my tongue cling to the roof of my mouth
>> if I do not remember you,
> If I do not consider Jerusalem my highest joy. . . .
> Daughter Babylon, doomed to destruction,
>> happy is the one who repays you
>> according to what you have done to us.
> Happy is the one who seizes your infants
>> and dashes them against the rocks. (Ps. 137:1–6, 8–9)

It was not unnatural or wrong for the Jewish people to long for their homeland, and to be angry that the Babylonians have ordered them to sing their songs about it, but note the anger that leads the people not only to long for home, but to desire the death of the Babylonian infants.[5]

It seems, though, that there was a third alternative to assimilation or bitterness and anger, and it came in the form of a letter from a Jew who was still in Jerusalem. In the letter, the prophet Jeremiah gave the exiles in Jerusalem God's instructions for how they were to live, which must have seemed counterintuitive and even shocking to many of the Jews exiled in Babylon: "Seek the peace and prosperity of the city to which I have carried you into exile. Pray to the Lord for it, because if it prospers, you too will prosper" (Jer. 29:7).

God, through Jeremiah, told the Jewish exiles not to be fooled by the so-called prophets and diviners among them, that they will be in exile in Babylon for seventy years, and that only then will God "come to you and fulfill my good promise to bring you back to this place"—since, God had said, it was *he* (albeit through Nebuchadnezzar) who had brought them to Babylon in the first place. So, God says "to all those *I carried into exile* from Jerusalem to Babylon . . . build houses and settle down" (Jer. 29:5, 8–10). It was this alternative that Daniel and his friends chose to follow in their training and work for King Nebuchadnezzar.

As we live in a culture in which many increasingly view Christianity with suspicion or hostility, should we still pray for the cities where we live, "seeking the peace and prosperity of the city"? We believe the answer is yes, but what does that look like today? Let's look carefully at what Jeremiah said in his letter and think about what the implications and applications for us might be.

First, God made clear that it was ultimately *he*, not Nebuchadnezzar, who had brought them to Babylon. He had a purpose (or purposes) in bringing them there, and despite what they may feel, he had not abandoned or forgotten them: "I know the plans I have for you, plans to prosper you and not to harm you, plans to give you hope and a future" (Jer. 29:11). Daniel accepted that his role was to serve Nebuchadnezzar and that God knew what he was doing in placing him there. Can we accept that God has placed us where we are in our work not just for our own self-fulfillment but also for *his* purposes? In asking this, we are not suggesting that Christians—or anyone else—should accept working in an *abusive* situation, but we should be careful about walking away from a job simply because it is hard or because the people we work with or for are hard to get along with. We are also not suggesting that God's plans for us means that we are destined to "prosper" in the sense used by some: that is, that God's plans for us are that we will become wealthy or have a life without problems.

Second, God tells the Jews living in Babylon that their hope and future is tied to the peace and prosperity of the Babylonian people among whom they live, and they are to pray for that peace and prosperity: "If Babylon prospers, you will prosper." This is, frankly, counterintuitive for many Americans, including Christians. We often assume that as long as we and our family maintain our personal morality and spend time with other Christians (and perhaps do some occasional evangelism), that's about as far as our responsibility to God goes. But the lesson the Jews living in exile needed to learn was that they were part of *communities* that went beyond their own tribe, and that seeking the well-being of all of Babylon would, ultimately, benefit the Jews as well.

We wonder what would have happened in Psalm 137 if the people had sought the peace of the city? Would the terrible thoughts about the captors still have been present? It seems the answer is clearly no.

Several churches in Hattiesburg have "adopted" local public elementary schools, with church members helping with tutoring after school, painting rooms and hallways in the summers, and providing school supplies for children whose parents cannot afford to buy them. One church, Ekklesia, pays the salary of a woman who coordinates the efforts of volunteers at one of those elementary schools; and each week in the worship service, the pastor prays for the parents, teachers, and students at Hawkins Elementary School. In 2018, the citizens of Hattiesburg voted overwhelmingly to renew a bond issue to provide needed repairs to district schools. In 2022, the Hattiesburg Public School District—and Hawkins Elementary itself—achieved an "A" rating from the Mississippi Department of Education, having previously been rated as a "D" school district. Though the mayor in Hattiesburg only appoints school board members and has no power to decide how the school district should be operated, he recognized that this achievement of moving from a "D" rating to an "A" affected the entire community: "It's the most significant accomplishment in the last five to ten years in our city. When our community steps up . . . when they support and they go arm-in-arm with our school district, there's no limit to what the city can do. And I'm so proud of the A, but I'm more excited about the future."[6]

———

When Daniel and his friends completed their training, "the chief official presented them to Nebuchadnezzar. The king talked with them, and he found none equal to [them]; so they entered the king's service" (Dan. 1:18–19). Daniel's friends—Shadrach, Meshach, and Abednego—were assigned as administrators in the Babylonian Empire (3:12), and they were later promoted by Nebuchadnezzar *after* they "defied the king's command" to worship an image of gold and survived being thrown into a furnace of fire by the enraged king (3:28, 30). Daniel himself applied the wisdom God gave him as someone who could "understand visions and dreams of all kinds" (:17). Like Joseph, he recognized that this particular gift of wisdom had been given to him as a "trustee" for the benefit of someone else (in Joseph's case, it was Pharaoh and ultimately his family and "many lives" as well [Gen. 50:20]).

One wonders how Daniel viewed Nebuchadnezzar. What did he think of him? The language Daniel used in addressing Nebuchadnezzar suggests that he recognized that despite his blustering and pontificating, the king was genuinely disturbed by the dreams he had been having. Daniel realized that with God's help he could use the gift of understanding dreams for Nebuchadnezzar's—and therefore Babylon's and his fellow Jews'—benefit. He asked Nebuchadnezzar for "time, so that he might interpret the dream for him," and he asked his friends to "plead for mercy from the God of heaven concerning this mystery, so that he and his friends might not be executed with the rest of the wise men of Babylon"[7] (2:18).

Like Joseph (Gen. 41:16), Daniel at the outset tells Nebuchadnezzar the source of his gift of understanding and explaining dreams: "No wise man, enchanter, magician or diviner can explain to the king the mystery he has asked about, but there is a God in heaven who reveals mysteries" (Dan. 2:27–28). Daniel's "secret weapon" of wisdom was something that none of the Babylonian wise men had: He *knew God*, and he knew that God is the one who controls history, including kingdoms and kings. After God revealed the king's dream to him in a vision at night, Daniel expresses his relief over God making the meaning of the dream known in a "spontaneous hymn of thanksgiving to the only God who could so answer prayer, but there was great awe because that same God, unseen and infinitely great, had been directly in touch with him personally."[8]

> "Praise be to the name of God for ever and ever;
>> Wisdom and power are his.
> He changes times and seasons;
>> He deposes kings and raises up others.
> He gives wisdom to the wise
>> And knowledge to the discerning.
> He reveals deep and hidden things;
>> He knows what lies in darkness,
>> And light dwells in him.
> I thank and praise you, God of my ancestors:
>> You have given me wisdom and power,
> You have made known to me what we have asked of you,
>> You have made known to us the dream of the king." (Dan. 2:20–23)

After Daniel tells King Nebuchadnezzar what his dream was and what it meant, Nebuchadnezzar "fell prostrate before Daniel and paid him honor and ordered that an offering and incense be presented to him," and he tells him, "'Surely your God is the God of gods and the Lord of kings and a revealer of mysteries, for you were able to reveal this mystery.' Then the king placed Daniel in a high position and lavished many gifts on him. He made him ruler over the entire province of Babylon and placed him in charge of all its wise men" (2:46–48).

In the end, the *most* essential way Daniel "took wisdom to work" was that he prayed over his work *before he went to work* (and, as mentioned previously, it wasn't just the urgent plea for help that he and his friends prayed before Daniel's audience with Nebuchadnezzar). We need to pray daily for our work as we pray for the rest of our lives: our families, our churches, our friends. Daniel's (and his friends') example encourages us to do so. Remember that "God first appears in Scripture—in Genesis 1:1—as a Worker,"[9] and that being made in the image of God (Gen. 1:27) means, at least in part, that our work "expresses something of who He is and what He wants done in the world."[10]

———

Daniel's friends continued to serve King Nebuchadnezzar even though Shadrach, Meshach and Abednego bore the wrath of the king when they refused to bow down and worship a huge golden image the king had made. After they came through a blazing furnace "without a hair on their heads singed," the king praised "the God of Shadrach, Meshach and Abednego, who sent his angel and rescued [them]," and gave *them* a promotion in his service as he had done Daniel in the earlier episode (Dan. 3).

Daniel himself had to deal with Nebuchadnezzar again when he interpreted yet another of Nebuchadnezzar's dreams at the conclusion of his great building projects recounted in Daniel 4. Even though Daniel told the king what was going to happen to him because of his pride (he was going to have his royal authority taken from him, and he would live like an animal, eating grass) and specifically why (he believed his magnificent building projects were entirely his doing and for his personal glory), Nebuchadnezzar ignored Daniel's warnings. After what Daniel told him would happen did indeed happen, Nebuchadnezzar repented, his "sanity was restored" (Dan. 4:34), and he breaks into praise to God for what he has finally realized: that "[God's] dominion is an eternal dominion; his kingdom endures from generation to generation."

No doubt Daniel was pleased with the fact that Nebuchadnezzar had come to recognize that God was the actual ruler of the universe, but when he was originally called on by the king to tell him the meaning of the king's dream involving a huge tree that was cut down, Daniel "was greatly perplexed for a time, and his thoughts terrified him" (Dan. 4:19). He tells Nebuchadnezzar that he wishes that the dream applied to the king's enemies rather than to him, and then proceeds to tell him the meaning of the dream.

It would be understandable if, when Daniel heard (and understood the meaning of) the king's dream, Daniel had said to himself, "Why should I interpret his dream? He brought me here against my will and forced me to work for him. He is arrogant and pompous. Let nature take its course." Instead, Daniel expressed sorrow at Nebuchadnezzar's fate. He seemed to actually *care* about Nebuchadnezzar *personally*; he regretted what was going to happen to him, but he realized that the humiliation the king was going to suffer was ultimately for his own good.

Do we see the leaders in the organizations we work in as *people* with genuine needs—regardless of the image they might be trying to project of "having it all together"?

—

"Without any explanation or indication of date the narrative leaps from the reign of Nebuchadnezzar to the very end of the Babylonian empire, the night on which its last ruler was killed and the city fell to the Medes and Persians."[11] A new king has come to power in Babylon; his name is Belshazzar.

Unlike Nebuchadnezzar, who had put "the articles from the temple of God" he had taken after conquering Jerusalem into "the treasure house of his god" (Dan. 1:2), Belshazzar, in the midst of a great drunken banquet with "a thousand of his nobles" orders the gold and silver goblets that were taken from the temple so that they could drink from them. As they did so, "they praised the gods of silver, of bronze, iron, wood and stone" (5:2–4).

Suddenly, "the fingers of a human hand appeared and wrote on the plaster of the wall," and the king's face "turned pale and he was so frightened that his legs became weak and his knees were knocking" (5:5–6). Belshazzar summons his magicians and astrologers and says that whichever of them could interpret the writing on the wall would be "clothed in purple and have a gold chain placed around his neck, and he will be made the third highest ruler in the kingdom," but none of them are able to "read the writing or tell the king what it meant" (5:7–8).

Finally, the queen mother enters the banquet hall, having heard the voices of the king and his nobles. After learning what the problem was, she tells Belshazzar about Daniel: a man "with insight and intelligence and wisdom like the gods" (5:11). Desperate to know the meaning of the writing on the wall, the king calls for Daniel and makes him the same offer of personal glory—being "clothed in purple" and having a "gold chain" placed around his neck if he could interpret the writing.

By now, Daniel is probably an old man. The question that Belshazzar asks Daniel—"Are you Daniel, one of the exiles my father the king brought from Judah?"—suggests that Daniel has been relegated to the "back office" in the palace after Nebuchadnezzar's death, and his best days as a counselor seem to be behind him. In light of the change in Babylon's leadership from Nebuchadnezzar to Belshazzar, Daniel "must have expected that the work God had so certainly begun in the previous generation [with Nebuchadnezzar] would prove more obviously lasting in its influence."[12]

Daniel refused the king's promise of lavish gifts for himself: "You may keep your gifts for yourself and give your rewards to someone else" (Dan. 5:17). He then interprets the mysterious writing: Because Belshazzar had praised and honored idols instead of God, God was bringing his reign to an end and his kingdom would be divided and given to the Medes and Persians. "That very night Belshazzar, king of the Babylonians, was slain, and Darius the Mede took over the kingdom" (5:30–31).[13]

After Belshazzar was deposed, we again see Daniel as a counselor to kings Darius and Cyrus, but we suspect he had learned a lesson, if he did not know it already, about the impermanence of leaders and of institutions, including governments, companies, and churches.

In *The ServiceMaster Story*, Al examines what might be called the life cycle of a company that from 1929 through 2000 focused "primarily on the growth and development of its employees."[14] ServiceMaster grew to be a $6 billion company operating in forty countries due to its four objectives: to honor God in all they do, to help people to develop, to pursue excellence, and to grow profitably. But beginning in 2002, with the retirement of former CEO Bill Pollard from the ServiceMaster board of directors, Al writes that ServiceMaster's annual reports "reflected a change in emphasis consistent with the new leadership of the company. The focus on the dignity of the work, and the dignity and importance of the worker, was largely gone from the discussions of the business. The focus instead shifted to financial growth and the importance of the customer."[15] ServiceMaster walked away from the values that tied them to a higher authority for the integrity and the deep commitment to the value of its workers and their development.[16]

———

After Darius became king, Daniel was made one of three administrators over the one hundred twenty local administrators who ruled throughout the kingdom. Daniel did such a good job in his work that the king put him in charge of the entire kingdom (in this, we are again reminded of what happened to Joseph in Egypt hundreds of years earlier). Perhaps not surprisingly, the other administrators resented this foreigner's success, and they attempted to find something they could use against him, but they were not able to come up with anything because Daniel "was totally exemplary and trustworthy" (6:4 MSG).[17] Given his character, they conclude, "We're never going to find anything against this Daniel unless we can cook up something religious." So, appealing to Darius's ego, they talk the king into issuing and enforcing a decree that "anyone who prays to any god or human being during the next thirty days, except you, Your Majesty, shall be thrown into the lions' den." Suitably flattered, Darius issues the decree.

Daniel learns of the decree, but he doesn't change his thrice-daily routine of "praying, thanking and praising God" in front an open window that faced toward Jerusalem. After the "conspirators . . . found him praying, asking God for help" they promptly went to Darius with the evidence of Daniel's law-breaking, and reminded the king of his ill-advised decree. Darius apparently realized his mistake and "tried his best to get Daniel out of the fix he'd put him in," but the conspirators again reminded the king of the fact that "it's the law of the Medes and Persians that the king's decree can never be changed." The king is forced to have Daniel thrown into the lions' den, but he tells him, "Your God, to whom you are so loyal, is going to get you out of this."

After fasting and not sleeping all night, Darius rushes the next morning to the lions' den and calls out, "Daniel, servant of the living God, has your God, whom you serve so loyally, saved you from the lions?" For the first time since he was arrested, we hear Daniel speak:

> "Oh king, live forever! My God sent his angel, who closed the mouths of the lions so that they would not hurt me. I've been found innocent before God and also before you, O king. I've done nothing to harm you." (6:21–22)

The king was delighted and had Daniel hauled up. "There wasn't a scratch on him. He had trusted his God." Darius then has the conspirators, their wives and children thrown into the lions' den, where they are promptly torn to pieces.

What are some takeaways from this most famous story from the book of Daniel for those of us living in "Babylon" in the twenty-first century?

First, we note that Daniel did not change his behavior when he learned of the king's decree. He did not start praying so that others could see him in an act of defiance; rather, as a Jew, he prayed "just as he had always done" with the "windows open toward Jerusalem." Do we ordinarily pray in public places like restaurants when we eat out with others? If the answer is yes, then what about when some of those eating with us are non-Christians? Daniel's example seems to be "just keep doing what you've always done. Don't make a show of it, but don't hide who you are loyal to, either."

Second, while Daniel did not change his behavior in response to Darius's decree, he did add to his prayers of thanksgiving and praise a request that God would help him in what he suspected was coming. He didn't want to die, and there is nothing wrong with asking God for help. While we believe God is sovereign in history (as the later chapters of Daniel certainly makes clear), that doesn't mean God doesn't listen to us when we pray for help and respond to our prayers—as he did for Daniel.

At the same time, as he was being thrown into the lions' den, Daniel did not know what would happen to him. He had done the right thing by continuing to pray to God each day with "the windows open," which was, in fact, in defiance of the king's decree. God rescued him from the lions, but he had no guarantee of the outcome—and neither do we when our faith is put to the test. God's purposes were fulfilled in Daniel's life, and on this occasion that meant he would be saved from the lions. But Daniel recognized that his future was in God's hands, whether or not he lived and continued to serve the king.

There are four words that seem to sum up Daniel's character: loyalty, trust, respect, and integrity. Darius recognized Daniel's loyalty was first to God (Darius remarks on this twice in chapter 6 [vv. 16, 20]), but that loyalty to God did not mean he could not also serve the king faithfully. And at the end of the lions' den story, the narrator offers this summary of Daniel: "He had trusted his God" (6:23).

Though he was brought to Babylon against his will, Daniel treated all those in authority over him with respect, even when he felt he could not eat or drink the royal food; and even after being thrown into the lion's den, the first thing he said to Darius was "May the king live forever!" (6:21). And if integrity means "the state of being whole and undivided," then Daniel did not change his habit of praying daily in the face of the threat of death: he was the same person under pressure as he was without that pressure.

What about us? What words will others—including people who do not worship God as we do—use to characterize us?

10 | Peter

"He is no fool who gives what he cannot keep, to gain what he cannot lose."
— Jim Elliott

"We have met the enemy and he is us."
— Pogo

Near the end of his life, Peter wrote,

> Dear friends, do not be surprised at the fiery ordeal that has come on you to test you, as though something strange were happening to you. But rejoice inasmuch as you participate in the sufferings of Christ, so that you may be overjoyed when his glory is revealed. If you are insulted because of the name of Christ, you are blessed, for the Spirit of glory and of God rests on you. If you suffer, it should not be as a murderer or thief or any other kind of criminal, or even as a meddler. . . . Therefore let those who suffer according to God's will entrust their souls to a faithful Creator while doing good. (1 Pet. 4:12–15)[1]

Peter tells us to expect persecution and rejoice because Jesus, the One we follow, was also persecuted. When we are treated well as Christians, that's great (unless we are hiding our faith), but it is not the norm. And when we are persecuted, we should not be surprised as if this were something unusual. This is to be expected.

Peter also reminds us that it doesn't count as persecution for Christ when we are ridiculed, or worse, for our own bad behavior. We ourselves are impacted by sin, and we need to be reminded that brokenness in this world does not come only from those "out there" but also from ourselves.

He concludes with the reminder that we are not simply enduring life but that we are also on assignment to do good. It would be easy to reduce even this instruction to "doing charitable works," but Peter is talking about a lifestyle. God has placed us here to make a difference for his kingdom in everything we do, whether working in the church, teaching in school, sweeping floors, leading a software company, raising a family, or simply living in a neighborhood. Peter sets the context for our suffering (the right kind) in the larger frame of our mission.

How did Peter come to these challenging and important insights? As we look at his life, we can see that he was drawing on his own experience. And if the great apostle was willing to see both sides of his persecution as well as his mission, we need to be willing to do so as well. He lived in his own polarizing world and can help us understand how to live in ours.

Our introduction to Peter comes in John 1. After John the Baptist pointed to Jesus as the Messiah, Andrew, Simon Peter's brother, heard this and began following Jesus. The first thing Andrew did was find Simon and tell him, "We have found the Messiah" (that is, the Christ). When Andrew brought Peter to Jesus, Jesus looked at him and said, "You are Simon son of John. You will be called Cephas." When translated, Cephas is "Peter" (John 1:40–42).

Andrew, of course, knew Peter best. When he saw who Jesus was, he knew this was an answer to everything Peter had been looking for, and he must have hoped that Peter would be helpful in this new movement. Eventually, Peter was drawn into Jesus' inner circle, along with James and John, going with him where no one else went. In the Gospel stories, it is often Peter who speaks up, helping us learn more about Jesus.

Drawing on David Gill's wonderful book on Peter, we can summarize the following key points about him.[2] Peter was from Bethsaida and Capernaum and a fisherman by trade. Though not schooled like the religious leaders of the day, he knew and understood Greek and had knowledge of Greek culture. But his Galilean accent and lack of formal training were contemptible from the perspective of the elite. He was married, and later took his wife on some of his missionary travels. He apparently remained active as a fisherman even when he was primarily a follower of Jesus, and he returned to his fishing business after the resurrection.

After being introduced to Jesus, he soon became a follower and later a prominent figure in the church.

Peter walked with Jesus, heard his teaching, and saw his miracles. This included when Jesus fed five thousand people with only five small loaves of bread and two fish. But it was the conclusion of that event that marked Peter forever. Jesus sent the disciples to the other side of the Lake of Galilee while he stayed behind to dismiss the crowd and then go off to pray. Before dawn, their boat was caught in a tumultuous storm, and Jesus came alongside the boat walking on the water. The disciples were afraid, thinking they had seen a ghost, but Jesus said, "Take courage. It is I. Don't be afraid" (Matt. 14:27). It was Peter who spoke up: "Lord, if it is you, tell me to come to you on the water." Here, Peter demonstrated his need to speak, his bias toward action, and his honest doubt as he qualified his comment with "if it is you." When Jesus invited him to come, he stepped out and walked on the water. But when Peter looked around and saw the wind and the waves, he immediately started to sink. Jesus reached out his hand and took him into the boat, asking, "Why did you doubt?" Not only was Peter saved, but the storm died down. The disciples could clearly see that it was Jesus, and they were all amazed at his power over the elements. Peter could now add personal experience to his observations of Jesus.

When Jesus came to the region of Caesarea Philippi, he asked his disciples, "Who do people say the Son of Man is?" (Matt. 16:13). The disciples all joined in with statements about what others were saying: Elijah, or Jeremiah, or one of the prophets. But then Jesus asked them, "Who do *you* say that I am?" Peter is the one who boldly answers: "You are the Messiah, the Son of the living God" (Matt. 16:16). Jesus commends him for his answer and adds, "Blessed are you, Simon son of Jonah, for this was not revealed to you by flesh and blood, but by my Father in heaven" (Matt. 16:17). This stood as a reminder to Peter, and it echoes down to us: real insight comes only from God.

After six days Jesus took with him Peter, James and John the brother of James, and led them up a high mountain by themselves. There he was transfigured before them. His face shone like the sun, and his clothes became as white as the light. Just then there appeared before them Moses and Elijah, talking with Jesus. (Matt. 17:1–3)

What an amazing scene. Moses had been dead for thirteen hundred years, and Elijah had quite dramatically been taken to heaven while still alive about nine hundred years earlier. How could Peter, James, and John make sense of this scene? Again, Peter speaks up to fill the silence. The Gospel of Mark records him as saying, "Rabbi, it is good for us to be here. Let us put up three shelters—one for you, one for Moses and one for Elijah." In Mark 9:5–6, we read: "(He did not know what to say, they were so frightened.)"

It is easy to be critical of Peter at this point. Without thinking, he appears to put Jesus on the same level as Moses and Elijah and wanted to do something to honor them. But this did not demonstrate what Jesus had tried to teach him. He needed to bring God's insight into the situation, not his own muddled thinking. God then clarified the picture for Peter, James, and John—and us—in what happened next:

> A bright cloud covered them, and a voice from the cloud said, "This is my Son, whom I love; with him I am well pleased. Listen to him!" When the disciples heard this, they fell facedown to the ground, terrified. But Jesus came and touched them. "Get up," he said. "Don't be afraid." When they looked up, they saw no one except Jesus. (Matt. 17:5–8)

God seems to say that it's not about the three; it's about Jesus.

As Jesus approached the time when he would go to the cross, the disciples were still thinking he had come as the Messiah to set up his position as earthly king.

> [Jesus] then began to teach them that the Son of Man must suffer many things and be rejected by the elders, the chief priests and the teachers of the law, and that he must be killed and after three days rise again. He spoke plainly about this, and Peter took him aside and began to rebuke him. But when Jesus turned and looked at his disciples, he rebuked Peter. "Get behind me, Satan!" he said. "You do not have in mind the concerns of God, but merely human concerns."
> (Mark 8:31–33)

Peter had again jumped ahead of what he knew, drawing conclusions that were not correct.

———

Peter's biggest failure started with overconfidence. After the Last Supper, when Jesus and his disciples left the upper room, Jesus said to them, "This very night you will all fall away from me" (Matt. 26:31). Again, Peter steps in to challenge that statement, saying, "Even if all fall away from you, I never will" (Matt. 26:33). And when Jesus told Peter he would deny him three times before the rooster crowed, Peter replied, "Even if I have to die with you, I will never disown you" (Matt. 26:35). We are certain Peter believed this. Like we often do, he was relying on his own faithfulness to carry out the promise—but it was not enough. Later that evening, while Jesus was standing trial, Peter was sitting in the courtyard when a servant girl came to him and said, "You were also with Jesus of Galilee." But he denied it saying, "I don't know what you're talking about" (Matt. 26:69–70). In rapid succession, Peter denied his Lord two more times. And then the rooster crowed.

Luke writes, "The Lord turned and looked straight at Peter. Then Peter remembered the word the Lord had spoken to him: 'Before the rooster crows today, you will disown me three times.' And he went outside and wept bitterly" (Luke 22: 61–62). It must have hurt Peter even more to know that Jesus himself witnessed his denial.

The next two days were challenging for Peter. He lived with his denial while Jesus lay dead in the tomb. But then on Sunday, the disciples heard that Jesus was missing from his tomb. In his Gospel, John records that he (a much younger man) outran Peter as they hurried to the tomb to investigate. Though John was hesitant to go into the empty tomb, Peter rushed right in and saw that though the grave clothes were there, Jesus was not. That evening, Jesus appeared to the disciples. They were overjoyed but still uncertain. It is indeed hard to make sense of things that don't fit our own paradigms.

———

The disciples had come together, and Jesus was not a constant part of the gatherings now. Unsure what to do, Peter (surprise, surprise) came up with a plan to go fishing, and the others agreed. They were out on the lake all night but caught nothing. Early the next morning, Jesus was standing on the shore of the lake, but they didn't recognize him. He asked them if they had caught any fish, and they said no, so he said, "Throw your net on the right side of the boat and you will find something" (John 21:6).

We wonder if even the instruction might have been the first clue that it was Jesus. This wasn't the first time Peter had been out fishing when Jesus had told him to put his nets out in the deep water for a catch (Luke 5:4–6). Peter had responded grudgingly then, perhaps thinking that he was the fishing expert, not Jesus. "Master, we've worked hard all night and haven't caught anything. But because you say so, I will let down the fishing nets" (Luke 5:5). That time, they hauled in a great catch of fish, and they did so again this time. When they caught a net full of fish, John said to Peter, "It is the Lord" (John 21:7). We can't miss the importance of the workplace in Peter's discipleship here. Peter grew in his trust of Jesus through his interaction with Jesus in the workplace.

As we have come to expect from Peter, he immediately jumped into the water to swim over to Jesus. He was still the man of action, even though a cloud hung over his relationship with Jesus. After breakfast, Jesus took Peter aside. Three times Jesus asked Peter if he loved him, and three times Peter responded fully. Each time Jesus called Peter to action, to feed his sheep. By doing this, Jesus reestablished Peter in the role he had for him.

—

After Jesus ascended into heaven, Peter took the lead with the early church. After the coming of the Holy Spirit at Pentecost, Peter stood up and gave a defense of who Jesus was and why he had died. His message demonstrated his knowledge of the Scriptures, drawing prophecies together and concluding, "Therefore let all Israel be assured of this: God has made this Jesus, whom you crucified, both Lord and Messiah" (Acts 2:36).

Peter's Spirit-filled presentation had a huge impact as about three thousand people were added to the church that day. The church continued to grow and gain structure, with Peter right in the middle of it all. The apostles were continuing the healing work of Jesus. Persecution of the church steadily increased as well, and the apostles were arrested and put in prison. But when an angel of the Lord opened the prison doors, they continued to preach about Jesus.

Though the Jewish leaders wanted to have all of the disciples put to death, one of their own, Gamaliel, stood up in defense of Jesus' disciples. He effectively argued that if their religion was of human origin, it would die like other religious or political sects. But if it was from God, then the religious leaders would be powerless to stop it. So the disciples were flogged and charged not to speak again in the name of Jesus. The apostles rejoiced because they had been counted worthy to suffer Jesus and went on speaking about him.

This is a good reminder for those in our day who believe they are being persecuted. Can we rejoice in the midst of persecution? Or are we angry that we are not given privileged status?

Up until this point, anyone who was a Christian, and hence the entire church, was Jewish. They therefore continued to follow many Jewish practices, which included being separate from Gentiles. Could Gentiles also be Christians? Did they need to follow Jewish practices to follow Jesus? Could these Jewish Christians regard Gentile Christians as equals? Little did Peter know that God was going to use him, a lifelong Jew who had never eaten anything unclean (not kosher) and had never entered the home of a Gentile, to bring about a transformation in the church. God did this in a dramatic, unambiguous fashion.

God sent an angel to a man named Cornelius in a dream, saying, "Your prayers and gifts to the poor have come up as a memorial offering before God. Now send men to Joppa to bring back a man named Simon who is called Peter. He is staying with Simon the tanner, whose house is by the sea" (Acts 10:4–5). So Cornelius sent two of his servants to Joppa to find Peter.

While the men from Cornelius were still on their way, it was noon in Joppa and Peter was hungry. He went up on the roof while lunch was being prepared and fell into a trance—perhaps even a nightmare. God gave Peter the same dream three times. In it, a sheet came down from heaven with all sorts of animals, reptiles, and birds that Peter, as an observant Jew, knew he could not eat. Each time a voice told him, "Get up, Peter. Kill and eat." Each time Peter responded, "Surely not Lord! I have never eaten anything pure or unclean!" Each time the voice came back to him with the statement, "Do not call anything impure that God has made clean" (Acts 10:13–16).

Peter didn't know what to make of the dream, but the Spirit of God told him that visitors were on their way to see him and that he should go with them when asked. When the two men arrived, Peter welcomed them into his home, a risky move since they were Gentiles. They told him about Cornelius, so Peter went with them, along with some other brothers from Joppa. When they arrived at Cornelius's house, they discovered a large gathering. Peter said to them all, "You are well aware that it is against our law for a Jew to associate with or visit a Gentile. But God has shown me that I should not call anyone impure or unclean. So when I was sent for, I came without raising any objection. May I ask why you sent for me?" (Acts 10:28–29).

Cornelius told Peter and his friends that an angel had said to invite Peter and then said, "Now we are all here in the presence of God to listen to everything the Lord has commanded you to tell us" (Acts 10:33). Peter then drew on sermons he had already given to tell the story of Jesus: who he was, why he came, and what our response to him needs to be. Peter and his fellow Jews were astonished to see how positively these Gentiles responded to the message. Their response was confirmed by signs from the Holy Spirit, which caused Peter to suggest that these Gentiles be baptized. What a dramatic result! The story, however, does not end there and continues in three parts.

First, when Peter returned to Jerusalem, the other Jewish Christians besieged him with questions and accusations. How could he go into a Gentile home? How could he eat with them? Peter then told them the whole story, with the clarity of God's obvious presence at each step. He closed with a powerful question: "So if God gave them the same gift he gave us who believed in the Lord Jesus Christ, who was I to think that I could stand in God's way?" (Acts 11:17). To their credit, the Jews in Jerusalem understood and believed. "When they heard this, they had no further objections and praised God, saying, 'So then, even to Gentiles God has granted repentance that leads to life'" (Acts 11:18).

Second, when there were disagreements in the church as to how to handle the growing Gentile population, they came together to resolve the matter. Some were fine with accepting the Gentile believers as long as they participated in all of the Jewish laws and ceremonial practices. Others argued that even the Jews couldn't keep all of their own practices and laws and that this would be an impossible burden on them.

Again, it was Peter who stood up to address the gathering, drawing on his dreams and his time with Cornelius. After much debate, they agreed that only a few requirements would become the common practice in the church in deference to the Jewish believers, yet they did not require Gentiles to observe most of the Jewish laws. The agreement was confirmed with the statement, "It seemed good to the Holy Spirit and to us" (Acts 15:28). This agreement had not come about by compromise or crafty people, but by the Holy Spirit and by the disciples responding to the Spirit.

———

The early church, led by Peter, had worked out the call for all humanity to be treated with dignity and respect. Before the watching world, they were living out Jesus' prayer in John 17:20–23:

"My prayer is not for them alone. I pray also for those who will believe in me through their message, that all of them may be one, Father, just as you are in me and I am in you. May they also be in us so that the world may believe that you have sent me. I have given them the glory that you gave me, that they may be one as we are one—I in them and you in me—so that they may be brought to complete unity. Then the world will know that you sent me and have loved them even as you have loved me."

What happened at the Jerusalem Council was a pivotal moment in the history of the church, and there are at least three key applications from this event for today.

First, the council concluded that Gentiles did not have to become ethnic Jews (particularly through circumcision) to become members of Jesus' family. To put that in the language of today, our fellowship as Christians should extend across ethnic boundaries, but that does not mean we become "monochrome" in our worship styles, our church leadership styles, and so on. We retain our ethnic and cultural identities. We should celebrate these cultural differences, learning from and appreciating the richness those differences bring to the body of Christ.

Second, friendship and relationships are keys—important keys—to crossing cultural and racial boundaries. Peter's role in the council was to tell them how God used his own experience in the home of the Gentile Cornelius—where he had spent several days enjoying their hospitality—to help him understand the reality that God "does not discriminate between Gentiles and Jews, for he purified their hearts by faith" (Acts 15:9). Going into the home of someone of a different race and eating with them there—as Peter did with Cornelius—or somewhere else seems like a simple act, like a "baby step," but acts of giving and receiving hospitality often result in someone becoming our friend. When that happens, we care about that person and want to see the best for our friend: we become, very practically, different parts of the same body.

Like many African Americans who grew up in the deep South, Dolphus Weary left Mississippi in 1967 for Los Angeles when he turned twenty-one, vowing never to return. Shortly before receiving his master's degree, he toured Asia with an evangelical basketball team. His coach encouraged him to "consider Asian missions as a lifetime calling,"[3] but Weary felt God was calling him to return to Mississippi, to leave his "safe space" and work in racial reconciliation. In 1971, he returned home and founded Mission

Mississippi, an organization "dedicated to promoting racial reconciliation among Christians in Mississippi." The key principle for Mission Mississippi is "bringing Christians together one relationship at a time," which is often worked out practically through Black and white Christians sharing meals together as a way of beginning friendships.[4]

Finally, we need to recognize that crossing racial and ethnic boundaries is not a one-and-done commitment. Just because the council made their decision about Gentile Christians joining the church, it did not mean that natural divisions between Jews and Gentiles were now gone forever and that everyone "lived happily ever after." The issues the council dealt with periodically resurfaced, as we will see later. Reconciliation and restoration with regard to racial tensions has always been and still is complex and, despite our best efforts, will always be a "work in progress." Nevertheless, we have a good model in Acts 15 of how the early church chose to be an *inclusive* rather than an *exclusive* fellowship.

For Al, this Acts 15 account challenges us to go one step further, beyond individual relationships and friendships as important as these are.

In *One Blood: Parting Words to the Church on Race and Love*, civil rights leader and preacher John Perkins wrote, "It was Billy Graham who said it first, and Martin Luther King Jr. echoed it from his jail cell in Birmingham: Sunday at 11:00 am in America is still the most segregated of times. This charge was made against the Church in the 1950s, and sadly is still true today."[5] Brian McCormick points to progress in this area, noting that "the share of churches with at least one out of five members from a minority background had grown from 6% in 1998 to 16% in 2019."[6] Yet, he notes that for historically white churches, this transition is challenging.

Al sees the need for multiethnic churches for several reasons. First, people of the kingdom of God should represent the coming kingdom as stated in in Revelation 7:9,

> After this I looked, and there before me was a great multitude that no one could number, from every nation, tribe, people and languages, standing before the throne and before the Lamb. They were wearing white robes and were holding palm branches in their hands.

Second, as Paul says in describing the body of Christ, we need one another: different perspectives, different gifts, different experiences. Having these gifts represented in the gathered as well as the scattered church is important.

Third, in speaking at Mars Hill in Athens, Paul says, "He has made from one blood every nation of men to dwell on all the face of the earth" (Acts 17:26 NKJV). Perkins argues from Paul's statement that distinctions by race, rather than by ethnic and cultural backgrounds, is an artificial construct that has led us to racism. The church is called by Christ to model reconciliation. Unfortunately, the church often mirrors the racial divides of culture.[7]

There will remain differences in worship style and doctrinal understanding in the church, which brings out the diversity of God's people. It is just that these divides need not be along racial lines. Changes in the church will not come from edicts, policies, or dictates. They will come only from the willingness of Christians to engage in conversation and the leading of the Holy Spirit, as demonstrated in the solution to the divide in the church between Jews and Gentiles in Acts 15.

—

The third part of the Cornelius story and the decision by the Council of Jerusalem is Peter's regression to the former ways. Even though he had been at the center while the early church worked out the importance of bringing all peoples together in the church, Peter found himself under pressure by the Jewish Christians. Here is what Paul says about this in his letter to the Galatians:

> When Cephas [Peter] came to Antioch, I opposed him to his face, because he stood condemned. For before certain men came from James, he used to eat with the Gentiles. But when they arrived, he began to draw back and separate himself from the Gentiles because he was afraid of those who belonged to the circumcision group. The other Jews joined him in his hypocrisy, so that by their hypocrisy even Barnabas was led astray. When I saw that they were not acting in line with the truth of the gospel, I said to Cephas in front of them all, "You are a Jew, yet you live like a Gentile and not like a Jew. How is it, then, that you force Gentiles to follow Jewish customs?" (Gal. 2:11–14)

How could Peter have done this? We have seen before that he, like us, wants to be appreciated by others. When he got with the wrong crowd, he stepped back from the bold step he had led through God's guidance. This stands as a sober reminder to us all. When God calls us to take a position built on his truth, this territory is not simply won once and then it is over. It takes perseverance. The writer to the Hebrews reminds us that we need one another in this battle: "And let us consider how we may spur one another on toward love and good deeds, not giving up meeting together, as some are in the habit of doing, but encouraging one another—and all the more as you see the Day approaching" (Heb. 10:24–25).

———

As we read Peter's letters written near the end of his life, we are struck by a person who has lived through the polarizing time when Jesus was on earth as well as all the challenges of the early church navigating through conflicts from society as well as within the church. Here is the way Peter draws this together:

> Dear friends, I urge you as foreigners and exiles, to abstain from sinful desires, which wage war against your soul. Live such good lives among the pagans that, though they may accuse you of doing wrong, they may see your good deeds and glorify God on the day he visits us. (1 Pet. 2:11–12)

Peter reflects here what Jesus said in the Beatitudes: "Let your light so shine before others that they may see your good deeds and glorify your father in heaven" (Matt. 5:16).

Peter also calls us to respect secular authority in our lives. We realize that this is not something that came easily to him when we remember that Emperor Nero would put to death a short time after he wrote this:[8]

> Submit yourselves for the Lord's sake to every human authority: whether to the emperor, as the supreme authority, or to governors, who are sent by him to punish those who do wrong and to commend those who do right. For it is God's will that by *doing good* you should silence the ignorant talk of foolish people. Live as free people, but do not use your freedom as a cover-up for evil; live as God's slaves. Show proper respect to everyone, love the family of believers, fear God, honor the emperor. (1 Pet. 2:13–17; italics added)

Peter also addresses differences from within the church. We can hear modern Christians say, "Does Peter have any idea what the people in my church are like?" Yet when we read of the early church, particularly in the epistles, we see that divisions were rampant over disputes of every imaginable thing. Paul had to remind the Galatian church, "If you bite and devour each other, watch out or you will be destroyed by each other" (Gal. 5:15). And in 1 Peter 3:8–9, Peter encourages us:

Finally, all of you, be like-minded, be sympathetic, love one another, be compassionate and humble. Do not repay evil with evil or insult with insult. On the contrary, repay evil with blessing, because to this you were called so that you may inherit a blessing.

His writing is a heartfelt call for us to navigate the world wherever God places us with purpose, kindness, humility, and love for one another, not merely to hang on through suffering. Peter wants us to radically reorient our lives (2 Pet. 2:9), follow Christ (2 Pet. 2:21), and "bless . . . to do good . . . to seek peace (2 Pet. 3:9–11). "The call of Christ means we are to bring the hope of his goodness to the world."[9]

Near the end of his second letter, Peter makes this personal. As we just read above, Paul had publicly called out Peter when he pulled back from eating with Gentile believers. Even though Peter was in the wrong, he could have carried a grudge or held on to his hurt. But Peter writes:

Our dear brother Paul also wrote you with the wisdom that God gave him. He writes the same way in all his letters, speaking in them of these matters. His letters contain some things that are hard to understand, which ignorant and unstable people distort, as they do the other Scriptures, to their own destruction. (2 Pet. 3:15–16)

In this letter, Peter challenges his readers, which include us, to hold onto Scripture as the final measure of what is good and right, and to do so without distortion.

11 | Paul

I draw on a theology of reconciliation that is holistic. It is rooted in a core of spiritual reconciliation with God. In the human sphere, it deals with our internal self and conflicts we may have within. Branching out, we move to relationships with those close to us—family, friends, and affinity groups. A greater bridge is to those quite different from us—"other people" with differences such as race, ethnicity, language, or even age, political positions, or religious identity. As humans work in groups, we encounter organizational and systemic issues that call us to the ministry of reconciliation, resolving conflicts and creating systems that contribute to the well-being of all. Finally, we live in a natural world where the ministry of reconciliation is expressed in care for the creation, both living and nonliving as well as its ecosystem.

— Bill Lowrey, former director of peacemaking,
World Vision International

Saul was blind. And though he had just been struck down with physical blindness, he now realized his whole life to this point had been characterized by an unwillingness to see what was right in front of him: the reality that God had kept his promise to rescue Israel, but in a way he could not possibly have imagined. That God himself came in the form of a man called Jesus and that he suffered, died, and then rose from the dead.

It wasn't quite true, of course, that Saul had never entertained the *possibility* that the Jesus story just might be true. There were, from time to time, little doubts about what he was doing to these followers of Jesus, and though he had absolutely approved of Stephen being stoned to death (Acts 7:58), the doubts kept creeping in (Acts 26:14,)[1] But those thoughts eventually always passed. Until three days ago.

The men who had accompanied Saul from Jerusalem to Damascus weren't quite sure what to do with him. In addition to being blind, he wouldn't eat or drink, and he spent much of his time praying (Acts 9:11). They wondered how long this could go on, and what would come next. Saul wondered, too. Then came a knock at the front door. A man who identified himself as Ananias asked to see the blind man, and he was taken to the room where the man sat in darkness.

Ananias was simply known as "a disciple" of Jesus (Acts 9:10), and he was initially reluctant to see Saul given Saul's reputation as a persecutor of Christians in Jerusalem. But when God told Ananias that he had chosen Saul to carry his message to the Gentiles, Ananias obeyed the Lord's instructions. When he arrived at Simon the Tanner's house, he placed his hands on Saul and called him "Brother Saul," or "Saul, my brother" (Acts 9:17 NEB).

In his letter to the Colossian church some years later, Paul encouraged them to "be wise in the way you act toward outsiders; make the most of every opportunity. Let your conversation be always full of grace, seasoned with salt, so that you may know how to answer everyone" (Col. 4:4–6). Ananias's words of grace and welcome laid the foundation for the rest of Paul's life and work. What words do non-Christians associate with the follows of Jesus today?

Perhaps we imagine that after his conversion to Christianity, Paul would be able to quickly move into a leadership position within the church. Where many of the original apostles were fishermen and former tax collectors, Paul had studied under the great Jewish teacher, Gamaliel, and was intellectually brilliant:

> Everything we know about him encourages us to think of the young Saul of Tarsus as an unusually gifted child. He spoke Hebrew fluently. He spoke the Aramaic of the Middle East . . . in addition to the ubiquitous Greek, which he spoke and wrote at great speed. . . . He gives every impression of having swallowed the Bible whole. . . . Whether Saul has read the non-Jewish philosophers of the day or the great traditions that go back to Plato and Aristotle, he knows the ideas.[2]

Paul may have learned with great zeal, but he had not followed his teacher in the way he presented his arguments. The Pharisee Gamaliel had been able to calm the storm of criticism of the new Christians at least temporarily with these words:

> "In the present case I advise you: Leave these men alone! Let them go! For if their purpose or activity is of human origin, it will fail. But if it is from God, you will not be able to stop these men; you will only find yourselves fighting against God." His speech persuaded them. (Acts 5:38–39)

At any rate, Paul immediately put his brilliant mind to work, preaching in all the synagogues in Damascus, proclaiming that "Jesus is the Son of God" (Acts 9:20). Everyone who heard Paul was astonished, particularly given his previous background, but because of his rhetorical gifts, he "grew more and more powerful and baffled the Jews living in Damascus by proving that Jesus is the Messiah" (Acts 9:9:21–22). Beginning a pattern that would be repeated many times, the Jewish authorities devised a plot to murder Paul but some of his followers helped him escape Damascus one night by lowering him in a basket through an opening in the wall that surrounded the city (Acts 9:23–25). He eventually made his way to Jerusalem, but not surprisingly, the disciples there "were all afraid of him, not believing that he was really a disciple" (Acts 9:26). However, a man named Barnabas stepped up and "brought him to the apostles," telling them Paul's story, beginning with his conversion on the road to Damascus and "how in Damascus he had preached fearlessly in the name of Jesus" (Acts 9:27).

We briefly met Barnabas earlier in Acts 4:36–37, where we learn that his given name is Joseph, that he is from the island of Cyprus, and that he "sold a field he owned and brought the money at the apostles' feet." Not surprisingly, given his generosity, the apostles gave him the nickname of "Barnabas," which means "Son of Encouragement." Barnabas's generosity and encouragement was not limited to his money. Having seen Paul in action in Damascus, he is willing to spend his personal capital and take the chance that Paul can be trusted, so he vouches for him to the apostles in Jerusalem. We wonder if Paul would have become the great leader had Barnabas not given him the benefit of the doubt and vouched for him when no one else in Jerusalem did?

There is no such person as a self-made person. All of us have benefited from someone taking a chance on us. Shortly before Randy graduated from college, Pete Hammond, who had been an InterVarsity Christian Fellowship staff worker during Randy's first year in the chapter at Southern Miss, invited him to apply to join the InterVarsity staff. That thought had never occurred to Randy for the simple reason that the InterVarsity staff he knew were, to him, "spiritual giants" and he clearly was not. Nevertheless, he agreed to apply and much to his amazement was hired. He spent the next three years working with students on college campuses in Tennessee before returning to Mississippi to attend law school. For two of those three years, Pete Hammond was Randy's supervisor. Though it was only a few years, Randy and Kathy found those years in Knoxville to be incredibly forma-tive for them in a multitude of ways—including their marriage (they had married a year before Randy graduated from college).[3] Pete Hammond took a chance on Randy, and while he recognized that he was far from Paul in terms of spiritual maturity, he continues to be thankful for the fact that someone believed he had potential.

Two key people shaping Al's life were Al Greene and Wayne Alderson. Dr. Al Greene was the superintendent and founder of Bellevue Christian School and introduced Al to an encompassing view of the transformation of life for the believer. He often quoted 2 Corinthians 5:17, "If any man be in Christ he is a new creation; old things have passed away, behold all things have become new" (KJV). He would put the emphasis on *all* things, showing that history, mathematics, and art were all different in light of the new set of glasses Christians were called to put on to see the world through Christ.

Wayne Alderson was a steel company vice president in Pittsburgh. When Al heard him interviewed on the radio and heard about the book on his life,[4] he bought it immediately, read it through in one night, and called Wayne the next day. They became friends for more than thirty years. Wayne's life verse was 2 Corinthians 5:19, "God was reconciling the world to himself in Christ . . . and he has committed to us the message of reconcili-ation." Wayne's lifelong commitment was to be an agent of reconciliation, which continues today through his Value of the Person organization.

———

Like Joseph, Moses, and Daniel, Paul had an excellent education that helped prepare him for his assignment to "proclaim [God's] name to the Gentiles and their kings" as well as to the people of Israel (Acts 9:15). Also like Joseph and Moses, Paul moved into the background of Scripture for a period of time. In Paul's case, after more attempts on his life, he was sent off to Tarsus for "a decade or so of silence: roughly 36 to 46."[5]

What did Paul do during this period of silence? N. T. Wright suggests that he likely did three things:

1. He earned his own living in the family business as a tentmaker.

2. He prayed and studied. His later letters reflected this deep study.

3. He had a particular spiritual experience that he could never talk about.[6]

During this time, he was also given a "thorn in the flesh" that he prayed God would take away, but the answer was no. Yet Paul, and we, are blessed by the discernment that came from this period. "Paul came to see that these two stories, Israel's story and God's story had merged together. . . . Both narratives were fulfilled in Jesus."[7]

In his first letter to the Christians in Corinth, Paul explained to a group of believers who were apparently enamored with some flashy philosophers and teachers that the person without the Spirit living in them—those not following Jesus—cannot accept and understand *reality*, even though they appear to be "wise." For Paul, it was only those who have the Spirit of God living in them who are, in fact, truly wise despite what the world may think, because the Christian has "the mind of Christ." It is really a breathtaking claim. To support his statement that "we have the mind of Christ," Paul quotes Isaiah 40:13, "Who has known the mind of the Lord so as to instruct him?" What exactly is Paul talking about when he makes this claim? How is it possible to "know the mind of the Lord"?

In his letter to the Roman Christians, Paul tells them to not "conform to the pattern of this world, but be *transformed by the renewing of you mind*. Then you will be able to test and approve what God's will is—his good, pleasing and perfect will" (Rom. 12:2). J. B. Phillips memorably translates this verse: "Don't let the world around you squeeze you into its own mold, but *let God re-mold your minds from within*, so that you may prove in practice that the plan of God for you is good, meets all his demands, and moves towards the goal of true maturity" (Rom. 12:2 PHILLIPS). Again, as Christians, how can our minds be "transformed" or "re-molded from within" so that we do not simply "conform to the pattern of this world"?

When Paul spent those years in Arabia and elsewhere after he met Jesus, he "renewed his mind" by rethinking what he had always assumed in light of the new fact of Jesus as the Messiah. We need to do the same. We need to put on some new "glasses" as we read and study Scripture, as we think and pray about the *implications* and *applications* of the gospel of Christ to our everyday lives, and as we work and interact with our colleagues at work and in the communities where we live. And, like Paul, this rethinking is not a quick process. It is gradual, but it is also intentional.

What about you? Are you willing to put on a different set of glasses as you read and study Scripture, being open to God renewing and remolding your thinking about your relationships, your work, your priorities? "We have the mind of Christ," so let's be willing to learn and think new thoughts as we study Scripture, as we turn over the implications and applications of what we see in Scripture in our minds, as we ask God for "eyes to see," and as we talk with those who are wiser about what it means to follow Jesus in our everyday lives.

————

The most thorny issue the early church faced was the question of how the Gentiles fit into the Jewish "story." When Jesus said that his (Jewish) disciples were to "go and make disciples of all nations" (Matt. 28:19) and that they were to be his "witnesses in Jerusalem, and in all Judea and Samaria, and to the ends of the earth" (Acts 1:8), how exactly would that work in practice? For God to assign Paul, who described himself as "circumcised on the eighth day, of the people of Israel, of the tribe of Benjamin, a Hebrew of Hebrews . . . [and] a Pharisee" (Phil. 3:5), the task of proclaiming God's name "to the Gentiles and their kings and to the people of Israel" (Acts 9:15) was not only a great ironic twist in the plot but also a huge intellectual—and personal—challenge for Paul. No wonder God told Ananias that he was going to show Paul "how much he must suffer for my name" (Acts 9:16). Paul had a hard assignment.

To begin with, Paul's basic personality and background—zealous, outspoken, with a brilliant mind steeped in the Old Testament Scriptures—would prove to be important in navigating this controversy, but he needed more than these tools to be successful in helping the young Christian community become a united fellowship of Jews *and* Gentiles. Paul needed to learn to be a bridge-builder for Christ between two distinct cultures. Perhaps this was what he learned during his decade-long period of silence in Tarsus. He had to have a foot in both camps, not abandoning his Jewish roots while at the same time helping his Jewish brothers and sisters understand that Jesus really meant what he said about "making disciples of all nations."

The beautiful unity of the church led by Peter, James, and Paul is a reminder that God can bring healing from great divides over difficult issues.

The final decisions, "after much discussion" (Acts 15:7),[8] came together in Acts 15, which we discussed in the chapter on Peter. It was an incredible triumph to bring ethnic and racial healing to a divided church. We would do well to listen carefully to their wisdom in addressing our own divides today.

In his letter to the Roman church, Paul portrays the Gentiles as branches grafted into a tree (Rom. 11:17). In his letter to the Ephesian believers, he says that Christ has "made the two groups one and has destroyed the barrier, the dividing wall of hostility" (Eph. 2:14). In 1 Corinthians 12, Romans 12, and Ephesians 4, he reminds Christians that whatever their background, they are dependent on one another; they are like different parts of the body, which means they need one another. As he wrote to the Galatian Christians,

> In Christ's family there can be no division into Jew and non-Jew, slave and free, male and female. Among us you are all equal. That is, we are all in a common relationship with Jesus Christ. Also, since you are Christ's family, then you are Abraham's famous "descendant," heirs according to the covenant promises. (Gal. 3:28–29 MSG)

How can we apply Paul's model of bridge-building today in our polarizing world that is, sadly, not only outside the church but within the church as well?

First, we have to decide that we *want* to be bridge-builders both to non-Christians and to other Christians. There are plenty of people—again, Christians and non-Christians—who promote division in our society through social media and cancel culture. Social media does not *have* to be divisive, however, though that often seems to be the case. Randy has a friend who has a Facebook account with more than three thousand friends. From the time she joined Facebook years ago, she made the deliberate choice to post only constructive things—posts that would encourage and build up rather than divide.

Second, we have to recognize and accept that being bridge-builders in the West today means moving out of our comfort zones. When God assigned Paul to go into Gentile territory, he could not have imagined what that would mean in terms of cultural disorientation. He would be misunderstood and attacked by his own people, repeatedly put in prison, often for long periods of time by the Gentile authorities and would spend a lot of time refereeing conflicts between Jews and Gentiles in the churches he founded. Before being called by God to *intentionally* take the message of Christ to the Gentiles, Paul was "safe": he was with his native people, doing his best to maintain the purity of Judaism by stamping out what he believed was a heretical sect.

Al's son Michael has worked for many companies as a senior human resources executive. He frequently gives a talk on what it means to learn and grow in your assignment. He pictures a person where they are with a box around them called "the comfort zone." He then pictures them where they aspire to be. Then he notes, "the only way to get from here to there is to get out of your comfort zone."[9]

What about us? Are we willing to be bridge-builders, creative agents of reconciliation in a society divided by race, politics, gender, and a host of other issues? As Paul wrote to the Corinthians, a group of Christians that had more than its share of internal divisions,

> We don't evaluate people by what they have or how they look. We looked at the Messiah that way once and got it all wrong, as you know. We certainly don't look at him that way anymore. . . . God put the world square with himself through the Messiah, giving the world a fresh start by offering forgiveness of sins. God has given us the task of telling everyone what he is doing. We're Christ's representatives. God uses us to persuade men and women to drop their differences and enter into God's work of making things right between them. (2 Cor. 5:16–19 MSG)

—

Sadly, shortly after the decision of the apostles and other leaders that the church would welcome Gentiles without forcing them to follow the law of Moses, particularly circumcision, Paul and Barnabas had a dispute. Barnabas, of course, had been an early encourager of Paul and had come to his aid when others would not trust him. Now Barnabas came to the aid of his nephew, John Mark. While on a previous journey with Paul, John Mark had deserted Paul and Paul no longer trusted him. "They had such a sharp disagreement that they parted company. Barnabas took Mark and sailed for Cyprus, but Paul chose Silas and left, commended by the brothers to the grace of the Lord" (Acts 15:39–40).

Two comments are in order for this challenging event in Scripture. First, some say that Paul was right to do what he did with Mark because we hear much more of Paul in the rest of Acts, but Barnabas disappears from the story. However, we must remember that Luke was writing this account and was traveling with Paul; and though we hear nothing more about Barnabas, we do hear more about John Mark. He wrote the Gospel of Mark and was later commended by Paul himself, who wrote, "Only Luke is with me. Get Mark and bring him with you, because he is helpful to me in my ministry" (2 Tim. 4:11). Apparently, Paul reconciled with Mark (and Barnabas?), but it seems that even after the two friends separated, Barnabas was still an encourager.

Second, too often, great difficulty follows on the heels of great success. The disciples had just come together over a highly contentious issue through a wonderful solution from God. It might have been tempting to rest on that success, not realizing the enemy was still at work. It is a humbling reminder for us to keep up our guard. At the end of Jesus' temptations in the wilderness, although Jesus had resisted all of them, Luke tells us that Satan "left him until an opportune time" (Luke 4:13). Satan wasn't done yet.

As we navigate our polarizing world, we may from time to time have success in breaking down barriers. The danger comes, though, when we somehow believe we accomplished this on our own, which makes us vulnerable to enemy attack.

—

Paul drew on his learning when he taught in the marketplace. When he was in Athens, a group of Epicurean and Stoic philosophers began to debate him. Eventually, they brought him to a meeting of the Aeropagus, which N. T. Wright suggests was not a philosophical debating society but "the highest court in the land."[10] The charge against Paul was that he was "advocating foreign gods" (Acts 17:18).

In his defense, Paul drew on his knowledge of Greek literature and poetry and the Jewish Scriptures to explain his understanding of how Jesus' death and resurrection is the fulfillment of what Greek culture was "groping" for in its stories and poetry *and* the Jewish story of God's determination to rescue the world. In the end, the Athenian response to Paul's defense was mixed: "When they heard about the resurrection, some of them sneered, but others said, 'We want to hear you again on this subject.' . . . Some of the people became followers of Paul and believed" (Acts 17:32–34). If Paul, in all of his wisdom and development through his time with God, can get a mixed response to his message, then should we be surprised when our own best insights are tossed aside?

Randy's wife, Kathy, participates in what are called "Peace Feasts": meals shared by Christians and Muslims, in which, after eating together, "parallel" passages from the Quran and the Bible are read aloud (if you haven't ever done this, you'll be surprised at how many similar passages there are in the two books!), and then the group discusses the similarities and differences in the two passages. Although there is no attempt to directly evangelize anyone, there is an opportunity to learn what the two faiths have in common and how they differ. For both Muslims and Christians, Kathy says, participating in these meals and discussions has allowed them to hear about the other's faith *from their own lips*, with the result that many of the misconceptions each group had about the other were found to be just that: misconceptions.

Paul wisely took what he knew to be true about Greek culture (as well as the Jewish Scriptures) and used that effectively to make his point about the reality of the resurrection. Rather than simply venting about the plethora of "gods" in Athens, and how much it disturbed him (which it obviously did; see Acts 17:16), he patiently and respectfully used his knowledge of Greek literature and culture to help him in his defense of Christianity. As we engage with people in our culture we believe to be wrong about this or that issue, are we willing to hold in tension our belief that, as St. Augustine says, "all truth is God's truth" as Paul did in Athens?

———

Though Paul was not formally trained as a lawyer, he often found himself in court—but as a defendant. Sometimes his appearance in court was the result of members of the Jewish community wanting the Roman authorities to punish Paul because he had been preaching what they considered blasphemy—that Jesus was the Messiah and had been raised from the dead—though they usually presented the charges in the form of him being a troublemaker and stirring up the people to riot (see, e.g., Acts 24:5–6). Once he was in court because some Gentiles believed Paul's message that "gods made with human hands are no gods at all" was potentially fatal to their business of making silver shrines for a Greek goddess—and to the tourist trade of an entire city: Ephesus, home of the "internationally acclaimed temple to Diana, one of the 'Seven Wonders of the Ancient World.'"[11] The Roman judicial authorities, however, consistently refused to be drawn into what they considered Jewish theological arguments when the Jews brought charges against Paul. In the case of Ephesus, the city clerk himself appealed to the Gentile crowd to not take the law into their own hands but to follow correct legal procedure if they wanted to bring a formal charge against Paul.

When Paul and Silas were beaten and thrown into jail for the night in Philippi, Paul refused to let the Roman authorities off the hook when they were prepared to release them the next morning. Instead, Paul said to the officers sent by the magistrates, "They beat us without a trial, even though we are Roman citizens, and threw us into prison. And now do they want to get rid of us quietly? No! Let them come themselves and escort us out [of town]" (Acts 16:37).

After Paul was arrested for the last time in Jerusalem, he again raised the fact that he was a Roman citizen and therefore entitled to be tried before the proper Roman authorities before he could be flogged (Acts 22:25).

It wasn't just the Romans who were after Paul but also the Jews—his own people. When the Roman commander wanted to find out why the Jews had accused Paul, they brought him before the Sanhedrin.

> Paul looked straight at the Sanhedrin and said, "My brothers, I have fulfilled my duty to God in all good conscience to this day." At this the high priest Ananias ordered those standing near Paul to strike him on the mouth. Then Paul said to him, "God will strike you, you whitewashed wall! You sit there to judge me according to the law, yet you yourself violate the law by commanding that I be struck!" (Acts 23:1–3)

This startled those standing by the high priest, and they challenged Paul asking him how he dared to insult God's highest priest. Paul realized he had lost his temper and apologized: "Brothers, I did not realize that he was the high priest; for it is written: 'Do not speak evil about the ruler of your people'" (Acts 23:5). In the heated times in which we live in the twenty-first century, are we willing—as Paul was—to acknowledge our own mistakes when we lash out at someone?

When Paul appeared before the local governor, Festus, in Caesarea, he refused to return to Jerusalem to stand trial on the charges the Jews had brought against him. Instead, as a Roman citizen, he appealed to Caesar.

> "I am now standing before Caesar's court, where I ought to be tried. I have not done anything wrong to the Jews, as you yourself know very well. If, however, I am guilty of doing anything wrong that deserves death, I do not refuse to die. But if the charges brought against me by these Jews are not true, no one has the right to hand me over to them. I appeal to Caesar." (Acts 25:10–11)

The way Paul handled himself in court is quite instructive for us. He was respectful of and willing to submit himself to the Roman judicial system, even if some of the people he would appear before were dishonest, played politics, and were morally corrupt: Felix left him in jail for two years after Paul presented his defense, hoping Paul would offer him a bribe (Acts 24:26–27); Festus offered Paul the opportunity to go to Jerusalem to stand trial as a favor to the Jews (Acts 25:9); King Herod Agrippa was married to his own sister, Bernice, and Paul made his final recorded defense before them (Acts 25:13–26:32).

One of the most precious rights we have in the American judicial system is the right to due process, the opportunity for people to present their side to an impartial tribunal before being deprived of life, liberty, or property. This right is so important that it actually appears twice in the United States Constitution. The Fifth Amendment says that "No person shall . . . be deprived of life, liberty, or property, without due process of law." The Fourteenth Amendment, passed after the American Civil War, extends that prohibition to states within the United States. This requirement of due process was apparently built into the Roman judicial system as well, and Paul as a Roman citizen was entitled to it. We all should follow the example of due process given to Paul by not rushing to judge someone as guilty before they have a chance to tell their side of the story, which is what due process actually means.

———

Paul's writing contained some powerful insights that directly address our current polarization. Perhaps reflecting on his early misguided zeal, he reminds us in his letter to the Philippians, "Do nothing out of selfish ambition or vain conceit. Rather, in humility value others above yourselves, not looking to your own interests but each of you to the interests of the others" (Phil. 2:3–4). To underscore this same point, he reminds the Corinthians, "For who makes you different from anyone else? What do you have that you did not receive? And if you did receive it, why do you boast as though you did not?" (1 Cor. 4:7). In a world of self-made experts, these are important and humbling reminders.

Paul also talks about how we fit in with others, painting a picture that undermines strict individualism. "Just as a body, though one, has many parts, but all its many parts form one body, so it is with Christ" (1 Cor. 12:12).

We are a part of the whole under Christ. We should not think less of what we have been given: "Now if the foot should say, 'Because I am not a hand, I do not belong to the body,' it would not for that reason stop being part of the body. And if the ear should say, 'Because I am not an eye, I do not belong to the body,' it would not for that reason stop being part of the body" (1 Cor. 12:15–16). Nor should we think more of our own position and put down others: "The eye cannot say to the hand, 'I don't need you!' And the head cannot say to the feet, 'I don't need you!' On the contrary, those parts of the body that seem to be weaker are indispensable, and the parts that we think are less honorable we treat with special honor" (1 Cor. 12: 21–23).

———

Paul understood that his work for God had an expiration date, but that the assignment from Jesus to "make disciples of all nations" to *all Christians* would continue "to the very end of the age" (Matt. 28:20); and so, as Paul approached the end of his life, he gave some directions to his young protégé Timothy on successfully continuing that work.

Paul explained to Timothy that *his* work would also come to an end, and so it was vital that "the things you have heard me say in the presence of many witnesses entrust to reliable people who will also be qualified to teach others" (2 Tim. 2:2). According to Paul in Galatians 1:11–12, he had the best teacher of them all: "I want you to know, brothers and sisters, that the gospel I preached is not of human origin. I did not receive it from any man, nor was I taught it; rather, I received it by revelation from Jesus Christ." Paul was also mentored by Ananias and Barnabas and probably Peter—having spent fifteen days getting acquainted with him—and James when he went to Jerusalem for the first time (Gal. 1:18). Paul in turn mentored Timothy, giving him the privilege of appearing as a co-author in several of his letters, (2 Cor. 1:1; Phil. 1:1; Col. 1:1) and calling him "my true son" (1 Tim. 1:2) and "my dear son" (2 Tim. 1:2). Now it was Timothy's turn to work with other, younger Christians who would faithfully pass on the "treasure" Paul had entrusted to Timothy: the gospel of Jesus Christ.

In our work, as well as in our family relationships, Christians today need to "recover the pattern of older believers working with younger ones."[12] Many churches form Sunday school classes or Bible studies based on age. While it may seem natural to separate age groups, always segregating Christians like this means that younger Christians will not have the benefit of gaining the perspective of older Christians who have seen and experienced much more in their lives, and older Christians will not experience the joy of watching younger Christians gradually develop into mature disciples of Jesus.

Paul recognized that Timothy's mentoring did not begin with himself; rather, Timothy had models who had been faithfully following Jesus from the time Timothy was born in his grandmother, Lois, and his mother, Eunice (2 Tim. 1:5; 3:15). Although we know very little about these two women, it apparently was they who gave Timothy his knowledge of the Scriptures, "which are able to make you wise for salvation through faith in Christ Jesus" since they are all "God-breathed" and "useful one way or another—showing us truth, exposing our rebellion, correcting our mistakes, training us to live God's way," with the result that through God's word, "we are put together and shaped up for the tasks God has for us" (2 Tim. 3:16–17 MSG). All Timothy had to do from this point on, Paul concluded, was to "stick with what you learned and believed, sure of the integrity of your teachers" (2 Tim. 3:14 MSG).

And so, Paul could take a minute before concluding his letter to Timothy and reflect on where *he* stood with the assignment God had given him: "I have fought the good fight, I have finished the race, I have kept the faith" (2 Tim. 4:7). He had played his part in the story of God. He had not played it perfectly, of course, but he had "run hard right to the finish" (2 Tim. 4:7 MSG).

In our experience, one characteristic of those who have mentored us—whether it was parents or work-related colleagues or mentors like Pete Hammond, Al Greene, or Wayne Alderson—is that they continued to serve God as long as they were physically or mentally able. Pete "retired" from his work with InterVarsity, but he continued working on a variety of projects, including traveling around the country visiting and encouraging people he had discipled on campus decades before. Al's last visit with Al Greene a few months before he died included a lively discussion of recent books each had read. When we asked Pete about his retirement from InterVarsity, he smiled and reminded us that there is no such thing as "retirement" as we think of it today in the Bible. "Redeployment, yes," he said "retirement, no." Al has learned that retirement is really "new tires for the next leg of the journey." May we, like Paul and our mentors, not stop short of the finish line in the work God has given us to do—whatever that work might be.

12 | Jesus

Let this mind be in you which is also in Christ Jesus.
— Philippians 2

Therefore be imitators of God, as beloved children. And walk in love, as Christ loved us and gave himself up for us.
— Ephesians 5

Jesus. We debated whether to include Jesus in the narrative of this book for two reasons.

First, there is so much written about him in the Gospels, the letters, and throughout the Old Testament that such a task would be impossible. (Of course, while Jesus is the central figure in the Gospels and the remainder of the New Testament, Luke 24:27 reminds us that he is central to the entire Bible.) Second, we didn't want to make the mistake Peter appeared to make at the Mount of Transfiguration. When Peter saw Jesus with Moses and Elijah, he said, "If you wish, I will put up three shelters, one for you, one for Moses, and one for Elijah" (Matt. 17:4). It was as if Peter thought the three were on equal footing. God made it clear in that situation that Peter was misguided. A cloud rolled in and soon they saw Jesus only. We therefore did not want to think of Jesus in the same way we have considered other narratives.

On the other hand, Jesus is the very embodiment of the path we are to follow as over and over again, he said, "Follow me." In Hebrews 12:2, we are reminded to "run with endurance the race marked out for you, looking to Jesus." We know we can't find this path by ourselves, and we can't run it by ourselves—only in his power. We also know that Jesus limited himself in order to walk on earth in human form, and that he "grew in wisdom and in stature and in favor with God and all of the people" (Luke 2:52).

We cannot leave his story out of this discussion, so we will highlight a few things from his life that underscore the path he calls us to walk in this polarizing world. We learn from him both in what he said and in how in interacted with others.

Like us, his society was also polarized. The Jews were under Roman rule. Jesus was only two years old when his parents had to escape to Egypt with him because of persecution. Others in his faith community, the Jews, were living in fear that what little freedom they had would be taken away by the Romans. One of the marks against Jesus from the Jewish leaders was that his disruption might cause them to lose their position in society, such as it was. After Jesus raised Lazarus from the dead, the Jewish leaders were worried.

> Then the chief priests and the Pharisees called a meeting of the Sanhedrin. "What are we accomplishing?" they asked. "Here is this man performing many signs. If we let him go on like this, everyone will believe in him, and then the Romans will come and take away both our temple and our nation."
> (John 11:47–48)

Jesus faced a battle from both the external world and from the religious leaders.

He even faced a battle with his disciples who had trouble understanding his message (perhaps we do as well!). Up until the time of the cross, the disciples were looking for him to set up an earthly kingdom in power. As Jesus began to explain the reality of the kingdom of God to his disciples, they couldn't believe him.

> From that time on Jesus began to explain to his disciples that he must go to Jerusalem and suffer many things at the hands of the elders, the chief priests and the teachers of the law, and that he must be killed and on the third day be raised to life. Peter took him aside and began to rebuke him. "Never, Lord!" he said. "This shall never happen to you!" (Matt. 16:21–22)

Jesus needed to rebuke Peter for this comment, even calling him Satan, for keeping him from the hard task he had to accomplish.

In his life and teachings, Jesus calls us to follow him as we seek to navigate where he has placed us in the world. We will focus our discussion on his life and statements regarding five common responses by Christians today:

1. Resignation and assimilation
2. Withdrawal and retrenchment
3. Fear
4. Seeking power
5. Anger

After this, we will look briefly at his own commitment to walk in a polarized world and what he had to say to us about ours.

Unlike the other narratives in which people did some things well and other things poorly, Jesus is the standard by which other actions are measured. His nuanced responses remind us that we are not evaluating what he did but looking carefully for our own response. We cannot just simply follow him as a model, carrying this out on our own once we figure it out. Only in his power can we live in his way as we endeavor to be imitators of Christ.

How might Jesus react to the response of either *resignation* or *assimilation*? We recognize these are two quite different reactions, though they share the concept of pulling back from the battle.

Jesus was not resigned to the world in the same way that we might be. He fully acknowledged the suffering of the world and the painful task before him, yet he still went forward with a commitment that demonstrated his focus on his special assignment in a broken world. In the hours before his death, we find Jesus in the Garden of Gethsemane: "Going a little farther, he fell with his face to the ground and prayed, 'My Father, if it is possible, may this cup be taken from me. Yet not as I will, but as you will'" (Matt. 26:39). His commitment to the will of his Father was clear, and it was a much different path than the way of resignation.

Even in the face of this reality, Jesus continued to remind his disciples of a future hope. At the death of his friend Lazarus, he spoke of hope to Martha, "I am the resurrection and the life. The one who believes in me will live, even though they die; and whoever lives by believing in me will never die. Do you believe this?" (John 11:25–26). For Jesus, the challenges are real and the hope is real. He calls us to live in both.

As to assimilation, we are not to let ourselves be defined by the world. Here is what Jesus said:

"I gave them your word;
The godless world hated them because of it,
Because they didn't join the world's ways,
Just as I didn't join the world's ways.
I'm not asking that you take them out of the world
But that you guard them from the Evil One.
They are no more defined by the world
Than I am defined by the world.
Make them holy—consecrated—with the truth;
Your word is consecrating truth.
In the same way that you gave me a mission in the world,
I give them a mission in the world." (John 17:14–17 MSG)

We have a mission in the world. We are pulled either to become a part of the world or to withdraw from it. Jesus says not to do either. We see this not only in Jesus' teachings but also in his actions. When Jesus called Matthew, a tax collector, to follow him as a disciple, he went to his home for dinner.

> While Jesus was having dinner at Matthew's house, many tax collectors and sinners came and ate with him and his disciples. When the Pharisees saw this, they asked his disciples, "Why does your teacher eat with tax collectors and sinners?" On hearing this, Jesus said, "It is not the healthy who need a doctor, but the sick. But go and learn what this means: 'I desire mercy, not sacrifice.' For I have not come to call the righteous, but sinners." (Matt. 9:10–13)

We are called to be engaged in the world but not to assimilate into its ways. This is one of those points of tension, holding two seemingly contradictory truths together, which Christians are called to live out. We are called to represent Jesus.

———

We find another nuanced response when it comes to *withdrawal* and *retrenchment*. Jesus frequently withdrew for a time of prayer. This is what kept him anchored in his purpose and in step with his Father. At the end of Mark 1, we see a good example of this. In verses 21–34, Jesus engaged with the people of Capernaum, healing the sick and driving out demons. A large crowd followed him, hoping to be healed.

> Very early in the morning, while it was still dark, Jesus got up, left the house and went off to a solitary place, where he prayed. Simon and his companions

went to look for him, and when they found him, they exclaimed: "Everyone is looking for you!" Jesus replied, "Let us go somewhere else—to the nearby villages—so I can preach there also. That is why I have come." So he traveled throughout Galilee, preaching in their synagogues and driving out demons.

(Mark 1:35–39)

We notice three things here. First, the demand was high, his work was good and productive, and people wanted him there. He could have stayed there for a long time. Second, after his time of prayer, he knew he needed to move on to another place. There is a difference between demand for our work and God's call, and it takes prayer to know the difference. If this was true for Jesus, then it is certainly true for us. We also need a time of rest to regain our focus. Third, Jesus didn't withdraw permanently; only for a time of discernment, connection with his Father, and rest for his bodily weariness. He then immediately went on to another village.

In these challenging times, there are some calling for a more radical withdrawal. Rod Dreher called for this in *The Benedict Option: A Strategy for Christians in Post-Christian Nations*.[166] A reviewer of the book writes,

> This book calls on Christians, struggling to live as Christians in our post-Christian world, to follow the model of the sixth-century founder of monasticism, St. Benedict of Nursia. It was Benedict, disgusted by a disintegrating Roman culture, who withdrew from his society in order to rebuild authentic Christian community. As followers of Jesus Christ, he asked, how could they reclaim orthodox faith and practice? His actions reshaped the future of Western civilization. Dreher believes we face such a choice as Christians for our own day.[2]

While there may be some people who feel called to this response, the pre-Christian world in Jesus' day was not any better than ours. But Jesus did not choose to withdraw, except for those times to prepare for the next battle.

———

What does Jesus have to say about a response of *fear*? Although we can read his response in many places, here is one example. From only five barley loaves and two fish, Jesus fed five thousand people with twelve baskets of food left over after all had eaten their fill. Surely this was a time when they would all realize that Jesus was not an ordinary person.

After this, he sent his disciples across Lake Galilee while he went off to pray. During their journey, a raging storm came up on the lake. In Matthew

14:25–27, we read, "Shortly before dawn Jesus went out to them, walking on the lake. When the disciples saw him walking on the lake, they were terrified. 'It's a ghost,' they said, and cried out in fear. But Jesus immediately said to them: 'Take courage! It is I. Don't be afraid.'" In the midst of a storm, when the disciples thought they were doomed, Jesus said, "Don't be afraid." When the God of the universe can feed five thousand people with so little and can walk on the water in a raging storm, perhaps we should trust him. But it remains hard.

Peter demonstrated this moments later when he said, "Lord if it is you, tell me to come to you on the water" (Matt. 14:29). So Peter walked on the water. Yet another confirmation of a well-placed confidence in the God who says, "Fear not." Do we also trust him? But we, like Peter, soon begin to look around at our circumstances, and "when he saw the wind, he was afraid and, beginning to sink, cried out, 'Lord, save me!'" (Matt. 14:30). Perhaps this is the problem. We trust God for a time, but then circumstances become too severe, and we grow fearful again.

Al remembers the time when his wife Nancy was diagnosed with cancer. Facing a significant surgery, the two of them arrived at the hospital at 6:00 am. Al was frightened, but Nancy was calm. They sat in the hospital parking lot and cranked up the Hillsong version of "Shout to the Lord."[3] At the end of the song, Nancy said, "God has this one; I am at peace." After an eight-hour surgery, followed by months of chemotherapy, Nancy came through it and was ultimately declared cancer free—though she said she had confidence in God regardless of the outcome. That was twenty-five years ago, and they are grateful.

It is somehow easy to think we are in control when we are not. And when we are not in control, we worry. Many are afraid when they fly in a commercial airplane and are more confident when they drive, though statistics show that driving is much more dangerous than flying. Often, both our confidence and our fear are misplaced.

This is not the only time when Jesus said, "Fear not." Jairus, a synagogue leader, approached Jesus because his daughter was sick. By the time Jesus arrived at the man's home, a friend approached Jairus with the message that his daughter had died. When Jesus heard the news, he said to Jairus, "Don't be afraid; just believe" (Mark 5:36).

Hundreds of times in the Bible, some variation of the statement "fear not" is recorded. This doesn't only apply to raging storms, ghosts, cancer, or death. Many are fearful of the state of the world today, but Jesus speaks to this as well when he says, "Fear not."

———

Jesus spoke and acted against the desire of those who seek to combat the evil in the world by *seeking power* for themselves. In his letter to the Philippians, Paul writes,

> Have the same mindset as Christ Jesus: Who, being in very nature God, did not consider equality with God something to be used to his own advantage; rather, he made himself nothing by taking the very nature of a servant, being made in human likeness. And being found in appearance as a man, he humbled himself by becoming obedient to death—even death on a cross! (Phil. 2:5–8)

Jesus did not come to this earth as a conquering king or a great leader, but as a servant. He not only lived this, but he also instructed his disciples how to live as a servant. Jesus was with his disciples when the mother of two of them (James and John) came to Jesus to ask to have her two sons seated on the left and right of him in his kingdom. The other disciples reacted strongly against such behavior—likely because they wanted these positions for themselves! But Jesus told them that leadership in his kingdom is different from the world:

> "You know that the rulers of the Gentiles lord it over them, and their high officials exercise authority over them. Not so with you. Instead, whoever wants to become great among you must be your servant, and whoever wants to be first must be your slave—just as the Son of Man did not come to be served, but to serve, and to give his life as a ransom for many." (Matt. 20:25–28)

Leadership in the kingdom is leadership from servanthood, not from power. This is the way Jesus lived, and his kingdom changed the world. Yet we still hear Christians say, "If only we could get the right people in power in the right positions, we could take back our society."

We see some of this kind of thinking even in the lives of the disciples. Some scholars suggest that this may have been what happened with Judas, Jesus' betrayer. Judas, like the other disciples, thought Jesus was an earthly king with his reign starting in Jerusalem. Perhaps Judas thought that if Jesus were taken by the authorities, he would respond in force and take his intended position. The tragic results of his betrayal must have surprised Judas.

Ironically, power has not been good for the church. When Constantine converted to Christianity in the early 300s, he made Christianity the official religion of the Roman Empire. Where the church had flourished under persecution, Christianity's influence waned after this. For more recent examples, when the church was driven underground in the Soviet Bloc and in China in the twentieth century (and in many parts of the world still today), it flourished during a time of severe persecution. As author Tony Campolo has often said, "The historical record is that whenever the Christian church gains power, it loses its influence."[4]

———

The principles of leading by serving, though often not practiced, apply well in other situations also. Bill Pollard was invited to interview for an executive position with ServiceMaster with the promise that he might become CEO at some point in the future. As he prepared for the interview, he decided to pursue what steps he needed to take for him to gain that position. As he began to ask questions, the current board chairman, Ken Hansen, stood up and said, "The interview is over" and ushered him to the door. Bill was surprised and disappointed.

Later that evening, he received a phone call from Hansen inviting him to breakfast the next morning. At breakfast, Ken asked Bill if he knew what had happened. When Bill said he assumed he was not a good fit, Ken said it wasn't that simple. "Bill, if you want to come to ServiceMaster and contribute, you will have a great career. But if you are coming to the Company for a title or a position or to promote yourself, you'd better forget it."[5]

Bill Pollard did take the position. For the first six weeks, he was introduced to the work of their people who scrubbed floors in a hospital. This experience changed his life and view of leadership as he learned to be a servant. He later said, "My leadership responsibility was not about me or my feelings. It was about what should be done for our business and for our people. Leadership is an awesome responsibility."[6]

———

Sometimes we see Christians justifying their *anger* toward society, pointing out that Jesus turned over the tables in the temple in anger. Is there a legitimate role for anger in response to the decline in society that seems so apparent?

Looking carefully at Jesus' life, we see two places where he clearly expressed anger. One was at the tomb of his friend Lazarus, as recorded in John 11. Jesus had just wept over the loss of his friend, and the people around wondered aloud, "Well, if he loved him so much, why didn't he do something to keep him from dying? After all, he opened the eyes of a blind man" (John 11:37 MSG). Eugene Peterson captures his response this way: "Then Jesus, the anger again welling up within him, arrived at the tomb. It was a simple cave in the hillside with a slab of stone laid against it. Jesus said, 'Remove the stone'" (John 11:38 MSG). On this incident, Francis Schaeffer wrote, "Jesus, standing in front of the tomb of Lazarus, was *angry* at death and at the abnormality of the world; the destruction and distress caused by sin."[7] The world is not as it should be, and it hurts. Only Jesus was able to do something about this brokenness, by going to the cross for the sins of the world.

A second time we see Jesus angry is in the temple. He had triumphantly entered into Jerusalem, with shouts of "Hosanna!" welcoming him as king. No doubt many thought this was the moment he would take power and bring them victory and peace over their enemies, but Jesus spotted a real enemy from within. Mark 11:15–17 tells us,

> On reaching Jerusalem, Jesus entered the temple courts and began driving out those who were buying and selling there. He overturned the tables of the money changers and the benches of those selling doves, and would not allow anyone to carry merchandise through the temple courts. And as he taught them, he said, "Is it not written: 'My house will be called a house of prayer for all nations'? But you have made it 'a den of robbers.'"

We see Jesus directing anger toward those religious leaders who stole from the people for personal gain, which is the very antithesis of God's law and the gospel.

Today, much of the anger comes from those whose personal positions have been challenged, rather than against a violation to the kingdom of God. Yet Jesus, when it came to his personal position, deferred. For example, at his trial, the chief priests were looking for false evidence against Jesus and brought two people who claimed they heard Jesus say he would destroy the temple and rebuild it in three days. When they asked Jesus what he had to say about this evidence, he remained silent.

Sometimes the anger we see displayed by Christians is toward the brokenness in the world—anger toward those in sexual sin, for example. In the

John 4 account, the woman at the well was one of these. Did Jesus know about her messed up marital life when he first met her? Of course he did. Yet he didn't start the conversation by straightening her out and telling her what was wrong with her. He offered her a drink of living water. After discussion, when he did get to the topic of her relationships, she said she had no husband, and their dialogue is instructive:

> Jesus said to her, "You are right when you say you have no husband. The fact is, you have had five husbands, and the man you now have is not your husband. What you have just said is quite true." "Sir," the woman said, "I can see that you are a prophet. Our ancestors worshiped on this mountain, but you Jews claim that the place where we must worship is in Jerusalem." (John 4:18–20)

Jesus had a higher purpose for this conversation. He didn't challenge her for changing the subject nor did he continue to talk about her brokenness. He wanted to offer life itself to her and the rest of her village.

Consider Zacchaeus. Here was a crooked businessman who had gained wealth by dishonest means. Jesus knew about this but wanted to have dinner in his home, which drew criticism from others who said, "He has gone to be the guest of a 'sinner'" (Luke 19:7). Jesus' very presence with the man convicted and changed him, transforming Zacchaeus into a follower.

There are so many other examples of people who encountered Jesus. For those who had all of the answers and deterred his followers, Jesus had strong words. For those who sought the way, the truth, and the life, Jesus held his arms wide open.

In addition to what Jesus had to say regarding our own common responses to polarization, we see the choices he made and the instruction he offers us for our walk. Luke 9:51 makes this startling observation about Jesus just before his death: "As the time approached for him to be taken up to heaven, Jesus resolutely set out for Jerusalem." Did he know what awaited him? Clearly yes, but still he faced the humiliation and painful death on the cross. He knew what he was called to do, and he "resolutely" set out to do it. Long before, Isaiah prophesied about this, pointing to Jesus but also calling to us:

> Because the Sovereign Lord helps me, I will not be disgraced. Therefore have I set my face like flint, and I know I will not be put to shame. He who vindicates

me is near. Who then will bring charges against me? Let us face each other! Who is my accuser? Let him confront me! It is the Sovereign LORD who helps me. Who will condemn me? (Isa. 50:7–9)

Do we view ourselves as people on an assignment where God chose to place us? Is it an accident that we live now in this polarizing twenty-first century? Even if our assignment is hard, we should remember that it was not as hard as the assignment of our Lord.

In the Garden of Gethsemane, Jesus asked God to take that cup of suffering and death away from him, hoping there was another way. He says to his disciples, "'My soul is overwhelmed with sorrow to the point of death. Stay here and keep watch with me.' Going a little farther, he fell with his face to the ground and prayed, 'My Father, if it is possible, may this cup be taken from me. Yet not as I will, but as you will'" (Matt. 26:38–39). Jesus' words to us echo through the ages: "I have told you these things, so that in me you may have peace. In this world you will have trouble. But take heart! I have overcome the world" (John 16:33).

In the Beatitudes, Jesus taught us what it means for his people to live in his kingdom. The first three Beatitudes provide our orientation: "Blessed are the poor in spirit, for theirs is the kingdom of heaven. Blessed are those who mourn, for they will be comforted. Blessed are the meek, for they will inherit the earth" (Matt. 5:3–5).

David Gill helps us understand these words.[8] He interprets "poor in spirit" as "openness and humility, "those who mourn" as "accountability and responsibility," and "the meek" as "power under control." In Jesus' kingdom, we start with humility, responsibility, and power under control. Only then do we get to the fourth of the Beatitudes, "Blessed are those who hunger and thirst for righteousness," which he interprets as "ethics and excellence." Too often in today's culture wars, we see people start with their claim of standing for truth (excellence and ethics) without any sense of humility, accountability, or living under the control of the Spirit of God.

But the conclusion of the Beatitudes is also an important reminder. In many culture wars, there is an assumption that all this will lead to a peaceful life. Rather, Jesus ends his Beatitudes with saying, "Blessed are those who are persecuted for righteousness," which Gill says calls for "courage and persistence." If we are persecuted for bypassing the first three Beatitudes, that is on us. But if we seek his kingdom, the persecution will still be there. There is no promise of an easy life for a Christian who follows in the way of Christ. Jesus concludes by calling us to do good anyway: "Let your light so shine before others that they may see your good deeds and glorify your father in heaven" (Matt. 5:17).

———

Jesus' life and teaching are reminders of what we are called to do in navigating a polarizing society. Since we are not Jesus, however, sometimes we will fail. Thankfully, we have God's word to help us in our walk:

> Therefore each of you must put off falsehood and speak truthfully to your neighbor, for we are all members of one body. "In your anger do not sin": Do not let the sun go down while you are still angry, and do not give the devil a foothold. . . . And do not grieve the Holy Spirit of God, with whom you were sealed for the day of redemption. Get rid of all bitterness, rage and anger, brawling and slander, along with every form of malice. Be kind and compassionate to one another, forgiving each other, just as in Christ God forgave you.
> (Eph. 4:25–27, 30–32)

Scripture also reminds us that the world will only grow more troubling and that we should carefully guard our response as how we act reveals our true selves.

Many people are on a dark spiral downward. But if you think that leaves you on the high ground where you can point your finger at others, think again. Every time you criticize someone, you condemn yourself. It takes one to know one. Judgmental criticism of others is a well-known way of escaping detection in your own crimes and misdemeanors. But God isn't so easily diverted. He sees right through all such smoke screens and holds you to what *you've* done.

> You didn't think, did you, that just by pointing your finger at others you would distract God from seeing all your misdoings and from coming down on you hard? Or did you think that because he's such a nice God, he'd let you off the hook? Better think this one through from the beginning. God is kind, but he's not soft. In kindness he takes us firmly by the hand and leads us into a radical life-change. (Rom. 2:1–4 MSG)

In one of his parables, Jesus talks about a person who himself was flawed but wouldn't forgive another (Matt. 18:23–35). A man had a great debt and was brought before his master. When he pleaded his case that he could not pay, his master forgave him. But rather than passing on this kind of forgiveness, he threw a man who owed him a small amount into prison even though the man pleaded for mercy. Hearing about this, the master brought judgment against him because though he was forgiven much, he refused to forgive another. Jesus concluded the story by saying, "This is how my heavenly Father will treat each of you unless you forgive your brother or sister from your heart" (Matt. 18:35). With this, Jesus has established the gold standard.

As we examine the various cases of Jesus encountering his world, we are tempted to build a model for behavior: in one situation, we should take one set of actions, and in another, we should follow a different set. There are no "12 Easy Steps to Being Like Jesus." Following Jesus is not only a challenge (which we often get wrong), but it's also an adventure with One who is patient, forgiving, and determined to mold us into people like himself. We should study Jesus' life, but we won't always get it right. Paul reminds us,

> I realize that I don't have what it takes. I can *will* it, but I can't *do* it. I decide to do good, but I don't *really* do it; I decide not to do bad, but then I do it anyway. My decisions, such as they are, don't result in actions. Something has gone wrong deep within me and gets the better of me every time.
>
> (Rom. 7:18–20 MSG)

But then Paul finds the solution to the problem: "The answer, thank God, is that Jesus Christ can and does." We can walk faithfully and expectantly in our polarizing society with the power of Jesus.

In conclusion, we think C. S. Lewis captures this expectant attitude in the face of opposition: in a passage from *Mere Christianity*:

> Imagine yourself as living in a house. God comes in to rebuild that house. At first, perhaps, you can understand what he is doing. He is getting the drains right and stopping the leaks in the roof, and so on; you knew those jobs needed doing and so you are not surprised. But presently he starts knocking the house about in a way that hurts abominably and does not seem to make sense. What on earth is he up to? The explanation is that he is building quite a different house from the one you thought of—throwing out a new wing here, putting on an extra floor there, running up towers, making courtyards. You thought you were going to be made into a decent little cottage: but he is building a palace. He intends to come and live in it himself.[9]

Conclusion | We Are Not Alone

While there are indeed pressures for those who seek to walk with Christ in a polarizing society, there is also "a great cloud of witnesses" who have walked this path before us. While there may be a temptation to assimilate into culture, to withdraw from culture, to be afraid, to be angry, or to seek power over our world, these responses do not define the path we are called to walk. Learning from both the successes and failures of those we have studied from the Bible, we have seen another way. Rather than seeing ourselves as victims, we can pursue another path that bears witness to the greatness of the God we serve. As Jesus put it, we can be "salt and light" in our world as he has called us to be.

The eleven case studies we chose for this book, plus the one on Jesus, are not isolated, unusual cases. We could learn similar lessons from many other scriptural narratives. Below are further examples.

Jacob often seems like one who is more focused on his own interests than the interests of others. But he desperately wanted the blessings of God, wrestling all night with an angel of God in his search, just as he seemed to wrestle all his life against his own desires.

Rahab, with a small amount of faith, chose to stand with God's people in spite of social pressure and her challenging past.

Deborah and *Barak* demonstrated how working together when faith is weak can support God's purposes.

Solomon was regarded as gifted by God and the wisest man, but he derailed in his walk by the desire to assimilate into his culture.

Nehemiah respectfully asked the king he was serving in Babylon for permission to rebuild Jerusalem and then dealt with conflicts from enemies from without and the people of God from within.

Jeremiah was called by God to a particularly difficult task, yet he faithfully endured hardship throughout his life while holding onto his resolve to serve his God.

Jonah thought he had a better picture of justice than God did and found himself angry and depressed when he tried to do it his way.

Lydia was a businesswoman in a man's world, walking faithfully and bringing leadership and support to the early church.

And there are many others.

———

What did we learn about the responses to polarization? The case studies we looked at in this book offer different illustrations of dealing with a polarizing world. Below, we will look at these common responses and how Jesus calls us to live.

Resignation and Assimilation. Jesus says that we are *in* the world but that we should not be *of* the world. Daniel brilliantly demonstrated this in his own walk with God. He was respectful even in opposition, yet he sought a path where he could engage without compromise. This is part of the story for each of those we described in the previous chapters. Think of Joseph or Moses standing before Pharaoh, or Esther with Xerxes, or Jesus engaging with sinners. Each of these offers a case study of what it means to be in the world and not of the world.

Withdrawal and Retrenchment. Jesus offers real insight into an appropriate use of withdrawal. We saw his frequent retreat from people for times of prayer and rest in order to reengage in his calling. Daniel and Esther illustrated this as well. Withdrawal, like keeping the Sabbath, is pulling back from the daily grind to a time of listening to God; it is not a way of protecting our lifestyles. All those we discussed were on an assignment from God, called to his purposes. So it is with us.

Fear. The stories we shared are filled with frightening situations. There is no denial of the reality of the challenges these individuals experienced. Think of David facing Goliath or Saul. Think about Job losing his fortune, family, and health and yet trying to take the next step. Consider Moses standing before mighty Pharaoh or the people he was trying to lead when they were in revolt. Think about Daniel thrown to the lions, or Esther approaching King Xerxes. Consider Paul being beaten, or Peter walking on the water in a storm. Fear is a natural reaction, and this hasn't changed for us today. Like them, we need to remember Jesus' statement, "Fear not!" Ponder the power of God demonstrated in the lives of every story we studied. Do we truly believe that we walk with a God more powerful than any force against us?

Seeking Power. Jesus showed and taught us that his ways are not found through our power plays. This most influential person in history never held public office. He taught that we should not lead as the world does through a position of power and might, but rather as a servant. Although God sometimes placed his people in a position of power (e.g., Joseph, Esther, David, Joshua), none of them achieved that position through their own strength. Paul and Peter had leadership positions in the church that were not achieved through their own cleverness or campaign. Rather, each went through an often humbling process and thus exercised whatever role they had with humility.

Anger. The world is broken by sin and is not as it should be. We can acknowledge this, and even be angry about it. We saw Jesus get angry at the tomb of Lazarus or with the money changers in the temple. We saw Moses get angry with a rebellious people in the wilderness. We saw Joseph demonstrate anger with his brothers who sold him into slavery. We saw Paul angry with the corrupt officials. Yet we need to observe the nature of this anger. With Jesus, and with Joseph, the anger came from the state of the world and the impact of sin in the world. There is a righteous acknowledgment of what sin has done to our world. Today, however, anger often flares up at problems we have to deal with, as if we should be immune to this brokenness. Jesus could accompany his anger with hope. Joseph could say, "You intended it for evil, but God intended it for good." And when it became about personal feelings or actions, we note that Paul apologized for his anger to the chief priest and Moses was not allowed to pass into the Promised Land.

Rather than these typical responses to cultural pressures, we have seen another way—a path characterized by a walk of true faith. This faith is characterized by love, humility, respect, and compassion for those around us. We have presented these imperfect examples from the narratives of Scripture to provide tangible illustrations of what it means to "seek justice, love mercy, and walk humbly before God" (Micah 6:8) in a hostile world. Our brief picture of Jesus, the only One who walked this path with perfection, underscored the same points. We have seen respectful truth in the face of power, a recognition that even angry powerful people are made in the image of God, and many examples of influence that came from a position of apparent weakness. We learned from each that while these are imperfect models, they are people who were deeply connected with God and made their choices in his power and not their own. We have seen illustrations of those who represented God in a winsome way that created change. We are called to do the same.

Often, as with those who have gone before, this challenge is made more difficult because of pressures from other believers who claim to have all of the answers. This was the conflict Joseph had with his brothers. This was the conflict Moses had with Miriam and Aaron. This was the conflict Jesus had with the Pharisees.

This conflict is troublesome in two different ways. First, perhaps because the Christian faith is characterized by truth, it is easy to believe that we are the author of that truth. But we must remember that "grace and truth came by Jesus Christ." It is not enough to be right, and we are not always right. We need to seek truth while remaining humble, offering grace, and demonstrating love. Sometimes we confuse truth with familiarity, not recognizing when God is doing a new thing in our world. This was central to the conflict Jesus had with the Pharisees. They were so sure they had the truth that they didn't recognize the author of truth, Jesus Christ, when he showed them another way.

The second reason why conflict with other Christians is troublesome is the witness this offers to the watching world of what it means to be a follower of Jesus. The world may point at the Christians they know and think they must not have an answer to the challenges of life because of the way they treat one another. It would be easy to argue with this conclusion by saying that the world is just not capable of understanding doctrinal purity, so their judgment doesn't count.

But that is not what Jesus said. In his prayer to the Father before going to the cross, Jesus said, "I have given them the glory that you gave me, that they may be one as we are one—I in them and you in me—so that they may be brought to complete unity. Then the world will know that you sent me and have loved them even as you have loved me" (John 17:21–22).

Imagine it: Jesus said the world would know that he is the Son of God by the way they saw Christians demonstrating love to one another! And he wasn't talking only to his disciples: "My prayer is not for them [the twelve disciples] alone. I pray also for those who will believe in me through their message" (John 17:20). That's us!

There are three more angles to this story that call for our attention: The first is how we can move beyond an individualistic perspective, challenging one another to work together; the second is what we can learn from Scripture about how to challenge one another; and the third is what we can learn about creating broader group action around these issues.

———

Walking with Christ through a polarizing world is not something we can do independently. The West is characterized by individualism, and this seeps into our daily life and even into our ways of living out our faith. But Scripture calls us together in community. A frequent misunderstanding of Scripture comes from seeing challenges to the church (or to Israel) as a body and reinterpreting them individualistically.[1]

While we looked at case studies of individuals who demonstrated what it means to walk with God in a hostile world, none did this alone. Certainly, the presence of God in each of their lives is a vital part of the story. But these stories often included other individuals who were an integral part of that story. Moses had Aaron with him. Joshua was trained and mentored by Moses. Ruth had both Naomi and Boaz. David had Jonathan as a colleague and friend. Esther had her uncle Mordecai as someone who helped her see alternatives along the way and supported her in challenging times. Job had three friends who were not ultimately helpful, but then Elihu came along and helped Job begin to gain a different perspective on his suffering. Daniel had his three friends Shadrach, Meshach, and Abednego who were in training with him. Paul went out with Barnabas and then Silas. Jesus counseled his disciples to go into the world two by two.

Growing up, Al learned a number of songs that have been helpful in his Christian life, but some less so. One of those is "Dare to be a Daniel":

Dare to be a Daniel
Dare to stand alone
Dare to have a purpose firm
Dare to make it known.[2]

The second one is "On the Jericho Road":

On the Jericho road,
There's room for just two

No more and no less
Just Jesus and you.[3]

Both songs look at the Christian life from a strongly individualistic perspective. There is no question that sometimes we do have to stand alone—just us and Jesus. But we can (and often do) delude ourselves since we are individually also impacted by sin. This is why we need one another.

In writing about the body of Christ, Paul reminds us that we should not say we don't belong to the body just because we are not in some exalted position: "Suppose the foot says, 'I am not a hand. So I don't belong to the body.' By saying this, it cannot stop being part of the body" (1 Cor. 12:15). In a similar way, Paul says we should not decide someone else is not important because they are not like us: "The eye can't say to the hand, 'I don't need you!' The head can't say to the feet, 'I don't need you!' In fact, it is just the opposite. The parts of the body that seem to be weaker are the ones we can't do without" (1 Cor. 12:21–22).

We need others to help us see things we cannot see and to support us. The writer of Hebrews said, "And let us consider how we may spur one another on toward love and good deeds" (10:24). Or as the writer of Ecclesiastes says,

> Two are better than one, because they have a good return for their labor: If either of them falls down, one can help the other up. But pity anyone who falls and has no one to help them up. Also, if two lie down together, they will keep warm. But how can one keep warm alone? Though one may be overpowered, two can defend themselves. A cord of three strands is not quickly broken.
> (Eccl. 4:9–12)

A large part of the reason we chose to write this book together is the challenge and correction we could provide to each other. That didn't make writing the book easier, but we believe the challenge was helpful.[4]

—

It's one thing when two people, like Randy and Al, agree to work together. But how might we encourage, challenge, or exhort other believers regarding issues at the heart of the kingdom of God that want to divide us?

Sometimes, it is necessary to simply confront someone. We saw an example of this when Paul challenged Peter, confronting him to his face when Peter stepped away from associating with the Gentile believers in the church. Paul probably confronted Peter this way because of the high risk of the whole church regressing, but this is not the norm.

More generally, Jesus tells us how we should deal with a Christian who is off track, laying out a three-step plan:

> "If your brother or sister sins, go and point out their fault, just between the two of you. If they listen to you, you have won them over. But if they will not listen, take one or two others along, so that 'every matter may be established by the testimony of two or three witnesses.' If they still refuse to listen, tell it to the church; and if they refuse to listen even to the church, treat them as you would a pagan or a tax collector." (Matt. 18:15–17)

The first step is vital because sometimes a perceived sin is a misunderstanding. Don't involve more than the particular person until it becomes clear that the fault is real and grievous, and that the person is unrepentant.

Here, we must carefully distinguish between a sin and a differing perspective. No one has the whole truth, and Jesus challenges us to be careful about judging others. There are some matters we should simply let go. As Peter said, "Above all, love each other deeply, because love covers over a multitude of sins" (1 Pet. 4:8). Jude also reminds us to consider the person's circumstances: "Be merciful to those who doubt; save others by snatching them from the fire; to others show mercy, mixed with fear—hating even the clothing stained by corrupted flesh" (Jude 22–23). If we learn anything from these examples, we need to know that we cannot simply use a formula. Prayer and the leading of the Holy Spirit are critical in making the right approach to another individual.

Two other stories offer footnotes to how this message should be delivered. First, it is important to know who we are talking with, seeking to communicate in love in a way that the other person can receive the message. Using the language of C. S. Lewis, we need to "get past the watching dragons"[5]—that is, the self-defense of the person who would find a way to block anything said.

An example of this kind of communication is found in 2 Kings 5. Naaman, the captain of the guard in nearby Aram, had leprosy and heard that the God of Israel had the power to heal even something as devastating as his disease. He sent a note to the king of Israel, who thought Naaman was trying to pick a fight. But when Elisha the prophet heard about the situation, he sent a messenger to Naaman's house with the simple message, "Go, wash yourself seven times in the Jordan, and your flesh will be restored and you will be cleansed" (2 Kgs. 5:10).

Unfortunately, Naaman did not receive the message well. He was an important person and was offended that a servant was sent and that he had to wash himself in the Jordan River. "He said, 'I thought that he would surely come out to me and stand and call on the name of the LORD his God, wave his hand over the spot and cure me of my leprosy. Are not Abana and Pharpar, the rivers of Damascus, better than all the waters of Israel? Couldn't I wash in them and be cleansed?' So he turned and went off in a rage" (2 Kgs. 5:11–12).

In modern language, one might say Naaman had been triggered[6] and he blew up, unable to properly assess the situation. Naaman's servants then arrived with the right words for their master. They simply reoriented Naaman's thinking with a reminder: "If he had asked you to do some great thing, surely you would have done it. You do want to get well. Why don't you try it?" And they broke through to Naaman!

In our communication with others, it matters not only *what* we say but also *how* we say it. It is not about saying whatever we want; it's about helping another person understand the message. Knowing how Naaman would react, as his servants did, allowed them to refocus the issue in a language Naaman could understand.

Sometimes the best way to communicate is through a story rather than a direct statement. This helps to get the other person on board with your perspective and move beyond the "watching dragons." Jesus told stories and asked questions to push past defenses. We saw Nathan confront David with this method after David had committed the grievous sins of sleeping with another man's wife and then trying to cover it up by having her husband killed. A direct confrontation with David may not have gone well, so Nathan told David a story instead.

Finally, we have to understand that we are never going to resolve all our differences. As Paul says,

> If it is possible, as far as it depends on you, live at peace with everyone. Do not take revenge, my dear friends, but leave room for God's wrath, for it is written: "It is mine to avenge; I will repay," says the Lord. On the contrary: "If your enemy is hungry, feed him; if he is thirsty, give him something to drink. In doing this, you will heap burning coals on his head." Do not be overcome by evil, but overcome evil with good. (Rom. 12:18:21)

It is one thing to try to get another person to change directions, but in our era we also need to have a broader impact in order to gather larger bodies of believers to a cause that would alter the course. It is clear that in this post-Christian world, by whatever definition, the church needs to change course. If we are to be agents of this change, then each of us must broaden our perspective.

A few years ago, Al had the opportunity of interviewing Lew Platt, then chairman of the board at Hewlett Packard. In the interview, Platt drew three concentric circles on a piece of paper.

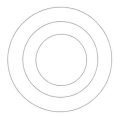

Then he said,

> The inner circle contains our values. The next circle out contains our objectives. The outer circle contains our practices. The values in the center circle (the importance of making a contribution, of good citizenship in the community, of valuing, trusting, and respecting people) are timeless. . . . We also have objectives in the second circle. These are not timeless but they change slowly. Finally, in the outer circle we have practices, and these change quickly. The pace of change in business forces us to change these practices even more quickly now than we did in the past. When we hold on to old practices and don't change them fast enough we get in trouble.[7]

The place we get into trouble, whether in business or the church, is when we begin treating practices as if they were sacred values. In helping an organization respond to changes in the world, we need to start by understanding the difference between practices and values.

There is an old story about the son watching his mother fix dinner and noticing that she cut off the tip of the roast before putting it in the pan. As children often do he asked, "Why did you do that?" Her reply was that her mother had always done that, so she suggested he ask Grandma the next time she came over. When Grandma arrived, the boy asked the question and she replied simply, "I never had a pan big enough for the whole roast!" The mother confused practice with a valuable cooking process.

A more serious example might be the dress code in the church. A few years ago, Al was in the Central African Republic, a hot, poor country with sporadic electricity and almost no air conditioning. Somehow, many of the pastors had come to associate proper dress with a Western three-piece suit made of wool. In the stifling heat, this form of dress was not nearly as appropriate as the more traditional African garb the pastors had previously worn. So we need to ask: Is a dress code a value or a practice?

———

We will look briefly at two examples from Scripture where change was necessary to get believers to come together to make that change. The first is a story of failure and the second, which was discussed earlier, is a success. We review it again briefly for contrast. These will inform our own conclusions about leading change in our world.

In John 9, Jesus healed a man who was born blind.[8] The religious leaders of the day, the Pharisees, came together to decide what to do about this unusual event that seemed to threaten their religious authority. They drew two conclusions from Jesus' act of healing the man, both seeming to be true. Jesus had healed on the Sabbath, so he must be a sinner. But the blind man was truly healed, and since only God can heal blindness, he must be from God. Which is it?

After a period of debate, we find that "they were divided" (John 9:16). It's like this today for the church over different issues. When two seeming truths come head to head, where do you go from there?

Ken Hansen, the former CEO of ServiceMaster, talked about this situation for leaders from a different context. The company had two objectives—helping people develop and growing profitably—that were often in conflict. Ken likened this to stretching an exercise band, where the conflicting objectives were at either end. "You had better hold on to both ends. The tension will drive creativity. But if you let go of one or the other, the tension will be released, and you will get hit on the head!"[9]

Unfortunately, the Pharisees did not carefully examine their first observation (that Jesus must be a sinner since he healed on the Sabbath) and ignored the second observation altogether (that the blind man was truly healed). In fact, they did more than let go of the second; they kicked the blind man out of the temple. They let go of the truth that could not be ignored and went with the one that preserved their legalistic perspective about work on the Sabbath. They completely missed a third truth: that this formerly blind man was indeed an image-bearer of God and of great worth. Jesus taught, "The Sabbath was made for man, not man for the Sabbath. So the Son of Man is Lord even of the Sabbath" (Mark 2:27–28). It appears they demonstrated confirmation bias, rationalizing their conclusion of rejecting Jesus rather than seeking truth.[10]

The story ends in a poignant way. "Jesus heard that they had thrown him out, and when he found him, he said, 'Do you believe in the Son of Man?' 'Who is he, sir?' the man asked. 'Tell me so that I may believe in him.' Jesus said, 'You have now seen him; in fact, he is the one speaking with you.' Then the man said, 'Lord, I believe,' and he worshiped him" (John 9:35–38). Jesus extends a hand to the one the religious community had tossed out. That's wonderful for this formerly blind person, but what does this say about the religious establishment? Is this where we are in Christendom? Do we have blind spots when we see practices or objectives competing with the fundamental values of our faith? Are the things we cling so tightly to foundational values or temporal practices?

We have already discussed (in the chapter on Peter and developed in Acts 15) the way the early church came together around the question of Gentile believers coming into the church. Here we point out two other things about this story.

First, when Paul and Barnabas were sent from Antioch to Jerusalem, they "told how the Gentiles had been converted." This was certainly a new thing for the church in Jerusalem, but they were welcomed with gladness. No doubt, because of the long journey, that welcome included hospitality and sharing meals together. It seems they approached this challenge by finding a common goal for the church rather than promoting their own opinions. Perhaps our own posture rooted in common goals and a desire for God's purposes rather than our own is the right place to start.

We have already observed that the conclusion from the Jerusalem Council did not require the Gentiles to become Jews, but they did lay out four things they wanted the Gentiles to do, including abstaining from meat sacrificed to idols. There is an important sequel to this story. Paul, in writing to the Corinthians, talked about whether believers could eat meat sacrificed to idols. It would seem from this conclusion of the Jerusalem Council that they should not. Yet here is what Paul said,

Eat anything sold in the meat market without raising questions of conscience, for, "The earth is the Lord's, and everything in it." If an unbeliever invites you to a meal and you want to go, eat whatever is put before you without raising questions of conscience. But if someone says to you, "This has been offered in sacrifice," then do not eat it, both for the sake of the one who told you and for the sake of conscience. I am referring to the other person's conscience, not yours. For why is my freedom being judged by another's conscience? If I take part in the meal with thankfulness, why am I denounced because of something I thank God for? So whether you eat or drink or whatever you do, do it all for the glory of God. (1 Cor. 10:25–31)

Was Paul defying the conclusion at the Jerusalem Council? Or was he recognizing it as a practice that was subservient to the foundational value of demonstrating love to others? How do we know the difference? Again, it is the guiding of the Spirit of God and the goal of demonstrating the love of God to his people and to a watching world. There is no doubt that these issues made the early disciples uncomfortable, but comfort was not the goal. Too often, we are not willing to discuss or debate these sensitive issues at all!

———

One final thought. It is too easy to reduce all of the examples we have considered to religious practice. These narratives went way beyond this. Each of the narratives we discussed featured people on assignment, accomplishing God's purposes in the world while preserving the testimony of God. Their lives were not simply characterized by the religious corner. Remember,

> Abraham was a tradesman and nation builder
> Joseph was a slave and a CEO of a food company
> Moses was a leader of people
> Joshua was a warrior
> Ruth was an immigrant laborer
> David was a shepherd and a king
> Esther was an outsider and a queen
> Job was a farmer
> Daniel was a government employee in a foreign land
> Peter was a fisherman

> Paul was a tent maker
> Jesus was a carpenter

Yes, Jesus was a builder working his trade for most of his life before becoming an itinerant preacher, teacher, and healer—and Savior of the world.

The discipleship we have been discussing is whole-life discipleship worked out at work, at home, in the neighborhood, and at church. The work assignments of the people we have studied are not incidental to their faithful walk but integral to it. We, too, are on assignment. That path marked out for us includes every aspect of our lives and is to be lived out with others before the watching world. We are called to be whole-life disciples.

> Therefore, since we are surrounded by such a great cloud of witnesses, let us throw off everything that hinders and the sin that so easily entangles. And let us run with perseverance the race marked out for us, fixing our eyes on Jesus, the pioneer and perfecter of faith. (Heb. 12:1–2)

Afterword | What *We* Learned

Polarization: A division into two sharply distinct opposites, especially a state in which the opinions, beliefs or interests or a group or society no longer range along a continuum but become concentrated at opposing extremes.

— *Merriam-Webster Dictionary*

Speaking well and listening well are not intuitive for everyone. They will often take practice and patience. They will require slowing down our social media impulses, making more drafts of the written word, and taking more pauses before the spoken word. None of this will be easy. But the coming years will give us plenty of opportunities to try.[1]

— John Inazu, *Confident Pluralism*

When we began discussing this project in the spring of 2022, it did not occur to either of us that *we ourselves* would have to learn to *practice what we preached*. Though we share a common faith in Jesus as Lord of all, and though we are alike in many other ways—our age (more or less!), our race, our gender, our marital status, and our love for our children and grandchildren—in other ways we are quite different. We have lived our entire lives in different parts of the country. Al lived in the Midwest for roughly the first thirty years of his life and then moved to the Seattle area where he has lived for some fifty years. Randy has lived all but three years in the state of Mississippi.

We also have different professional backgrounds: Al, with a PhD in applied mathematics, worked for the Boeing Company for more than thirty years with the last ten being the director of R&D for computing and mathematics for the company. His orientation is to analyze a problem and then seek an answer—even if the process of reaching an answer takes a long time.

Randy studied history as an undergraduate and then went to law school. At this point, he has practiced law for over forty-five years. In his work as a lawyer, one of his jobs is to parse words (in evaluating or creating contract documents, for example). Both of us look for patterns and often think in terms of analogies. The cultures we have lived in and the work we have engaged in during our lives have played significant roles in shaping how we think.

Co-writing a book—particularly a book focusing on how to be faithful to Jesus while navigating a culture that seems to be headed in a direction away from traditional assumptions and values—has highlighted some of our cultural differences and has challenged us, as we said, to put into practice what we are suggesting to our readers.

We made the decision early in the project that while one of us would be the primary author of a chapter, we wanted the other person to also make a significant contribution so that each chapter in the book would reflect the thoughts and ideas of both of us. After one of us finished a draft of a chapter, we sent these drafts back and forth, offering comments and suggestions as well as illustrations that might be appropriate. The original author then took those suggestions into account and incorporated most of them into the final draft.

Some chapters were easier to come to an agreement on as to what we needed to say than others, but with parts of a few chapters we wrestled back and forth for quite a while over a few issues before ultimately reaching a resolution. Having gone through this experience, we wondered whether it might not be helpful to let others "peek behind the curtain" and watch, so to speak, how we wrestled with one of these issues and how we reached a decision: a "case study," if you will, illustrating what we are encouraging in the book.

By no means do we want to suggest that we have it all figured out when it comes to navigating our differences. It's likely that, if we were writing the book as individuals, we might have said a few things differently from how the book ultimately turned out. Both of us would have missed out on the other's insights that both sharpened and shaped the book. Both of us agree with Al's early comment to Randy that the book is better having *both* our perspectives contribute to each chapter rather than just one or the other of us. As the quote from John Inazu at the start of the chapter suggests, we believe this experience of co-writing has required us to do just what he counsels: speak and listen well, practice and exercise patience. We decided to expose some of the conversations we had in the hope that it will be helpful to you as you navigate a culture that often makes us all feel like exiles. We don't have all the answers and do not see all things the same, but we remain friends with an appreciation of and commitment to each other.

———

Al was the primary author of the chapter on Ruth. In the original draft that Al sent to Randy, he described Boaz as "woke" because he advocated for Ruth who was in a disadvantaged position. Al also described himself as "woke" when he had, years earlier, advocated for a female co-worker who had only a high school education by reminding the men on the staff at Boeing to respect her new area of work. In the draft, Al used an early definition of "woke" as "aware of and actively attentive to the vulnerable (especially as related to issues of race and ethnicity)."

In response, Randy commented that he was "very reluctant to wade into the whole 'woke' controversy," and pointed out that *Merriam-Webster* actually had a second definition for "woke": "politically liberal (as in matters of racial and social justice) especially in a way that is considered unreasonable or extreme." He also pointed out that, while the original meaning of "woke" may have been as Al (and Esau McCauley,[2] whom Al quoted) defined it, the word no longer had a single meaning. Telling people the original meaning of this term was unlikely to cause those accustomed to a different definition to change their ideas about what it meant. Al's counter to this focused on the emphasis of the book: that is, dealing with polarization in in our world. "If we can't directly address issues of polarization, how do we get to our goal?"

We discussed this issue more than once over video conferencing, and Randy expressed his concern that many would have trouble seeing Boaz as "woke," given the definition they were accustomed to—whether or not it had been "co-opted by the political right to refer to any left-leaning policy that it wanted to condemn," as Esau McCauley wrote in an essay for the *New York Times*. Al suggested that there are those he knew who would appreciate the use of "woke" since they understood the original definition of the word. We seemed to be at an impasse.

Al still teaches occasionally at Seattle Pacific University; and one weekend after we had a conversation about this issue, he had lunch with three students who were in his class that day. He explained to them what we were writing about and the issue we were dealing with, and they told him that they agreed with his definition of "woke," but given the fact that the word means different things to different people, it may be distracting to readers. After that conversation, Al and Randy talked again, and Al suggested that rather than including the "woke" discussion in the Ruth chapter, we could use our discussion of "woke" as a case study of how we might still raise the issue and present both sides of our thinking, but at the same time make it clear that it was an issue one of us was not comfortable including in the body of the book. And so that is what we did.

In retrospect, Al reflected on the story of Nathan confronting David about his sin with Bathsheba. Nathan did not make this confrontation directly, but through a related story in order to get past David's "watchful dragons."[3] Al concedes that Randy was right (on this one!). In the end, our goal was communication not confrontation. Recognizing triggers that may block the conversation before it starts must be part of the strategy for dealing with polarization. To this we both agreed.

Unfortunately, our language is now littered with trigger words and terms and "woke" is only one of many fraught with misunderstanding. Others include critical race theory (CRT), evangelical, pro-life, marriage, and many more. How did we get to this point in the middle of the information age? Several factors may be at work here.

First, let's consider "location." In 1976, fewer than 25 percent of Americans lived in a place where the presidential election was decided by a landslide.[4] But in 2016, 80 percent of Americans lived in US counties that gave landslide victories to either Donald Trump or Hillary Clinton. This is likely the result of people moving to locations where they can live with more likeminded people. When we live in a bubble, it becomes harder to communicate with those outside it.

A second factor is that words naturally change meaning with use, often rendering these words unhelpful. C. S. Lewis discussed this on his radio program in the 1940s, which later became his book *Mere Christianity*:

> The word *gentleman* originally meant something recognizable; one who had a
> coat of arms and some landed property. When you called someone a gentle-

man you were not paying him a compliment, but merely stating a fact. If you said he was not a gentleman, you were not insulting him but giving information. There was no contradiction in saying that John was a liar and a gentleman; any more than there now is in saying James is a fool and an M.A. But then there came people who said—so rightly, charitably, spiritually, sensitively, so anything but useful—"but surely the important thing about a gentleman is not the coat of arms and the land, but the behavior?" . . . They meant well. But it is not the same. Worse still, it is not a thing everyone will agree about. To call a man "a gentleman" in this new, refined sense, becomes, in fact, not a way of giving information about him, but a way of praising him; to deny that he is "a gentleman" becomes simply a way of insulting him.[5]

Since technology plays the role of amplifier or accelerant, it is not surprising that words in our day change meaning much more rapidly.

A third factor is social media, which thrives on controversy and division. This is another way we can gather with like-minded people, reinforcing our own biases. Social media can also be the platform for driving division. The factors for polarization remain strong.

—

These factors can come together in an interesting way around what is known as the "motte-and-bailey fallacy."[6] Let's start with the picture of where this idea comes from. In medieval times, a group would claim a large amount of desirable territory (the bailey) that they could not defend but would build a well-protected castle (motte) in the center of the land they could defend. When an enemy attacked them, they retreated to the motte where they would be safe; and when the enemy backed off, they returned to the bailey. When this idea is applied to discourse, it is the strategy of using a term very broadly until challenged. After receiving the challenge, the defender retreats to a narrow and fully defensible meaning of the term. When the argument wanes, they return to the broader application. Thus the term changes meaning with the intention to deceive.[7] Arguments over almost any of the terms of tension at the heart of polarization seem to follow this pattern.

Of course, this pattern of deception can be used in two ways. It is usually presented as a strategy to claim territory that has little to do with the defensible core of the meaning. But a similar deception can take place if it is used to deny the defensible part of the meaning by seeking to associate that part with the indefensible argument, thus nullifying a truth.

At the core of CRT is the belief that structural racism exists. That is, laws and practices of the past have integrated discrimination into our society, including issues of red-lining, lack of educational opportunities, health insurance and medical care, home ownership, and the like. There are some who deny that any form of structural racism exists, and they attribute racial prejudice to individual acts. How does the discussion ensue? CRT has been used to claim a great deal of territory that doesn't fit under its definition, and proponents tend to retreat to demonstrating examples of structural racism in policy and practices.

But the reverse use of the motte-and-bailey fallacy fits here as well. Conservative activist Christopher Rufo decided to use social media to color all of CRT with its least defensible attributes. Here is his position as described in a 2021 *Washington Post* article:

> We have successfully frozen their brand—"critical race theory"—into the public conversation and are steadily driving up negative perceptions. We will eventually turn it toxic, as we put all of the various cultural insanities under that brand category," Rufo wrote. "The goal is to have the public read something crazy in the newspaper and immediately think 'critical race theory.' We have decodified the term and will recodify it to annex the entire range of cultural constructions that are unpopular with Americans." Rufo said in an interview that he understands why his opponents often point to this tweet, but said that the approach described is "so obvious." "If you want to see public policy outcomes you have to run a public persuasion campaign," he said. Rufo says his own role has been to translate research into programs about race into the political arena.[8]

Either approach—extending the territory of the meaning of a term and then retreating or using deception to destroy the legitimate meaning of that term—uses deception to gain advantage rather than seeking truth.

A better strategy calls us to seek truth and build trust. As Christians, we believe this is the path we are called to follow independent of the outcome. We seek truth and seek to build trust because it is right, not only because it provides benefit. Francis Fukuyama makes the case for trust in his 1995 book:

> If people who work together in an enterprise trust one another because they are all operating according to a common set of ethical norms, doing business

costs less. . . . By contrast, people who do not trust one another will end up cooperating only under a system of formal rules and regulations that have to be negotiated, agreed to, litigated, and enforced, sometimes by coercive means. . . . Widespread distrust in a society, in other words, imposes a kind of tax on all forms of economic activity, a tax that high trust societies do not have to pay.[9]

Back in the 1990s, Al experienced this at Boeing. Some people in his lab were conducting a joint research project with another party, and Al wanted to make sure that neither Boeing nor the other party would be restricted from using the results of the research. So he asked their in-house lawyer to draw up the paper work so that both of the parties could do what they wanted to do with the results. A month or so later, the lawyer brought back a forty-page document, explaining, "This is so we can do what we want with the results and so can they. But we don't trust them, so we had to tie everything down."

Trust is hard to build and easy to destroy, but it is essential to seek to build it because it is right and because it also brings great results.

When it came to writing this book, Al and Randy never stopped trusting each other, even when disagreements arose over this or that issue. Looking back, that trust was built up over several years of spending time together in each other's homes, traveling together with our wives, bouncing ideas off each other, and learning from each other. When the disagreements came as we worked on the book, both of us were instinctively determined not to let those disagreements derail either the book or our friendship. We had built up a reservoir of trust in each other that we were able to draw on when those disagreements arose.

———

We could go on to explore other terms of tension, but this is enough. What does this mean for us? First, we are not all going to agree on everything. In some cases, we might want to walk away rather than dealing with things, and sometimes we should. But can we also think of calmly exploring the differences, sometimes *celebrating* the differences? There was a time early in Al's life when he thought rather mechanistically about the world and wondered aloud why God made the diversity of trees, flowers, animals, and people. It took some maturity to come to appreciate the diversity—that it was all part of the beauty of God's creation. There are differing expressions of work, worship, talents, and expressions, which could be a source of joy rather than pain. Instead of seeking to align others with ourselves, let's offer grace, love, and admiration!

Second, we should grow in our understanding of those things that may trigger others and be cautious with our own use of words. Paul said this when he talked about eating meat offered to idols: "So then, about eating food sacrificed to idols: We know that 'an idol is nothing at all in the world' and that 'there is no God but one.' . . . Be careful, however, that the exercise of your rights does not become a stumbling block to the weak" (1 Cor. 8:4, 9). Or as he says to the Philippians, "Do nothing out of selfish ambition or vain conceit. Rather, in humility value others above yourselves, not looking to your own interests but each of you to the interests of the others" (Phil. 2:3–4).

Third, we should be careful about allowing ourselves to be triggered. When we hear a word or expression or opinion with which we disagree, can we seek clarification, ask questions, and look for common ground? Although we won't always find it, if we truly believe the other person is made in the image of God, then we should try. A common tendency of our culture is to label and dismiss: that is, to effectively put another person in a box thinking we know all about them when we do not. People are complicated, and there is much we can learn from one another. None of us know everything. When we "cancel" or attack a *person* rather than actually discussing and dealing with the ideas themselves, we have put that other person in a very small box, thinking we know them when we do not.

Engaging our polarizing culture does not mean we somehow need to become "moderate" on every issue, but it does mean following Paul's wise counsel to the Colossian Christians:

> Use your heads as you live and work among outsiders. Don't miss a trick. Make the most of every opportunity. Be gracious in your speech. The goal is to bring out the best in others in a conversation, not put them down, not cut them out.
> (Col. 4:5–6 MSG)

Appendix 1 | The Decline of Christianity

There are numerous markers suggesting the decline in Christianity in the West. These include the sheer number of people who self-identify as Christians and the number of churches that are closing due to lack of attendance. In addition, while being a Christian in the United States used to be a positive thing, data suggests this to has shifted from positive to neutral to negative in the past few decades. What the data does not show is whether this decline is simply the secularization of culture or a perception that what has been called Christianity in the United States has been perceived as merely Christendom, a form of Christianity lacking the substance to deal with the realities of the world where we find ourselves. In either case, those continuing to identify as Christians are feeling the change.

Pew Research data[1] projects that the 2020 number for self-reporting Christians in the United States (64 percent) will fall below 50 percent in the next 20–50 years. That number was 90 percent as recently as 1980.

Perhaps even more troubling is the decline in younger people identifying as Christians reported in the same study.

This trend is not restricted to the US. In 2022, it was reported that the percent of Christians in England and Wales dropped below 50 percent for the first time.[4] Also in 2022, Australia reported the percent of Christians had also dropped below 50 percent for the first time.[5] The figure had been over 50 percent in 2016 and over 60 percent in 2011.

While these are self-reporting numbers, they do offer a strong signal regarding the decline of Christianity in the West. The perception of Christians by the rest of United States society is highlighted by Aaron Renn.[6] He looks at the ways evangelicals are perceived by culture as:

Positive (pre-1994), Neutral (1994–2014), and Negative (2014–present).
He characterizes the relationship between culture and Christianity in this
Negative World:

> Society has come to have a *negative* view of Christianity. Being known as a
> Christian is a social negative, particularly in the elite domains of society. Chris-
> tian morality is expressly repudiated and seen as a threat to the public good and
> the new public moral order. Subscribing to Christian moral views or violating
> the secular moral order brings negative consequences.

**The rise of religious 'nones' looks similar in data from
Pew Research Center and the General Social Survey**

*General Social Survey (darker) and Pew Research Center (lighter) estimates
of U.S. religious composition, among U.S. adults*

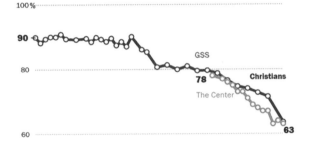

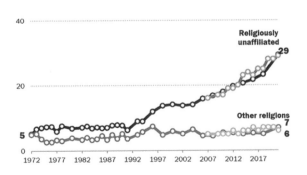

Note: Those who did not answer are not shown.
Sources: General Social Survey (1972-2021) were conducted primarily in person until
2021, when data was collected online. Pew Research Center survey data from 2020-21 is
based on the Center's National Public Opinion Reference Surveys (NPORS), conducted
online and by mail. All of the Center's data from 2019 and earlier come from random-digit-
dial telephone surveys. See Methodology for details.
"Modeling the Future of Religion in America"

PEW RESEARCH CENTER

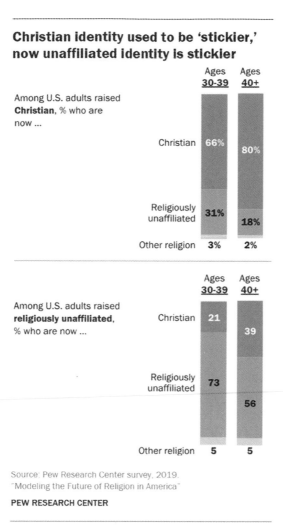

Christian identity used to be 'stickier,' now unaffiliated identity is stickier

Among U.S. adults raised **Christian**, % who are now ...

	Ages 30-39	Ages 40+
Christian	66%	80%
Religiously unaffiliated	31%	18%
Other religion	3%	2%

Among U.S. adults raised **religiously unaffiliated**, % who are now ...

	Ages 30-39	Ages 40+
Christian	21	39
Religiously unaffiliated	73	56
Other religion	5	5

Source: Pew Research Center survey, 2019.
"Modeling the Future of Religion in America"

PEW RESEARCH CENTER

Renn also highlights the difference among Christians: "American evangelicalism is deeply divided."

The net of these measures is: the number of self-identifying Christians is declining, the number of Christians attending church is declining, the number of younger people who leave Christianity is increasing, the decline is similar in some other parts of the world, and the perception Christians by society is becoming more negative. In addition, the oneness of the church that Christ calls for is also in retreat.

Together, we see that the path for Christians to navigate in this world looks very different than it did even a decade ago.

Appendix 2 | Learning from the Stories of Scripture

We acknowledge that some care is required in drawing lessons from the narratives of Scripture for two quite different reasons.

First, we run the risk of drawing wrong conclusions from the stories when we miss the cultural differences between the subjects of these stories and our own culture. We make assumptions, almost unknowingly, based on our own cultural backgrounds, and we too easily assume that others follow our own cultural assumptions. John Medina, a developmental molecular biologist who specializes in the human brain, put it well when he said, "What is obvious to you is . . . obvious to you."[1]

The subjects of the Bible stories operated from different assumptions. In their book *Misreading Scripture with Western Eyes*, E. Randolph Richards and Brandon J. O'Brien caution,

> The question about how our cultural and historical context influences our reading of Scripture has practical and pastoral implications. If our cultural blind spots keep us from *reading* the Bible correctly, then they can also keep us from *applying* the Bible correctly. If we want to follow Jesus faithfully and help others do the same, we need to do all we can to allow the Scriptures to speak to us on their own terms. [2]

Second, we need to be reminded that the Bible is written to tell us about God and his ways. Often, there is a tendency to try to draw lessons from Scripture that are far from the main purpose of the text. Haddon Robinson, former president of Denver Seminary and one of the founders of the Theology of Work Project put it very clearly:

It's one thing to say, "Love God and love your neighbor." It's another to show people what that looks like. But the more specific you try to be, the more likely you are to say things that God never intended. I heard someone preach a sermon from Ruth on how to deal with in-laws. Now, it's true that in Ruth you have in-laws. The problem is, Ruth was not given to address in-law problems. The sermon had a lot of practical advice, but it didn't come from the Scriptures.[3]

John and Kim Walton make a similar case when they write:

We tell Bible stories so that students of all ages can know God better. This means our primary concern in teaching any story from the Bible is to explain what the story tells us about God. . . . We can only attach authority to the lesson the text is intentionally teaching, and must look to the text to determine what that teaching is. . . . The Bible's teachings about God convey certain implications for us. What in my life must change? What attitudes must be adjusted? How does my worldview need to conform?[4]

These reminders of caution in the application of narratives tell us we cannot simply use them as models and blindly follow them. We should carefully observe these narratives as ways people connected with God and know that they are more than models to imitate.

Yet we know they are there for our instruction, bringing insight to our lives when applied with care. Dallas Willard offers good insight about the narratives of Scripture when he suggests that these stories build a bridge to their lives through our shared humanity:

If we are really to understand the Bible record, we must enter into our study of it on the assumption that the experiences recorded there are basically of the same type as ours would have been if we had been there. Those who lived through those experiences felt very much as we would have if we had been in their place.[5]

We tried to consider all of these factors when studying the stories for this book.

Acknowledgments

Many thanks to Malcolm Guite for the use of his poem "A Tale of Two Gardens," written at Christmastime 2022. Malcolm Guite is a beloved English poet-priest, renowned for his thoughtful and popular revival of the sonnet form. Having served as chaplain at Girton College, Cambridge, he is the author of more than six books and is a popular presenter around the world. We chose this poem because it captures the spirit of what we seek to convey in this book. As followers of Jesus, we need to see our call to walk with him by starting with how he walked among us.

We are both grateful for the support of Hendrickson Publishers in this project. Before his retirement, Paul Hendrickson offered kind support and encouragement. And Patricia Anders continues to be the excellent editor who can help us say what we wanted to say. The final product is so much better thanks to her strong hand and her engagement with this project. Remaining errors we own, but the book would not be the same without her guidance.

Al would like to thank Westminster Chapel and the adult Sunday school class where he went through an early version of this material. Their engagement and feedback were helpful in shaping the resulting chapters. The Christians in the business group in Seattle, KIROS, were also helpful in providing feedback on an early presentation of these ideas. Al would add a special thanks to his friend and co-author Randy Pope, whose perspective brought new light to many of the topics, and whose life experiences opened brand-new windows on this material. Special thanks to numerous colleagues who offered helpful suggestions after reading portions of this material as it was being developed, including Luke Bobo, Cheryl Broetje,

Caleb Breaky, Steve Brock, Henry Calhoun, Gina Casey, Tori Dabasinskas, and Mark Neuenschwander.

Finally, and continuously, Al is grateful to his wife Nancy for bearing with, encouraging, and offering insight to this project. He is forever grateful for their shared passions and lives together. Al and Nancy have three children and their spouses and seven grandchildren. He trusts this will be meaningful to them.

Randy is grateful for the opportunity to work on this project with his friend and mentor, Al Erisman. He appreciates Al's kindness and generosity toward him particularly as they worked through sometimes prickly issues in applying the Scripture to everyday life in the twenty-first century. Their friendship was deepened through the process of writing the book together.

Randy had fruitful discussions about different aspects of the book with his daughters, Lucy Schultze and Valerie Cullaton, and their respective husbands, Robert and Clay. It is a joy to watch and learn from each of them as they serve others in their respective places of work, including the work of parenting Randy and Kathy's four grandchildren.

Since 2017, a professional pleasure for Randy has been to work with and be challenged by many coworkers at the City of Hattiesburg, Mississippi, whose work ethic and love for the city embodies what Jeremiah was talking about when he encouraged the Jewish exiles in Babylon to "seek the peace and prosperity of the city" (Jer. 29:7).

Finally, we talked a lot in this book about "whole-life discipleship," trying to follow Jesus in every aspect of life. Randy's constant role model for that kind of discipleship for more than fifty years has been his wife, Kathy. Many of the points offered in this book are the result of long conversations between them. Among the many roles she plays in their marriage is that of sounding board and ideas editor. "Her husband trusts her without reserve, and never has reason to regret it" (Prov. 31:11 MSG).

Bibliography

Alter, Robert. *The Hebrew Bible, A Translation With Commentary*. New York: W. W. Norton, 2019.

Andersen, Francis I. *Job: An Introduction and Commentary*. TOTC 14. Downers Grove, IL: InterVarsity Press, 1974.

Arnold, Bill T., and H. G. M Williamson, eds. "Saul and Saul's Family." In *Dictionary of the Old Testament: Historical Books*. Downers Grove, IL: InterVarsity Press, 2005.

Baldwin, Joyce. *Daniel: An Introduction and Commentary*. TOTC 22. Downers Grove, IL: InterVarsity Press, 1978.

Baldwin, Melinda, "*Hidden Figures* Effectively Portrays Brilliant Women Making Scientific History." *Physics Today*, January 5, 2017.

Banks, Robert, and R. Paul Stevens. "Walking" In *The Complete Book of Everyday Christianity*. Downers Grove, IL: InterVarsity Press, 1997.

Barkas, Craig B. "How to Use Power, Influence, and Persuasion for Good." *Psychology Today*, January 15, 2021. https://www.psychologytoday .com/us/blog/power-and-influence/202101/how-use-power -influence-and-persuasion-good.

Bell, Steve. "Making Cabinets, Changing the World." *Ethix*, August 1, 2008. https://ethix.org/2008/08/01/making-cabinets-changing-the-world.

Broetje, Cheryl. "An Orchard with Fruit That Lasts." *Ethix*, December 1, 2005. https://ethix.org/2005/12/01/an-orchard-with-fruit-that-lasts.

Brown, Bréne. *Braving the Wilderness: The Quest for True Belonging and the Courage to Stand Alone*. London: Random House, 2017.

Carpenter, Humphrey, ed. *The Letters of J. R. R. Tolkien*. Boston: Houghton Mifflin, 1981.

Carroll, Craig. "What Is Motte & Bailey?" *The Bigger Picture*, December 2, 2020. https://medium.com/bigger-picture/what-is-a-motte-bailey -aad572eacc37.

Carter, Marshall. "Making Sense of the Financial Mess." *Ethix*, August 13, 2010. https://ethix.org/2010/08/13/making-sense-of-the-financial-mess.

Casper, Jayson. "Where It Is Hardest to Be a Christian: The Top 50 Countries Where Persecution Is Worst." *Christianity Today*, January 21, 2022.

Christensen, Clayton. *The Innovator's Dilemma: When Technologies Cause Great Firms to Fail.* Brighton: HBS Press, 1997.

Cole, R. Alan. *Exodus: An Introduction and Commentary. TOTC* 2. Downers Grove, IL: InterVarsity Press, 1973.

Crouch, Andy. *Playing God: Redeeming the Gift of Power.* Downers Grove, IL: InterVarsity Press, 2013.

Douthat, Ross. "A Gentler Christendom." *First Things*, June 2022. https://www.firstthings.com/article/2022/06/a-gentler-christendom.

Dreher, Rod. *The Benedict Option: How Christians Can Thrive in a Post-Christian World.* Grand Rapids: Brazos Press, 2020.

Eaton, Phil. "Reclaiming Christian Community?" *From My Study* (blog), March 14, 2017. https://www.peatonblog.com/.

Erisman, Albert M. *The Accidental Executive: Lessons on Business, Faith and Calling from the Life of Joseph.* Peabody, MA: Hendrickson, 2015.

———. *The ServiceMaster Story: Navigating Tension between People and Profit.* Peabody, MA: Hendrickson, 2020.

Erisman, Albert, and David Gautschi. "Profit Maximization Must Fall." In *The Purpose of Business.* London: Palgrave Macmillan, 2015.

Flow, Don. "Engaging the World: Vocation, Eschatology, and *Shalom.*" Seattle Pacific University (talk), 2008.

Fukuyama, Francis. *Trust: The Social Virtues and the Creation of Prosperity.* Glencoe: Free Press, 1995.

Gill, David W. "Eight Traits of an Ethically Healthy Culture: Insights from the Beatitudes." *Journal of Markets and Morality* (Fall 2013).

———. *Peter the Rock: Extraordinary Insights from an Ordinary Man.* Downers Grove, IL: InterVarsity Press, 1986.

———. *Workplace Discipleship 101: A Primer.* Peabody, MA: Hendrickson, 2020.

Gjelten, Tom. "Multiracial Congregations May Not Bridge Racial Divide." *NPR*, July 17, 2020.

Hagan, Lowell. *Second Sight: Renewing the Vision of Bellevue Christian School for the New Century.* Bellevue, WA: Bellevue Christian School, 2003.

Hill, Alec. *Living in Bonus Time: Surviving Cancer, Finding New Purpose.* Downers Grove, IL: InterVarsity Press, 2020.

Hill, Austin, and Scott Rae. *The Virtues of Capitalism: A Moral Case for Free Markets*. Chicago: Northfield, 2010.

Hollinger, Dennis. *Head, Heart, Hands: Bringing Together Christian Thought, Passion and Action*. Downers Grove, IL: InterVarsity Press, 2005.

Hunter, James Davison. *To Change the World*. Oxford: Oxford University Press, 2010.

Inazu, John. *Confident Pluralism: Surviving and Thriving through Deep Differences*. Chicago: University of Chicago Press, 2018.

Kass, Leon. *The Beginning of Wisdom: Reading Genesis*. Chicago: University of Chicago Press, 2003.

———. *Founding God's Nation: Reading Exodus*. New Haven: Yale University Press, 2021.

Keller, Tim. *Generous Justice: How God's Grace Makes Us Just*. New York: Penguin Random House, 2010.

———. "An Immigrant's Courage." 1997. Video, 10:42. https://www.youtube .com/watch?v=WF1CgX6ZcrE.

———. *Walking with God through Pain and Suffering*. New York: Penguin Random House, 2015.

Keller, Timothy, and Katherine Alsdorf. *Every Good Endeavor*. New York: Penguin Random House, 2012.

Lewis, C. S. *A Grief Observed*. San Francisco: Harper One, 2015.

———. *Mere Christianity*. New York: Macmillan, 1981.

———. *On Stories: And Other Essays on Literature*. San Diego: Harcourt Brace, 1982.

———. *Perelandra*. New York: Scribner, 1996.

———. *Prince Caspian*. New York: Macmillan, 1951.

———. *Reflections on the Psalms*. San Diego: Harcourt Brace Jovanovich, 1958.

———. *The Screwtape Letters*. New York: Touchstone, 1996.

———. "The World's Last Night." In *The World's Last Night and Other Essays*. San Diego: Harcourt Brace Jovanovich, 1987.

McAllister, Edwin. "Dolphus Weary," in *Mississippi Encyclopedia* (2017). https://mississippiencyclopedia.org/entries/dolphus-weary/.

McCauley, Esau. "The Racial Justice Needs Civil Discourse, Not Straw Men." *Christianity Today*, August 10, 2021. https://www.christianitytoday .com/ct/2021/august-web-only/critical-race-theory-racial-justice -debate-civil-discourse.html.

McCormick, Brian Robert. "The Possible Church: Stories of Those Who Have Led White Congregations into a Multi-Ethnic Reality." Diss., Duke Divinity School, Duke University, April 2022.

McGrath, Alister. *Eccentric Genius, Reluctant Prophet: C. S. Lewis: A Life.* Carol Stream, IL: Tyndale, 2013.

Medina, John. *Brain Rules: 12 Principles for Surviving and Thriving at Work, Home and School.* West Edmonds, WA: Pear Press, 2008.

Melfi, Theodore, dir. *Hidden Figures.* Burbank, CA: 20th Century Fox, 2017.

Mencken, H. L. *Prejudices: Second Series.* New York: Knopf, 1920.

Messenger, William, ed. *Theology of Work Bible Commentary.* Peabody, MA: Hendrickson, 2016. https://www.theologyofwork.org/resources/the -theology-of-work-biblecommentary/.

Motyer, J. S. *The Message of Exodus.* Downers Grove, IL: InterVarsity Press, 2005.

Parker, Tripp. "Who Matters More Than Why." KIROS (talk), November 2021. https://kiros.org/audio-2021/tripp-parker-nov2021/.

Perkins, John. *One Blood: Parting Words to the Church on Race and Love.* Chicago: Moody, 2017.

Peterson, Eugene. *A Long Obedience in the Same Direction: Discipleship in an Instant Society.* Downers Grove, IL: InterVarsity Press, 1980.

Platt, Lewis E. "Sharing Insight from 33 Years at Hewlett Packard." *Ethix,* April 1, 2000. https://ethix.org/2000/04/01/sharing-insight-from-33 -years-at-hewlett-packard.

Renn, Aaron. "The Three Worlds of Evangelicalism." *First Things,* February 2022. https://www.firstthings.com/article/2022/02/the-three-worlds -of-evangelicalism.

Richards, E. Randolph, and Brandon J. O'Brien. *Misreading Scripture with Western Eyes: Removing Cultural Blinders to Better Understand the Bible.* Downers Grove, IL: InterVarsity Press, 2012.

Richards, E. Randolph, and Richard James. *Misreading Scripture through Individualistic Eyes.* Downers Grove, IL: InterVarsity Press, 2020.

Robinson, Haddon. "The Heresy of Application." *Christianity Today,* Fall 2017.

Roche, Bruno, and Jay Jakub. *Completing Capitalism: Heal Business to Heal the World.* Oakland, CA: Berrett-Koehler, 2017.

Ryken, Leland, James C. Wilhoit, and Tremper Longman, III, eds. *Dictionary of Biblical Imagery.* Downers Grove, IL: InterVarsity Press, 1998.

Sample, Steven. *Contrarian's Guide to Leadership*. San Francisco: Jossey-Bass, 2003.

Schaeffer, Francis. *The Church at the End of the 20th Century*. Downers Grove, IL: InterVarsity Press, 1970.

———. *The God Who Is There*. Downers Grove, IL: InterVarsity Press, 1968.

Shugart, Sandy. *Leadership in the Crucible: Discovering the Interior Life of an Authentic Leader*. Altamonte Springs: Florida Hospital, 2013.

Solzhenitsyn, Alexander. *One Day in the Life of Ivan Denisovich*. New York: Penguin, 1991.

Sproul, R. C. *Stronger than Steel: The Wayne Alderson Story*. New York: Harper and Row, 1980.

Stevens, R. Paul. *The Kingdom of God in Working Clothes: The Marketplace and the Reign of God*. Eugene, OR: Cascade Books, 2022.

Stott, John R. W. "Power through Weakness." Video, 4:56. https://www.youtube.com/watch?v=cpY-C8hJO-4.

Tolkien, J. R. R. *The Fellowship of the Ring*. Boston: Houghton Mifflin, 1965.

———. "On Fairy Stories." *Tree and Leaf*. London: HarperCollins, 1988.

Wallace, Ronald S. *The Message of Daniel*. Downers Grove, IL: InterVarsity Press, 1978.

Waltke, Bruce K., and Cathi J. Fredricks. *Genesis: A Commentary*. Grand Rapids: Zondervan, 2001.

Walton, John H., and Kim E. Walton. *Bible Story Handbook: A Resource for Teaching 175 Stories from the Bible*. Wheaton, IL: Crossway, 2010.

Warren, Tish Harrison. *Liturgy of the Ordinary: Sacred Practices in Everyday Life*. Downers Grove, IL: InterVarsity Press, 2016.

Willard, Dallas. *Hearing God: Developing a Conversational Relationship with God*. Downers Grove, IL: InterVarsity Press, 2012.

Williams, Paul. *Exiles on Mission: How Christians Can Thrive in a Post-Christian World*. Grand Rapids: Brazos Press, 2020.

Word in Life Study Bible. Nashville: Thomas Nelson, 1990.

Wright, Christopher J. H. *Old Testament Ethics for the People of God*. Downers Grove, IL: InterVarsity Press, 2004.

Wright, N. T. *Paul: A Biography*. New York: HarperCollins, 2018.

———. *Surprised by Scripture*. New York: HarperOne, 2014.

Youngblood, Alice. "Only One-Third of Young Adults Feel Cared for by Others." Barna Study, October 2019. https://www.barna.com/research/global-connection-isolation/.

Notes

Introduction

1. Paul Williams, *Exiles on Mission: How Christians Can Thrive in a Post-Christian World* (Grand Rapids: Brazos Press, 2020), xiv.

2. Jayson Casper, "Where Is It Hardest to Be a Christian?: The Top 50 Countries Where Persecution Is Worst," *Christianity Today* (January 21, 2022).

3. J. R. R. Tolkien, *The Fellowship of the Ring* (New York: Houghton Mifflin, 1965), ch. 2.

4. James Davison Hunter, *To Change the World* (Oxford: Oxford Press, 2010), 95.

5. Ross Douthat, "A Gentler Christendom," *First Things* (June 2022), https://www.firstthings.com/article/2022/06/a-gentler-christendom.

6. Williams, *Exiles on Mission*, 31.

7. "Moralistic Therapeutic Deism," *Wikipedia*, last edited November 19, 2022, https://en.wikipedia.org/wiki/Moralistic_therapeutic_deism#Definition.

8. Rod Dreher, *The Benedict Option: A Strategy for Christians in a Post-Christian World* (New York: Sentinel, 2017), 93.

9. Williams, *Exiles on Mission*, 12.

10. Alice Youngblood, "Only One-Third of Young Adults Feel Cared for by Others," *Barna Study*, October 2019, https://www.barna.com/research/global-connection-isolation/.

11. Hunter, *To Change the World*, 171.

12. English Anglican cleric and theologian who was noted as a leader of the worldwide evangelical movement. He was one of the principal authors of the Lausanne Covenant in 1974. In 2005, *Time* magazine ranked Stott among the hundred most influential people in the world.

13. John Stott, "Power through Weakness," beginning at 4:56, https://www.youtube.com/watch?v=cpY-C8hJO-4.

14. *Word in Life Study Bible* (Nashville: Thomas Nelson, 1990), 1310.

15. *Word in Life Study Bible*, 1529.

16. Personal communication with Steven Garber, who is currently completing a book dealing with this topic tentatively titled *Glimpses of Hope: Living Proximately*.

17. In the appendix, "Learning from the Stories of Scripture," we describe in greater detail what it means to us to "carefully and honestly apply" what we can learn from these biblical narratives.

18. N. T. Wright, *Surprised by Scripture* (New York: HarperOne, 2014), 143.

19. C. S. Lewis, *Reflections on the Psalms* (San Diego: Harcourt, 1958), 1–2.

20. Lewis, *Reflections on the Psalms*, 2.

Chapter 1

1. Robert Alter, *The Hebrew Bible, Vol. 1: The Five Books of Moses* (New York: W. W. Norton, 2019), 37–38. Bioethicist Leon Kass writes that "the founders of Babel aspire to nothing less than self-*re*-creation" through technology; Leon Kass, *The Beginning of Wisdom: Reading Genesis* (Chicago: University of Chicago, 2003), 231.

2. J. R. R. Tolkien, "On Fairy Stories," *Tree and Leaf* (London: George Allen and Unwin, 1964), 54–55.

3. Bruce K. Waltke with Cathi J. Fredricks, *Genesis: A Commentary* (Grand Rapids: Zondervan, 2001), 200, quoting Walter Bruggemann, *Genesis: A Bible Commentary for Teaching and Preaching* (Atlanta: John Knox, 1982), 116.

4. Tolkien, "On Fairy Stories," 81.

5. "In the ancient Near East, a name was not merely a label but a revelation of character. Thus a great name entails not only fame but high social esteem 'as a man of superior character.'" Waltke, *Genesis*, 205.

6. Kass, *The Beginning of Wisdom*, 252.

7. Sarah is, in fact, apparently more than Abraham's wife. In Genesis 20:12, Abraham calls her his half-sister and explains to a foreign king that she is the daughter of his father, Terah, but not his mother. That fact does not change the fact that he was using her to protect himself.

8. The fact that Sarah made no response to Abraham's plan to pass her off as his sister does not indicate she was simply a passive, robot-like woman: it was she, after all, who told Abraham that he should have a child through her slave, Hagar, and it was she who laughed when God told Abraham that they would have a child even though they were very old.

9. Waltke, *Genesis*, 221.

10. Waltke, *Genesis*, 267.

11. Will Messenger, ed., *Theology of Work Bible Commentary* (Peabody, MA: Hendrickson, 2016), 47.

12. Waltke, *Genesis*, 268.

13. As a side note, we see Lot in Sodom as one who has largely assimilated into a corrupt culture. Rather than being an influence there, he seems to have blended into all the ways of the people there. When he gives a warning to his family to leave Sodom, his sons-in-law assume he must be joking about God's intention to destroy the city (Gen. 19:14).

14. Genesis 18:20–21 makes clear that God will not rely on hearsay to decide what to do with Sodom, nor will he prejudge the case, and he seems inclined not to believe the worst ("Innocent until proven guilty"?): "I will go down and see if what they have done is as bad as the outcry that has reached me. If not, I will know."

15. *Theology of Work Bible Commentary*, 49–50.

16. It is interesting that Genesis 25:8 describes Abraham as "an old man and full of years" when he died. Bruce Waltke comments on this phrase that "by the time of his death [Abraham] has enjoyed both abundant quantity and quality of life." Waltke, *Genesis*, 340.

17. "No greater compliment could be paid someone in the Old Testament than to say that he or she 'walked with God' (Gen. 6:9). . . . We find similar language in the New Testament. Here too walking is a key metaphor for depicting the way Christians should conduct themselves." Robert Banks and R. Paul Stevens, eds., "Walking," *The Complete Book of Everyday Christianity* (Downers Grove, IL: Inter-Varsity Press, 1997), 1098.

Chapter 2

1. Joseph is introduced to us at his birth recorded in Genesis 30:22–24. His recorded story begins in Genesis 37–50 when he is seventeen years old. He is mentioned numerous times through the rest of Scripture, notably in Psalm 105 where his suffering in prison is described.

2. Alexander Solzhenitsyn, *One Day in the Life of Ivan Denisovich* (1962; repr., Penguin, 1991), 76.

3. Solzhenitsyn, *One Day in the Life of Ivan Denisovich*, 76.

4. Albert Erisman, *The Accidental Executive: Lessons on Business, Faith, and Calling from the Life of Joseph* (Peabody, MA: Hendrickson, 2015), 59.

5. Al recalls listening to this interview sometime in the 1960s but has been unable to find a formal reference to it.

6. Marshall Carter, "Making Sense of the Financial Mess," interview by David Gautschi and Al Erisman, *Ethix Magazine,* Conversation, Issue 71 (May 7, 2010), https://ethix.org/2010/08/13/making-sense-of-the-financial-mess.

7. Erisman, *The Accidental Executive*, 93–94.

8. Carter, "Making Sense of the Financial Mess."

9. Albert M. Erisman, *The ServiceMaster Story: Navigating Tension between People and Profit* (Peabody, MA: Hendrickson, 2020), 6.

10. Eugene Peterson, *A Long Obedience in the Same Direction: Discipleship in an Instant Society* (Downers Grove, IL: InterVarsity, 1980).

11. Book cover copy from Sandy Shugart, *Leadership in the Crucible of Work: Discovering the Interior Life of an Authentic Leader* (Altamonte Springs: Florida Hospital, 2013).

12. Erisman, *The Accidental Executive*, 132.

13. See also Erisman, *The Accidental Executive*, 126.

Chapter 3

1. R. Alan Cole, *Exodus: An Introduction and Commentary*, *TOTC* 2 (Downers Grove, IL: InterVarsity Press, 1973), 53.

2. We learn not only the names of the two Hebrew midwives who refuse to carry the king's infanticide order, but because they "feared God," God "was kind" to them and "gave them families of their own" (Exod. 1:20–21). Their role in the story is quite small, but they played their part perfectly. Pharaoh, on the other hand, is one of main characters in the first half of the book of Exodus, but his name is never given. Alec Motyer comments that "there is a wealth of irony running through these opening chapters. Here, e.g., for all his 'greatness,' Pharaoh is left unnamed, while the midwives (whom he regarded as mere tools of his policy) are remembered individually." J. A. Motyer, *The Message of Exodus* (Downers Grove, IL: InterVarsity Press, 2005), 29n4. Alan Cole suggests that the decisions of the two midwives "for life sprang from reverence for God, the life-giver" and "the relevance of this to modern controversy about abortion should be carefully pondered." Cole, *Exodus*, 55.

3. *Theology of Work Bible Commentary*, 77.

4. *Theology of Work Bible Commentary*, 45.

5. "If the Pharaoh [who was king when Moses was adopted by his daughter] is Ramesses II, he had close to sixty daughters." Cole, *Exodus*, 58.

6. *Theology of Work Bible Commentary*, 79.

7. See R. Paul Stevens, *The Kingdom of God in Working Clothes: The Marketplace and the Reign of God* (Eugene, OR: Cascade Books, 2022).

8. C. S. Lewis, "The Efficacy of Prayer," *Fern-seed and Elephants* (London: HarperCollins, 1975), 83.

9. The RSV and ESV translate the Hebrew word here as "meek"; the NIV, *The Message*, and Jewish scholar Robert Alter translate it "humble." Alter comments that "his humble or unassuming character is reflected here in the fact that he has not troubled to listen, or has paid no attention, to the malicious rumors about him that Miriam and Aaron have initiated." Alter, *The Hebrew Bible,* vol. 1, 518.

10. *Dictionary of Biblical Imagery*, ed. Leland Ryken, James C. Wilhoit, and Tremper Longman III (Downers Grove, IL: InterVarsity Press, 1998), 546.

Chapter 4

1. "University of Iowa Campus Ministry Upheld in Court," Press Room, InterVarsity, October 19, 2019, https://intervarsity.org/news/university-iowa-campus-ministry-upheld-federal-court. In this case, InterVarsity Christian Fellowship had been on the University of Iowa campus for more than twenty-five years before it was banned for not allowing non-Christians to serve as officers of the campus chapter, but other campus groups—including Muslim, Sikhs, and Mormons—were banned for the same reason.

2. We might wonder why the Amalekites attacked the Israelites in the first place. It's true that the Israelites had "plundered" the Egyptians as they left that nation, taking with them much silver and gold, and perhaps the Amalekites had

heard about this and were intent on getting some of the plunder for themselves. But there was likely something deeper involved in this decision. Amalek, the ancestor of the Amalekites, was the grandson of Esau, the brother of Jacob, from whom the Israelites had descended (and even bore his name of Israel). Although Esau and Jacob had apparently reconciled many years after Jacob cheated Esau out of their father Isaac's blessing, we suspect that that reconciliation was incomplete and temporary, and as Leon Kass notes, "Tribes carry smoldering grudges from generation to generation, waiting for an opportunity to get even." Leon Kass, *Founding God's Nation: Reading Exodus* (New Haven: Yale University Press, 2021), 245.

3. Melissa Rademaker, "Sealy Makes History as Hattiesburg's First Female Police Chief," August 19, 2021, https://www.wdam.com/2021/08/20/sealy-makes -history-hattiesburgs-first-female-police-chief/.

4. In *The Hebrew Bible,* vol. 1, 516–17, Robert Alter comments:

> The prophesying of the other sixty-eight elders in the designated place of sanctity, near the Tent of Meeting, is one thing, but the manifestation of prophecy in the midst of the Israelite camp is quite another, for it could turn into a dangerously contagious threat to Moses's leadership, [but] Moses, having just surrendered a portion of the spirit invested in him to the seventy elders, now hyperbolically expresses the sense that holding on to a monopoly of power (equated with access to the divine spirit) is not at all what impels him as a leader. Although he knows that there is scarcely any prospect that the entire people will become prophets, he nevertheless points to an ideal of what we might call spiritual egalitarianism. Access to the realm of the spirit is granted by God, in principle to anyone God chooses.

5. Numbers 12 recounts the opposite problem from what Joshua was rebuked for in Numbers 11. In Numbers 12:1, Moses' sister and brother, Miriam and Aaron, "began to talk against Moses because of his Cushite wife, for he had married a Cushite."

6. "Numbers 12:8 explains the meaning of this phrase. God will speak to Moses . . . not in dreams and visions, but clearly and directly. Moses had the gift of clarity of spiritual insight: he shared the very counsels of God." Cole, *Exodus*, 224.

7. Little is known about the Anakim, but most likely they were "an extremely large and tall people, not unlike the Philistine champion Goliath. . . . The Anakim were settled in the hill country of southern Canaan, . . . [and] most of them were killed or driven out during the early campaigns of Joshua's conquest (Josh. 11:21–22), and Caleb finished the job when he was allotted Hebron (Josh. 21:11–12; Judg. 1:20). Appropriately, the only two spies who trusted God and refused to be intimidated by the Anakim were the one who eventually inherited their lands." *Word in Life Study Bible*, 343.

8. Although Joshua has not been mentioned yet in this incident, in the next chapter it is apparent that he stood with Caleb at this point.

9. "Vision," in *New Oxford American Dictionary*, 3rd ed. (New York: Oxford University Press, 2010), 1933.

10. Clayton Christensen, *The Innovator's Dilemma: When New Technologies Cause Great Firms to Fail* (Brighton: HBS Press, 1997).

11. C. S. Lewis, *The Screwtape Letters* (New York: Touchstone, 1996), 91.

12. Alister McGrath, *Eccentric Genius, Reluctant Prophet: C. S. Lewis: A Life* (Carol Stream, IL: Tyndale House, 2013), 130. After Lewis's death, Tolkien wrote that Lewis's "influence" on him was not as that concept is ordinarily understood. Rather, "The unpayable debt that I owe to him was . . . sheer encouragement. He was for long my only audience. Only from him did I ever get the idea that my 'stuff' could be more than a private hobby. But for his interest and unceasing eagerness for more I should never have brought *The L. of the R.* to a conclusion." Humphrey Carpenter, ed., *The Letters of J. R. R. Tolkien* (Boston: Houghton Mifflin, 1981), 362.

Chapter 5

1. "Whither Thou Goest," by Earl Chalmers Guisinger, 1954, and recorded by multiple artists.

2. *Theology of Work Bible Commentary*, 223.

3. Christopher J. H. Wright, *Old Testament Ethics for the People of God* (Downers Grove, IL: InterVarsity Press, 2004), 313.

4. Tim Keller, "An Immigrant's Courage," 1997, from 10:42 onward, https://www.youtube.com/watch?v=WF1CgX6ZcrE.

5. Albert Erisman, "Profit Maximization Must Fail," in Albert Erisman and David Gautschi, *The Purpose of Business* (London: Palgrave MacMillan, 2015), 53.

6. Austin Hill and Scott Rae, *The Virtues of Capitalism: A Moral Case for Free Markets* (Chicago: Northfield, 2010).

7. Bruno Roche and Jay Jakub, *Completing Capitalism: Heal Business to Heal the World* (Oakland, CA: Berrett-Koehler, 2017).

8. Tim Keller, "An Immigrant's Courage," from 14:07 onward, https://www.youtube.com/watch?v=WF1CgX6ZcrE.

9. Keller, "An Immigrant's Courage," from 10:42 onward.

10. *Hidden Figures,* directed by Theodore Melfi, written by Margot Lee Shetterly (20th Century Fox, January 2017), DVD

11. *Theology of Work Bible Commentary*, 228.

12. Cheryl Broetje, "An Orchard with Fruit That Lasts," interview by Al Erisman and Kenman Wong, *Ethix Magazine*, Issue 44 (November 2005), https://ethix.org/2005/12/01/an-orchard-with-fruit-that-lasts.

13. Broetje, "An Orchard with Fruit That Lasts."

14. Broetje, "An Orchard with Fruit That Lasts."

15. Broetje, "An Orchard with Fruit That Lasts."

16. Personal communication, Cheryl Broetje, Al Erisman, and Peter Dill, May 2014.

17. Broetje, "An Orchard with Fruit That Lasts."

18. Robert Alter, *The Hebrew Bible, A Translation with Commentary, Vol. 2: The Writings* (New York: W. W. Norton, 2019), 632–34.

19. Alter, *The Hebrew Bible*, vol. 2, 634.

20. Alter, *The Hebrew* Bible, vol. 2, 636.

21. The reference to Tamar is interesting, since she also entered the history of Israel as a Canaanite woman who tricked her father-in-law into marrying her. God turned this into a blessing as a prominent member of the line of David and Jesus.

Chapter 6

1. Did Samuel anticipate the need for a more stable line of succession than the ad hoc nature of the judges prior to him? The narrator tells us that "when Samuel grew old, he appointed his sons as Israel's leaders." Unfortunately, they "did not follow his ways. They turned aside after dishonest gain and accepted bribes and perverted justice" (1 Sam. 8:1–2).

2. Samuel tells the Israelites in detail "the way the kind of king you're talking about operates," and ends the description with this prediction: "You'll end up no better than slaves. The day will come when you will cry in desperation because of this king you so much want for yourselves" (1 Sam. 8:10–18 MSG).

3. Whether Saul was actually intended by God to be Israel's king or whether he was intended to be more of a transitional figure between the judges and an actual king is a question scholars continue to debate. See "Saul and Saul's Family," *Dictionary of the Old Testament: Historical Books*, ed. Bill T. Arnold and H. G. M. Williamson (Downers Grove, IL: InterVarsity Press, 2005), 881–82.

4. When David is brought in to appear before Samuel and his family, he is described as "the very picture of health—bright-eyed, good-looking" (1 Sam. 16:12). While good looks alone should not be the criteria for choosing a future king of Israel, they also do not automatically disqualify someone for leadership.

5. Sometimes the "organization" is the country, and advisors or family members who refuse to address an obvious physical or mental problem with the president can put the entire country in danger. Two obvious examples are the decision by Woodrow Wilson's wife and close advisors to keep the fact that he had suffered a severe stroke a secret from most people for several months after his stroke, and the decision of Franklin Roosevelt's advisors not to discourage him from running for a fourth term in 1944 even though his physical health was in severe decline. Roosevelt died three months after being sworn in for that fourth term.

6. Erisman, *The ServiceMaster Story*, 25–26.

7. See https://www.theodorerooseveltcenter.org/Learn-About-TR/TR-Encyclopedia /Culture-and-Society/Man-in-the-Arena.aspx.

8. C. S. Lewis, "Sometimes Fairy Stories May Say Best What's to Be Said," in *On Stories* (San Diego: Harcourt Brace, 1982), 47.

9. "A workplace discipleship posse has two main functions: first, it is to help us *figure out*—that is, discern the right thing to do, the will of God, that which God

will call "good." Second, this posse will help us *carry out*, execute, what we together have decided is the best way to go. It's about discernment, support, encouragement, and accountability." David W. Gill, *Workplace Discipleship 101: A Primer* (Peabody, MA: Hendrickson, 2020), 59.

10. Jesus describes himself as "humble in heart" (Matt. 11:29), and Paul urges the Philippians in "humility [to] value others above yourselves" by imitating the same mindset as Christ Jesus who "humbled himself by becoming obedient to death even death on a cross" (Phil. 2:3–5, 8).

11. Dennis Hollinger, *Head, Heart, Hands: Bringing Together Christian Thought, Passion and Action* (Downers Grove, IL: InterVarsity Press, 2005), 82.

Chapter 7

1. Tim Keller and Kathryn Alsdorf, *Every Good Endeavor* (New York: Penguin Random House, 2012), 118.

2. C. S. Lewis, *Perelandra* (repr., New York: Scribner, 1996), 120–21.

3. Tish Harrison Warren, *Liturgy of the Ordinary: Sacred Practices in Everyday Life* (Downers Grove, IL: IVP, 2016), 113.

4. Steven Sample, *Contrarian's Guide to Leadership* (San Francisco: Jossey-Bass, 2003), 71–72.

5. *Theology of Work Bible Commentary*, 246.

6. Francis Schaeffer, *The Church at the End of the 20th Century* (Downers Grove, IL: InterVarsity Press, 1970), 138–39.

7. The 2022 Corruption Perception Index, Transparency International, https://www.transparency.org/en/cpi/2022.

8. *Ethix* interview with Jack van Hartesvelt, November 2012, https://ethix.org/category/archives/issue-82.

Chapter 8

1. Francis I. Andersen, *Job: An Introduction and Commentary*, TOTC 14 (Downers Grove, IL: InterVarsity Press, 1974), 86.

2. Steve Bell, "Making Cabinets, Changing the World," interview by Al Erisman, *Ethix Magazine*, Issue 60 (September/October 2008), https://ethix.org/2008/08/01/making-cabinets-changing-the-world.

3. Bell, "Making Cabinets, Changing the World."

4. Bell, "Making Cabinets, Changing the World."

5. Timothy Keller, *Walking with God through Pain and Suffering* (New York: Penguin Random House, 2015), 138.

6. Leah MarieAnn Klett, "Tim Keller Shares Cancer Update, Says Facing Mortality has Transformed His Prayer Life," *The Christian Post*, January 7, 2023.

7. H. L. Mencken, *Prejudices: Second Series* (New York: Knopf, 1920), ch. 3, "The Divine Afflatus."

8. C. S. Lewis, *A Grief Observed* (San Francisco: Harper One, 2015), 4–5.

9. Lewis, *A Grief Observed*, 20.

10. Malcolm Guite, https://malcolmguite.wordpress.com/2020/03/07/lent -with-herbert-day-9-reversed-thunder/.

11. Timothy Keller, *Generous Justice: How God's Grace Makes Us Just* (New York: Penguin Random House, 2010), 16.

12. Francis I. Andersen, *Job, TOTC 14*, 231, quoted in Keller, *Generous Justice*, 12.

13. Tripp Parker, "Who Matters More Than Why," KIROS talk, November 2021, https://kiros.org/audio-2021/tripp-parker-nov2021/.

14. Erisman, *The ServiceMaster Story*, xxx.

15. Alec Hill, *Living in Bonus Time: Surviving Cancer, Finding New Purpose* (Downers Grove, IL: InterVarsity Press, 2020), 2.

Chapter 9

1. *The Word in Life Study Bible*, 1449.

2. Joyce Baldwin, *Daniel: An Introduction and Commentary, TOTC 22* (Downers Grove, IL: InterVarsity, 1978), 88.

3. It appears that Daniel's decision not to eat the food and wine from the king's table was temporary. In Daniel 10:3, Daniel says that during the time he was given a revelation concerning "a great war," he "mourned for three weeks," "used no lotions at all," and "ate no choice food . . . meat or wine." There is no reference to not eating from "the king's table" as there was in ch. 1.

4. Craig B. Barkacs, "How to Use Power, Influence, and Persuasion for Good," *Psychology Today* (January 15, 2021), https://www.psychologytoday.com/us/blog /power-and-influence/202101/how-use-power-influence-and-persuasion-good.

5. Jewish scholar Robert Alter comments:

> No moral justification can be offered for this notorious concluding line. All one can do is to recall the background of outraged feeling that triggers the conclusion: the Babylonians have laid waste to Jerusalem, exiled much of its population, looted and massacred; the powerless captives, ordered—perhaps mockingly—to sing their Zion songs, respond instead with a lament that is not really a song and ends with this bloodcurdling curse pronounced on their captors, who, fortunately, do not understand the Hebrew in which it is pronounced. Alter, *The Hebrew Bible*, vol. 3, 314.

6. Caroline Wood, "Hattiesburg Schools Make Major Jump in MDE Accountability Ratings; HHS No Longer 'F-Rated'" October 3, 2022, https://www.wdam .com/2022/10/04/hattiesburg-schools-make-major-jump-mde-accountability -ratings-hhs-no-longer-f-rated/.

7. We see nothing inconsistent with Daniel's wanting to not be executed along with all the wise men in Babylon and his willingness to genuinely help Nebuchadnezzar understand his dream.

8. Baldwin, *Daniel TOTC 22*, 100.

9. *Word in Life Study Bible*, 5.

10. *Word in Life Study Bible*, 917.

11. Baldwin, *Daniel TOTC 22*, 132.

12. Ronald S. Wallace, *The Message of Daniel* (Downers Grove, IL: InterVarsity Press, 1978), 89.

13. Even though Daniel's message to Belshazzar was perhaps the ultimate in bad news, Belshazzar still promotes him to be the "highest ruler in the kingdom" (Dan. 5:29).

14. Erisman, *The ServiceMaster Story*, 1.

15. Erisman, *The ServiceMaster Story*, 172.

16. Erisman, *The ServiceMaster Story*, 183.

17. The entire story can be found in Daniel 6. The quotations in the text are, with one exception, from Eugene Peterson's *The Message*.

Chapter 10

1. The epistle of 1 Peter is dated between AD 62 and 64. Peter was martyred under Nero a year or two later according to some sources. The narrative for Peter's life can be found throughout all four Gospels, in Acts (particularly Acts 1–15), and in his two letters (1 and 2 Pet.).

2. David W. Gill, *Peter the Rock: Extraordinary Insights from an Ordinary Man* (Downers Grove, IL: InterVarsity Press, 1986), 14–15.

3. Edwin McAllister, "Dolphus Weary," *Mississippi Encyclopedia* (July 11, 2017), https://mississippiencyclopedia.org/entries/dolphus-weary/.

4. McAllister, "Dolphus Weary." We recognize that some Christian leaders like Jemar Tisby believe that "a mainly intrapersonal, friendship-based reconciliation [is] virtually powerless to change the structural and systemic inequalities along racial lines in this country." Emma Green, "The Unofficial Racism Consultants to the White Evangelical World," *The Atlantic*, July 5, 2020, https://www.theatlantic.com/politics/archive/2020/07/white-evangelicals-black-lives-matter/613738/. Dolphus Weary recognized that "intrapersonal, friendship-based reconciliation" is not the end-all and be-all solution to the problems of racial division in Mississippi, but it is certainly part of the answer to the issues of racial divisions. From our experience, actually getting to know a person of a different race *as a person,* learning who that person *is* and what he or she has experienced, is often the first step to gaining an understanding of those "structural and systemic inequalities along racial lines" that do, in fact, exist. "Intrapersonal, friendship-based reconciliation" and working to change systemic inequalities are not mutually exclusive approaches.

5. John Perkins, *One Blood: Parting Words to the Church on Race and Love* (Chicago: Moody, 2017), 69.

6. Brian Robert McCormick, "The Possible Church: Stories of Those Who Have Led White Congregations into a Multi-Ethnic Reality" (diss., Duke Divinity School, Duke University, April 2022). Source: Tom Gjelten, "Multiracial Congregations May Not Bridge Racial Divide," *NPR*, July 17, 2020, https://www.npr.org/2020/07/17/891600067/multiracial-congregations-may-not-bridge-racial-divide.

7. Perkins, *One Blood*, 46.

8. "The first extra-biblical witness to it is Clement of Rome. He also leaves the place of the martyrdom unspecified (Ad Cor. 5). . . . On the tradition reported by Origen, that Peter was crucified head downward, see below, Bk. III. chap. 1, where Origen is quoted by Eusebius." Bible Hub, Church History—Eusebius Pamphilius, "The Persecution under Nero in which Paul and Peter were Honored at Rome with Martyrdom in Behalf of Religion," note 542, https://biblehub.com/library/pamphilius/church_history/chapter_xxv_the_persecution_under_nero.htm#1.

9. Don Flow, "Engaging the World: Vocation, Eschatology, and *Shalom*," talk given at Seattle Pacific University, May 2008.

Chapter 11

1. Admittedly, we are speculating here, but we agree with N. T. Wright that "this moment [of Saul's conversion on the road to Damascus] shattered Saul's wildest dreams and, at the same split second, fulfilled them. . . . Saul had been absolutely right in his devotion to the One God, but absolutely wrong in his understanding of who that One God was and how his purposes would be fulfilled." Wright, *Paul* 52–53.

2. N. T. Wright, *Paul: A Biography* (New York: Harper Collins, 2018), 15–16.

3. Pete Hammond continued to encourage both Randy and Al—and many others—even after he "retired" from InterVarsity in the early 2000s. One of the early pioneers in the Faith at Work movement, Pete died in 2008. Alec Hill, "Remembering Pete Hammond," InterVarsity, *News*, January 15, 2009, https://intervarsity.org/news/remembering-pete-hammond.

4. R. C. Sproul, *Stronger Than Steel: The Wayne Alderson Story* (New York: Harper and Row, 1980)

5. Wright, *Paul*, 68.

6. Wright, *Paul*, 68–69.

7. Wright, *Paul*, 71.

8. Eugene Peterson's *The Message* renders what happened a little more colorfully:

> The apostles and leaders called a special meeting to consider the matter. The arguments went on and on, back and forth, getting more and more heated. Then Peter took the floor: "Friends, you well know from early on God made it plain that he wanted the pagans to hear the Message of this good news and embrace it. . . . So why are you now trying to out-god God, loading these new believers down with rules that crushed our ancestors and crushed us, too? Don't we believe that we are saved because Master Jesus amazingly and out of sheer generosity moved to save us just as he did those from beyond our nation? So what are we arguing about?" There was dead silence. No one said a word. (Acts 15:6–12)

9. Michael Erisman, personal communication.

10. Wright, *Paul*, 194–95.

11. "The Ephesus Approach: How the Gospel Penetrated a City," *Word in Life Study Bible*, 1993.

12. "Mentoring Kingdom-Style," *Word in Life Study Bible*, 2197.

Chapter 12

1. Rod Dreyer, *The Benedict Option: A Strategy for Christians in a Post-Christian Nations* (New York: Sentinel, 2017).

2. Phil Eaton, "Reclaiming Christian Community?," *Blog*, March 14, 2017, https://www.peatonblog.com/blog/reclaiming-christian-community.

3. Darlene Zschech, "Shout to the Lord," Hillsong Music Australia, 1993.

4. Quoted in Lowell Hagan, *Second Sight: Renewing the Vision of Bellevue Christian School for the New Century* (Clyde Hill, WA: Bellevue Christian School, 2003), 76.

5. Erisman, *The ServiceMaster Story*, 89.

6. Erisman, *The ServiceMaster Story*, xvi.

7. Francis Schaeffer, *The God Who Is There* (Downers Grove, IL: InterVarsity Press, 1968), 107.

8. David W. Gill, "Eight Traits of an Ethically Healthy Culture: Insights from the Beatitudes," *Journal of Markets and Morality* (Fall 2013): 615–33.

9. Lewis, *Mere Christianity*, 205.

Conclusion

1. See E. Randolph Richards and Richard James, *Misreading Scripture through Individualistic Eyes* (Downers Grove: InterVarsity, 2020).

2. P. P. Bliss, "Dare to be a Daniel," 1873.

3. Don and Marguerete McCrossan, "On the Jericho Road," 1928.

4. See the afterword for some discussion of examples of how we wrestled with issues where our views were quite different.

5. Lewis, *On Stories*, 47

6. According to www.dictionary.com, when a person is "triggered," they're being provoked by a stimulus that awakens or worsens the symptoms of a traumatic event or mental health condition (https://www.dictionary.com/browse/Triggered). A person's strong reaction to being triggered may come as a surprise to others because the response seems out of proportion to the stimulus. In its popular use, the event interferes with their ability to listen, causing them to react emotionally.

7. Lewis E. Platt, Al Erisman, and David Gill, "Sharing Insight From 33 Years at Hewlett Packard," *Ethix*, Conversation, Issue 10 (April 2000), https://ethix.org/2000/04/01/sharing-insight-from-33-years-at-hewlett-packard.

8. The insight for this example comes from a sermon given by Jeff Van Duzer at Bethany Presbyterian Church, March 19, 2023, https://subsplash.com/bethanypc/media/mi/+9whsvzg.

9. Erisman, *The ServiceMaster Story*, 7.

10. The dilemma of the Pharisees is drawn from a sermon by Jeff Van Duzer, "Darkness to Light/Light to Darkness," Bethany Presbyterian Church, Seattle, March 19, 2023, https://subsplash.com/bethanypc/media/mi/+9whsvzg.

Afterword

1. John Inazu, *Confident Pluralism: Surviving and Thriving through Deep Difference* (Chicago: University of Chicago Press, 2018), 103.

2. Esau McCauley, "The Racial Justice Debate Needs Civil Discourse, Not Straw Men," *Christianity Today*, August 10, 2021, https://www.christianitytoday.com/ct/2021/august-web-only/critical-race-theory-racial-justice-debate-civil-discourse.html.

3. Unlike Nathan, we were not telling stories to get past the "dragons." But avoiding words that block the communication of the message because they raise the defenses of the listener is almost the same thing.

4. Bréne Brown, *Braving the Wilderness: The Quest for True Belonging and the Courage to Stand Alone* (New York: Random House, 2017), 51.

5. Lewis, *Mere Christianity*, xiii–xiv.

6. Craig Carroll, "What Is Motte & Bailey?," *The Bigger Picture* (December 2, 2020), https://medium.com/bigger-picture/what-is-a-motte-bailey-aad572eacc37.

7. Thanks to Tripp Parker who pointed out this fallacy.

8. Laura Meckler and Josh Dawsey, "Republicans, Spurred by an Unlikely Figure, See Political Promise in Targeting Critical Race Theory," *The Washington Post*, June 21, 2021, https://www.washingtonpost.com/education/2021/06/19/critical-race-theory-rufo-republicans/.

9. Francis Fukuyama, *Trust: The Social Virtues and the Creation of Prosperity* (Glencoe: Free Press, 1995), 27–28.

Appendix 1

1. Pew Research Study, "U.S. Christians Projected to Fall Below 50% of Population If Recent Trends Continue," September 8, 2022, https://www.pewresearch.org/religion/2022/09/13/modeling-the-future-of-religion-in-america/pf_2022-09-13_religious-projections_00-01/.

2. This graph was produced by the Pew Research Center and is used with permission.

3. This graph was produced by the Pew Research Center and is used with permission.

4. William Booth, "England and Wales No Longer Majority Christian Nations, Census Reveals," *The Washington Post*, November 29, 2022, https://www.washingtonpost.com/world/2022/11/29/uk-religion-census-christian/.

5. "2021 Census Shows Changes in Australia's Religious Diversity," *Australian Bureau of Statistics*, June 28, 2022, https://www.abs.gov.au/media-centre/media-releases/2021-census-shows-changes-australias-religious-diversity.

6. Aaron Renn, "The Three Worlds of Evangelicalism," *First Things* (February 2022), https://www.firstthings.com/article/2022/02/the-three-worlds-of-evangelicalism.

Appendix 2

1. In a personal conversation, John Medina stated this to summarize "Every Brain Is Wired Differently," a chapter in his book *Brain Rules: 12 Principles for Surviving and Thriving at Work, Home, and School* (West Edmonds: Pear Press, 2008), 51.

2. E. Randolph Richards and Brandon J. O'Brien, *Misreading Scripture with Western Eyes: Removing Cultural Blinders to Better Understand the Bible* (Downers Grove, IL: InterVarsity, 2012), 17.

3. Haddon Robinson, "The Heresy of Application," *Christianity Today* (Fall 1997).

4. John H. Walton and Kim E. Walton, *Bible Story Handbook: A Resource for Teaching 175 Stories from the Bible* (Wheaton, IL: Crossway, 2010), 16–18.

5. Dallas Willard, *Hearing God: Developing a Conversational Relationship with God* (Downers Grove, IL: InterVarsity, 2012), 35.

Index